# Good Housekeeping

# HOME *for the* HOLIDAYS

## Classic Family Recipes

*Edited by Susan Westmoreland*

FOOD DIRECTOR
GOOD HOUSEKEEPING

HEARST BOOKS
A division of Sterling Publishing Co., Inc.

New York / London
**www.sterlingpublishing.com**

## Good Housekeeping

EDITOR IN CHIEF: Rosemary Ellis
FOOD DIRECTOR: Susan Westmoreland
NUTRITION DIRECTOR: Samantha Cassetty
LIFESTYLE EDITOR: Sara Lyle

### *Good Housekeeping Great Home Cooking* Credits

WRITER: Beth Allen
CULINARY CONSULTANT/EDITOR: Deborah Mintcheff
CULINARY HISTORIAN: Jan Longone
COPY EDITOR: Brenda Goldberg
PROOFREADERS: Synde Matus, Diane Boccadoro,
Barbara Machtiger, and Loisina Michel

## Photo Credits

Angelo Caggiano: pg. 4, 91; Brian Hagiwara: 22, 29, 32,
76; Rita Maas: 5, 77, 94, 116; Simon Metz: 110; Steven
Mark Needham: 60, 96, 105, 121, 132, 138, 146, 155;
Ann Stratton: 15, 41, 124, 133; Mark Thomas: 23, 46,
48, 49, 69, 74, 97, 129, 140, 141, 143, 145, 149, 152, 156,
165, 167.

## Hearst Books

PUBLISHER: Jacqueline Deval
EDITORIAL DIRECTOR: Marisa Bulzone
ART DIRECTOR: Chris Thompson
COVER DESIGN: Bonnie Naugle

*Good Housekeeping Home for the Holidays* is an abridge-
ment of *Good Housekeeping Great Home Cooking,* which
was previously published by Hearst Books in hardcover,
under the title *Good Housekeeping Great American
Classics Cookbook.*

The Library of Congress has cataloged the previous
edition of this book as follows:
Good Housekeeping great American classics cookbook /
edited by Susan Westmoreland.
    p. cm.
    Includes index.
    ISBN 1-58816-280-X
    1. Cookery, American.  I. Title: Great American
classics cookbook. II. Westmoreland, Susan. III. Good
Housekeeping (New York, N.Y.)
TX715.G6542 2004
641.5973--dc22
                                        2004000933

10  9  8  7  6  5  4  3  2  1

Published by Hearst Books
A Division of Sterling Publishing Co., Inc.
387 Park Avenue South, New York, NY 10016

Good Housekeeping and Hearst Books are trademarks
owned by Hearst Communications, Inc.

The Good Housekeeping Cookbook Seal guarantees
that the recipes in this cookbook meet the strict stan-
dards of the Good Housekeeping Research Institute.
The Institute has been a source of reliable information
and a consumer advocate since 1900, and established its
seal of approval in 1909. Every recipe has been triple-
tested for ease, reliability, and great taste.

www.goodhousekeeping.com

Distributed in Canada by Sterling Publishing
c/o Canadian Manda Group, 165 Dufferin Street,
Toronto, Ontario, Canada M6K 3E7

Distributed in Australia by Capricorn Link
(Australia) Pty. Ltd.
P.O. Box 704, Windsor, NSW 2756 Australia

Manufactured in China

ISBN 978-1-58816-819-1

# Contents

# Chapter 1

# Hors D'oeuvres

The Age of Elegance was at its height in America during the last half of the nineteenth century. Formal seven-course dinners were common in some upper-class homes. The food was served in the latest style: *a la russe*. Instead of bringing it to the table all at once (in true English style), the butlers plated each course in the kitchen and presented them to each guest from gold and silver servers.

After the 1920s, despite Prohibition, this elaborate style of entertaining gave way to the cocktail party: those warm and friendly gatherings at home, where guests sipped, dipped, dunked, and nibbled, often well past the cocktail hour and long into suppertime. With this social phenomenon came finger foods that could be eaten without muss or fuss. Hostesses began stuffing celery, potting meats and seafood, broiling clams and oysters, baking cheese puffs, and creating dips for everything from raw oysters to crunchy vegetable crudités. By the 1930s, women's magazines and cookbooks were featuring recipes for fancy ribbon sandwiches, quick dips, spicy nuts, and cream cheese balls rolled in everything imaginable.

Popular, too, was the cocktail buffet table, which was often adorned with a chafing dish (which had been very popular at the turn of the century) to keep such favorites as cheese fondue, meatballs, or crab cakes warm for an hour or two. Punch bowls frequently made an appearance at these parties. In the '30s, punch bowls were filled with fruit juice, sometimes alcohol, slices of fresh fruit, and a simple ice ring, which floated on top and kept it all cold. During the holidays, fruit punch was replaced by festive eggnog sprinkled with ground nutmeg or by hot wassail. By the late '40s and through the '50s, fruit punches became dressier. Ice rings were tinted a pretty pink and fresh fruit was decoratively arranged within the ice, turning a simple fruit punch into a real showstopper. Today bite-size foods are classics, so nibble away to your heart's content!

◀ *Chafing-Dish Meatballs, Hot Cheddar Puffs, and Half-Moon Empanadas*

# Classic Onion Dip

In 1952, the Lipton Soup Company developed a dehydrated onion-soup mix, but a consumer, created the first dip using the soup mix, which Lipton has featured ever since. "Just open a couple of packages and fold into a cup of sour cream." Soon it became known as California Dip. Our onion dip is even better, for it's made the old-fashioned way: from slow-simmered onions folded into—of course—sour cream.

**PREP:** 10 minutes plus cooling ★ **COOK:** 30 minutes
**MAKES** 1²/₃ cups

2 large onions (12 ounces each), finely chopped (2 cups)
2 cups canned chicken broth
1 tablespoon minced garlic
½ bay leaf
¼ teaspoon dried thyme
1 teaspoon red wine vinegar
1 cup sour cream
⅛ teaspoon salt
⅛ teaspoon ground black pepper
crackers or potato chips

1. In 2-quart saucepan, combine onions, broth, garlic, bay leaf, and thyme; heat to boiling over high heat. Reduce heat and cook until liquid has almost completely evaporated, about 25 minutes.

2. Transfer mixture to medium bowl; stir in vinegar. Cool to room temperature.

3. Stir in sour cream, salt, and pepper. Cover and refrigerate up to overnight. Serve with crackers or potato chips.

**EACH TABLESPOON:** About 27 calories, 1g protein, 2g carbohydrate, 2g total fat (1g saturated), 4mg cholesterol, 93mg sodium.

# Maryland Crab Dip

In the 1950s, hostesses coast to coast entertained friends at fancy cocktail parties and informal backyard barbecues. This hot dip, made with chunks of crab, a hint of curry, and slivers of almonds, was often served regardless of what else was on the menu. Our recipe uses Old Bay seasoning in place of curry powder.

**PREP:** 5 minutes ★ **BAKE:** 23 minutes
**MAKES** 1½ cups

⅓ cup slivered almonds
½ pound lump crabmeat, picked over
½ cup mayonnaise
⅓ cup sour cream
2 tablespoons minced onion
2 tablespoons chopped fresh parsley
1 teaspoon Old Bay seasoning
crackers

1. Preheat oven to 350°F. Grease 9-inch pie plate.

2. Spread almonds on cookie sheet. Bake, stirring occasionally, until lightly browned and fragrant, about 8 minutes; cool.

3. In medium bowl, combine crabmeat, mayonnaise, sour cream, onion, parsley, and seasoning. Turn into prepared pie plate and spread evenly.

4. Bake until heated through, about 15 minutes. Sprinkle with almonds. Serve with crackers.

**EACH TABLESPOON:** About 62 calories, 2g protein, 1g carbohydrate, 6g total fat (1g saturated), 14mg cholesterol, 82mg sodium.

# Potted Shrimp

Lacking refrigeration, the early settlers preserved seafood and meats by "potting" them. They first cooked the food, then potted and sealed it with plenty of fat, often butter. Potting food is still quite popular throughout the Deep South, especially in the Carolinas.

**PREP:** 15 minutes plus chilling ★ **COOK:** 3 minutes
**MAKES** about 2 cups

8 tablespoons (1 stick) unsalted butter, softened (do not use margarine)
1 pound medium shrimp, shelled and deveined
¾ teaspoon salt
¼ teaspoon ground red pepper (cayenne)
2 tablespoons dry sherry
sesame crackers or toast

1. In 10-inch skillet, melt 1 tablespoon butter over medium-high heat. Add shrimp, salt, and ground red pepper. Cook, stirring frequently, until shrimp are opaque throughout, about 2 minutes. Add sherry and cook 30 seconds.

2. Transfer shrimp and pan juices to food processor with knife blade attached and pulse until shrimp is finely chopped. Add remaining butter; process until blended.

3. Transfer shrimp mixture to serving bowl. Cover and refrigerate up to 24 hours. Let stand 30 minutes at room temperature before serving. Serve with sesame crackers or toast.

**EACH TABLESPOON:** About 39 calories, 2g protein, 0g carbohydrate, 3g total fat (2g saturated), 25mg cholesterol, 72mg sodium.

# South-of-the-Border Guacamole

From south of the border down Mexico way comes an avocado dip that is heated up with chile peppers. Its name comes from the Spanish word *ahuacamolli* (avocado sauce). One recipe appeared in a 1942 *Good Housekeeping Cook Book*. As ethnic and regional specialties took over dinner parties in the 1950s, guacamole caught on quickly and remains a cocktail-party standby.

**PREP:** 5 minutes ★ **MAKES** about 1½ cups

2 medium or 1 large ripe Hass avocado*
2 tablespoons minced onion
2 tablespoons chopped fresh cilantro
1 tablespoon fresh lime juice
2 serrano or jalapeño chiles, seeded and minced
½ teaspoon salt
¼ teaspoon coarsely ground black pepper
1 ripe plum tomato, chopped
tortilla chips

Cut each avocado lengthwise in half; remove each pit. With spoon, scoop flesh from peel into medium bowl. Add onion, cilantro, lime juice, chiles, salt, and pepper. With potato masher, coarsely mash mixture; stir in tomato. Transfer to small serving bowl and serve or cover and refrigerate up to 2 hours. Serve with tortilla chips.

*Choose perfectly ripened avocados that yield to gentle pressure when lightly squeezed in the palm of the hand.

**EACH TABLESPOON:** About 35 calories, 1g protein, 2g carbohydrate, 3g total fat (1g saturated), 0mg cholesterol, 45mg sodium.

# Seven-Layer Tex-Mex Dip

You can assemble the bean and cheese layers of this dip and chill them until ready to serve, then warm them through in the oven and top with guacamole and sour cream.

**PREP:** 35 minutes ★ **BAKE:** 15 minutes
**MAKES** 24 servings

I can (15 to 19 ounces) pinto beans, rinsed and drained

I cup mild to medium salsa

2 green onions, finely chopped

I small garlic clove, minced

4 ounces Monterey Jack cheese, shredded (I cup)

I can (2.25 ounces) sliced ripe black olives, rinsed and drained

2 ripe medium Hass avocados

¹⁄₃ cup chopped fresh cilantro

3 tablespoons finely chopped red onion

2 tablespoons fresh lime juice

¹⁄₂ teaspoon salt

I cup sour cream

tortilla chips

1. Preheat oven to 350°F. In medium bowl, combine beans, 3 tablespoons salsa, half of green onions, and garlic. Mash until well combined but still slightly chunky. Spread in bottom of 9-inch glass pie plate.

2. Sprinkle Jack cheese over bean mixture, then spread with remaining salsa and sprinkle with olives. Bake until hot, about 15 minutes.

3. Meanwhile, cut each avocado in half; remove each pit. With spoon, scoop flesh from peel into same medium bowl. Mash avocados until slightly chunky. Stir in ¹⁄₄ cup cilantro, red onion, lime juice, and salt. Spoon avocado mixture over hot dip; spread sour cream on top. Sprinkle with remaining green onions and remaining cilantro. Serve with tortilla chips.

**EACH SERVING:** About 83 calories, 3g protein, 4g carbohydrate, 6g total fat (2g saturated), 9mg cholesterol, 206mg sodium.

# Chicken Liver Pâté

Our silky smooth version of a French pâté is seasoned the traditional way: with a splash of brandy, some black pepper, and dried thyme.

**PREP:** 25 minutes plus chilling ★ **COOK:** 23 minutes
**MAKES** about 1¹⁄₂ cups

2 tablespoons butter or margarine

I small onion, finely chopped

I garlic clove, finely chopped

I pound chicken livers, trimmed

2 tablespoons brandy

¹⁄₂ cup heavy or whipping cream

¹⁄₂ teaspoon salt

¹⁄₄ teaspoon dried thyme

¹⁄₄ teaspoon ground black pepper

assorted crackers, toast, or thinly sliced apples

1. In 10-inch skillet, melt butter over medium-high heat. Add onion; cook, stirring frequently, until tender and golden, about 10 minutes. Stir in garlic and livers; cook until livers are lightly browned

but still pink inside, about 5 minutes. Stir in brandy; cook 5 minutes longer.

**2.** In blender or in food processor with knife blade attached, puree chicken-liver mixture, cream, salt, thyme, and pepper until smooth, stopping blender occasionally and scraping down sides with rubber spatula.

**3.** Spoon mixture into small bowl; cover and refrigerate at least 3 hours or up to overnight. Let stand 30 minutes at room temperature before serving. Serve with crackers, toast, or apples.

**EACH TABLESPOON:** About 54 calories, 4g protein, 1g carbohydrate, 4g total fat (2g saturated), 92mg cholesterol, 75mg sodium.

# Bite-Size Quiche Lorraine

In the 1960s, Julia Child started a gourmet revolution by giving women the skills and recipes with which to cook classic French cuisine. Bacon-and-cheese pie from the south of France, called quiche Lorraine, quickly became an American standard. Julia called it "just a custard in a fancy dress."

**PREP:** 1 hour plus chilling ★ **BAKE:** 20 minutes
**MAKES** 36 mini quiches

**Pastry Dough for a 2-Crust Pie**

**1 tablespoon butter or margarine, melted**

**1 package (8 ounces) bacon, finely chopped**

**1 cup half-and-half or light cream**

**2 large eggs**

**¼ teaspoon salt**

**3 ounces Swiss cheese, shredded (¾ cup)**

**1.** Prepare Pastry Dough for 2-Crust Pie. Grease and flour thirty-six 1¾-inch mini-muffin-pan cups.

**2.** On lightly floured surface, with floured rolling pin, roll dough until ⅛ inch thick. Using 3-inch fluted round cookie cutter, cut pastry dough into 36 rounds, rerolling trimmings.

**3.** Line muffin-pan cups with dough rounds; brush lightly with melted butter. Cover the pan and refrigerate.

**4.** Preheat oven to 400°F. In 12-inch skillet, cook bacon over medium heat until browned. Transfer bacon to paper towels to drain.

**5.** In small bowl, beat half-and-half, eggs, and salt. Divide bacon and cheese evenly among pastry cups. Spoon about 1 tablespoon egg mixture into each cup. Bake until knife inserted in center of quiche comes out clean, 20 to 25 minutes. Remove quiches from pan and serve hot, warm, or at room temperature.

**EACH QUICHE:** About 111 calories, 3g protein, 7g carbohydrate, 8g total fat (4g saturated), 26mg cholesterol, 118mg sodium.

# Nachos

The story goes that, in the 1940s at the Victory Club in Piedras Negras, Mexico, Chef Ignacio "Nacho" Anaya ran out of his usual specials, so he melted cheese on toasted tortillas, topped each with a jalapeño slice, and called them *Nacho's Especiales*.

**PREP:** 30 minutes ★ **BAKE:** 5 minutes per batch
**MAKES** 36 nachos

36 unbroken large tortilla chips

3 large ripe plum tomatoes, cut into ¼-inch pieces

⅓ cup chopped fresh cilantro

¼ teaspoon salt

1 tablespoon vegetable oil

1 fully cooked chorizo sausage (3 ounces), finely chopped, or ¾ cup finely chopped pepperoni (3 ounces)

1 medium onion, finely chopped

1 garlic clove, finely chopped

½ teaspoon ground cumin

1 can (15 to 19 ounces) black beans, rinsed and drained

4 ounces Monterey Jack cheese, shredded (1 cup)

2 pickled jalapeño chiles, very thinly sliced

1. Preheat oven to 400°F. Arrange as many tortilla chips as will fit in single layer on two ungreased large cookie sheets. In small bowl, combine tomatoes, cilantro, and salt.

2. In 10-inch skillet, heat oil over medium heat. Add chorizo, onion, garlic, and cumin; cook, stirring, until onion is tender, about 5 minutes. Stir in beans, mashing with back of spoon; cover and cook until heated through.

3. Place 1 tablespoon mashed bean mixture on each tortilla chip. Sprinkle Jack cheese over beans and top each nacho with 1 slice jalapeño. Bake until cheese begins to melt, about 5 minutes.

4. Spoon about 1 teaspoon tomato mixture on each nacho. Transfer nachos to platter; keep warm. Repeat with remaining chips, bean mixture, cheese, and tomato mixture. Serve warm.

**EACH NACHO:** About 51 calories, 2g protein, 4g carbohydrate, 3g total fat (1g saturated), 5mg cholesterol, 112mg sodium.

# Firecracker Party Mix

In 1955, Ralston Purina in St. Louis created a party snack using Chex cereal squares to bolster sales. The cereal was tossed with pretzel sticks, nuts, and spicy butter spiked with Worcestershire sauce. Since then, numerous variations have evolved. This recipe mirrors the original with one exception: the nuts have been replaced with popped corn.

**PREP:** 10 minutes plus cooling
**BAKE:** 30 minutes per batch
**MAKES** about 25 cups

¼ cup Worcestershire sauce

4 tablespoons butter or margarine

2 tablespoons brown sugar

1½ teaspoons salt

½ to 1 teaspoon ground red pepper (cayenne)

12 cups popped corn (about ⅓ cup unpopped)

1 package (12 ounces) oven-toasted corn cereal squares

1 package (8 to 10 ounces) thin pretzel sticks

1. Preheat oven to 300°F. In 1-quart saucepan, combine Worcestershire, butter, brown sugar, salt, and ground red pepper; heat over low heat, stirring often, until butter has melted.

2. Place half each of popped corn, cereal, and pretzels in large roasting pan; toss with half of Worcestershire-butter mixture.

**3.** Bake popcorn mixture 30 minutes, stirring once halfway through baking. Cool mixture in very large bowl or on surface covered with waxed paper. Repeat with remaining ingredients.

EACH ½ CUP: About 65 calories, 1g protein, 13g carbohydrate, 1g total fat (0 g saturated), 0mg cholesterol, 245mg sodium.

# Half-Moon Empanadas

*(pictured on page 4)*

In Spanish *empanar* means "to wrap in dough." These half-moon pastry turnovers are filled with *picadillo,* the Mexican-spiced beef filling. Recipes for empanadas first appeared here in print in the 1920s, and these savories are now a staple in Mexican-American fare.

PREP: 1 hour 15 minutes ★ BAKE: 15 minutes per batch
MAKES about 54 turnovers

**Flaky Turnover Pastry (opposite)**
**2 teaspoons vegetable oil**
**1 small onion, finely chopped**
**1 large garlic clove, minced**
**¼ teaspoon ground cinnamon**
**¼ teaspoon ground red pepper (cayenne)**
**4 ounces ground beef chuck**
**¼ teaspoon salt**
**1 cup canned tomatoes with juice**
**3 tablespoons chopped golden raisins**
**3 tablespoons chopped pimiento-stuffed olives (salad olives)**
**1 large egg beaten with 2 tablespoons water**

**1.** Prepare Flaky Turnover Pastry. Wrap in plastic wrap; set aside.

**2.** In 10-inch skillet, heat oil over medium heat.

Add onion; cook, stirring frequently, until tender, about 5 minutes. Stir in garlic, cinnamon, and ground red pepper; cook 30 seconds. Increase heat to medium-high. Add ground beef and salt; cook, breaking up meat with side of spoon, until beef begins to brown, about 5 minutes. Stir in tomatoes with their juice, raisins, and olives, breaking up tomatoes with side of spoon. Cook over high heat until liquid has almost evaporated, 7 to 10 minutes. Remove from heat.

**3.** Preheat oven to 425°F. Divide dough into four equal pieces. On floured surface, with floured rolling pin, roll one piece of dough until ¹⁄₁₆ inch thick. Keep remaining dough covered. With 3-inch round biscuit cutter, cut out as many rounds as possible, reserving trimmings. On one half of each dough round, place 1 level measuring teaspoon of filling. Brush edges of rounds with some egg mixture. Fold dough over to enclose filling. With fork, press edges together to seal dough; prick tops. Brush tops of empanadas lightly with egg mixture. With spatula, lift turnovers and place, 1 inch apart, on ungreased large cookie sheet.

**4.** Bake turnovers just until golden, 15 to 17 minutes. Repeat with remaining dough, filling, and egg mixture. Press together dough trimmings and reroll.

## Flaky Turnover Pastry

In large bowl, combine *3 cups all-purpose flour, 1½ teaspoons baking powder,* and *¾ teaspoon salt.* With pastry blender or two knives used scissor-fashion, cut in *1 cup vegetable shortening* until mixture resembles coarse crumbs. Sprinkle with about *6 tablespoons cold water,* 1 tablespoon at a time, mixing with fork after each addition, until dough is just moist enough to hold together. Shape into ball. Refrigerate pastry if not assembling turnovers right away.

EACH TURNOVER: About 70 calories, 1g protein, 6g carbohydrate, 5g total fat (2g saturated), 5mg cholesterol, 80mg sodium.

# Hot Cheddar Puffs

*(pictured on page 4)*

As cocktail parties became the rage in the '50s, every good hostess began collecting recipes for favorite finger foods to serve at parties. Often some form of cheesy puffs appeared. Ours are special: hot, spicy, crispy, and melt-in-your-mouth delicious!

**PREP:** 20 minutes ★ **BAKE:** 25 minutes
**MAKES** about 8 dozen puffs

2 teaspoons curry powder

½ teaspoon ground coriander

½ teaspoon ground cumin

¼ teaspoon ground red pepper (cayenne)

6 tablespoons butter or margarine,
   cut into pieces

½ teaspoon salt

I cup water

I cup all-purpose flour

4 large eggs

4 ounces Cheddar cheese, shredded (I cup)

1. Preheat oven to 400°F. Grease two large cookie sheets.

2. In 3-quart saucepan, combine curry powder, coriander, cumin, and ground red pepper. Cook over medium heat, stirring constantly, until very fragrant, about 1 minute. Stir in butter, salt, and water; heat to boiling over high heat. Remove from heat. With wooden spoon, stir in flour all at once. Return pan to medium-low heat, stirring constantly, until mixture forms a ball and leaves side of pan. Remove from heat.

3. Stir in eggs, one at a time, beating well after each addition, until batter is smooth and satiny. Stir in Cheddar. Spoon batter into large pastry bag fitted with ½-inch plain tip. Pipe batter, about 1 inch apart, on cookie sheets, forming 1-inch-wide and ¾-inch-high mounds. Alternatively, drop teaspoons of dough on cookie sheets. With fingertip dipped in cool water, smooth peaks.

4. Bake puffs until deep golden, 25 to 30 minutes, rotating cookie sheets between oven racks halfway through baking. Transfer to wire racks to cool. Repeat with remaining batter.

5. Serve puffs at room temperature or reheat in 400°F oven 5 minutes to serve hot.

**EACH PUFF:** About 20 calories, 1g protein, 1g carbohydrate, 1g total fat (0g saturated), 10mg cholesterol, 30mg sodium.

# Peppery Nuts

During the 1950s, bowls of spiced nuts, flavored with Worcestershire sauce and a dash of hot pepper, were popular offerings at suburban soirées. Walnuts and almonds were popular in California, while pecans were the nut of choice in the Deep South.

**PREP:** 5 minutes plus cooling ★ **BAKE:** 20 minutes
**MAKES** about 2 cups

8 ounces walnuts (2 cups)

2 tablespoons sugar

I tablespoon vegetable oil

I½ teaspoons Worcestershire sauce

½ teaspoon ground red pepper (cayenne)

¼ teaspoon salt

**1.** Preheat oven to 350°F. Place walnuts in jelly-roll pan. Bake, stirring occasionally, until toasted, about 20 minutes.

**2.** Meanwhile, in small bowl, combine sugar, oil, Worcestershire, ground red pepper, and salt.

**3.** Drizzle spice mixture over hot nuts and toss until thoroughly coated. Spread nuts in single layer; cool completely in pan on wire rack. Store at room temperature in tightly covered container up to 1 month.

EACH ¼ CUP: About 210 calories, 4g protein, 9g carbohydrate, 19g total fat (2 g saturated), 0mg cholesterol, 80mg sodium.

# Sausage-Stuffed Mushrooms

American settlers frequently found mushrooms growing wild but avoided eating them, fearing they might be poisonous. It wasn't until the nineteenth century that cultivated mushrooms from France were imported. By the 1920s, white mushrooms were being cultivated here. They rapidly grew in popularity, and by the 1960s, stuffed mushrooms had become a popular hors d'oeuvre.

PREP: 50 minutes ★ BAKE: 15 minutes
MAKES 30 appetizers

1½ **pounds medium white mushrooms (about 30)**

8 **ounces sweet or hot Italian-sausage links, casings removed**

½ **cup shredded mozzarella cheese**

¼ **cup seasoned dried bread crumbs**

**1.** Remove stems from mushrooms; chop stems. Set mushroom caps and chopped stems aside.

**2.** Heat 10-inch skillet over medium heat. Add sausage; cook, breaking up meat with side of spoon, until well browned, about 8 minutes. With slotted spoon, transfer sausage to paper towels to drain. Spoon off all but 2 tablespoons drippings from skillet.

**3.** Add mushroom stems to hot drippings in skillet. Cook, stirring, until tender, about 10 minutes. Remove from heat; stir in sausage, mozzarella, and bread crumbs.

**4.** Preheat oven to 450°F. Fill mushroom caps with sausage mixture. Place stuffed mushrooms in jelly-roll pan. Bake until heated through, about 15 minutes. Serve hot.

EACH APPETIZER: About 39 calories, 2g protein, 2g carbohydrate, 3g total fat (1g saturated), 6mg cholesterol, 90mg sodium.

# Texas Cheese Straws

In the mid-1950s, fancy tea parties, complete with turn-of-the-century elegance, were popular in Texas cities. These crisp, flaky, twisted cheese straws were often present, displayed in a circular pattern on a cut-crystal platter.

**PREP:** 30 minutes ★ **BAKE:** 20 minutes per batch
**MAKES** about 48 cheese straws

1 tablespoon paprika

½ teaspoon dried thyme

¼ to ½ teaspoon ground red pepper (cayenne)

¼ teaspoon salt

1 package (17¼ ounces) frozen puff-pastry sheets, thawed

1 large egg white, lightly beaten

8 ounces sharp Cheddar cheese, shredded (2 cups)

1. Grease two large cookie sheets. In a small bowl, combine the paprika, thyme, ground red pepper, and salt.

2. Unfold 1 puff-pastry sheet. On lightly floured surface, with floured rolling pin, roll pastry into 14-inch square. Lightly brush with egg white. Sprinkle pastry with half of paprika mixture. Sprinkle half of Cheddar over half of pastry. Fold pastry over to enclose cheese, forming rectangle. With rolling pin, lightly roll over pastry to seal layers together. With pizza wheel or knife, cut pastry crosswise into ½-inch-wide strips.

3. Preheat oven to 375°F. Place strips, ½ inch apart, on prepared cookie sheets, twisting each strip twice to form spiral and pressing ends against cookie sheet to prevent strips from uncurling during baking. Bake cheese straws until golden, 20 to 22 minutes. With spatula, carefully transfer straws to wire racks to cool.

4. Repeat with remaining puff-pastry sheet, egg white, paprika mixture, and cheese. Store in airtight container up to 1 week.

**EACH STRAW:** About 75 calories, 2g protein, 5g carbohydrate, 6g total fat (2g saturated), 9mg cholesterol, 65mg sodium.

# Oysters Rockefeller

This dish, created in 1899, is truly "as rich as Rockefeller himself." The original chef's recipe was never revealed, though legend has it that one is instructed to "Take the tail and tips of small green onions. Take celery, take chervil, take tarragon leaves and the crumbs of stale bread. Take Tobasco sauce and the best butter obtainable. Pound all these into a mixture in a mortar, so that all the fragrant flavorings are blended. Add a dash of absinthe. Force the mixture through a fine-meshed sieve. Place one spoonful on each oyster as it rests in its own shell and in its own juice on the crushed rock salt, the purpose of which is to keep the oyster piping hot . . . " Numerous versions followed over the years. Here fresh oysters on the half shell are cooked until sizzling hot under a bed of seasoned chopped spinach and buttered bread crumbs.

---

**PREP:** 30 minutes ★ **BAKE:** 10 minutes
**MAKES** 4 first-course servings

---

I dozen oysters, shucked, bottom shells
    reserved

kosher or rock salt (optional)

I bunch spinach (10 to 12 ounces), tough
    stems trimmed, washed, and dried very well

I tablespoon plus 2 teaspoons butter or
    margarine

2 tablespoons finely chopped onion

pinch ground red pepper (cayenne)

¼ cup heavy or whipping cream

I tablespoon Pernod or other anise-flavored
    liqueur

pinch salt

2 tablespoons plain dried bread crumbs

I. Preheat oven to 425°F. Place oysters in shells in jelly-roll pan lined with ½-inch layer of kosher salt to keep them flat, if desired; refrigerate.

2. In 2-quart saucepan, cook spinach over high heat until wilted; drain. Rinse spinach with cold running water; drain well. Finely chop spinach. Wipe saucepan dry with paper towels.

3. In same clean saucepan, melt 1 tablespoon butter over medium heat. Add onion; cook until tender, about 3 minutes. Stir in ground red pepper. Stir in spinach, cream, Pernod, and salt. Cook over high heat, stirring, until liquid has reduced and thickened. Remove from heat.

4. In small saucepan, melt remaining 2 teaspoons butter over low heat. Remove from heat; stir in bread crumbs until evenly moistened.

5. Spoon spinach mixture evenly on top of oysters. Sprinkle with buttered bread crumbs. Bake until edges of oysters curl, about 10 minutes.

---

**EACH SERVING:** About 166 calories, 6g protein, 9g carbohydrate, 12g total fat (7g saturated), 57mg cholesterol, 228mg sodium.

# Clams Casino

The year was 1917, and Mrs. Paran Stevens was hosting her society friends at the Casino at Narragansett Pier in New York City. Maitre d'Hotel Julius Keller created a dish for the occasion featuring clams on the half shell baked with bacon and seasonings.

**PREP:** 30 minutes ★ **BAKE:** 10 minutes
**MAKES** 6 first-course servings

**2 dozen littleneck clams, scrubbed and shucked, bottom shells reserved**

**kosher or rock salt (optional)**

**3 slices bacon**

**1 tablespoon olive oil**

**½ red pepper, very finely chopped**

**½ green pepper, very finely chopped**

**¼ teaspoon coarsely ground black pepper**

**1 garlic clove, finely chopped**

**1 cup fresh bread crumbs (about 2 slices bread)**

**1.** Preheat oven to 425°F. Place clams in shells in jelly-roll pan lined with ½-inch layer of kosher salt to keep them flat, if desired; refrigerate.

**2.** In 10-inch skillet, cook bacon over medium heat until browned; transfer to paper towels to drain. Discard drippings from skillet. Add oil, red and green peppers, and black pepper to skillet. Cook, stirring occasionally, until peppers are tender, about 5 minutes. Stir in garlic and cook 30 seconds; remove from heat.

**3.** Finely chop bacon; stir bacon and bread crumbs into pepper mixture in skillet. Spoon crumb mixture evenly over clams. Bake until crumb topping is light golden, about 10 minutes.

**EACH SERVING:** About 107 calories, 9g protein, 6g carbohydrate, 5g total fat (1g saturated), 23mg cholesterol, 122mg sodium.

# Dilly Shrimp

Pickling foods not only preserves them but also adds extra flavor. The food is first boiled, then pickled with vinegar, spices, and fresh dill. Pickled shrimp is best made a day ahead and refrigerated overnight, making it great for parties.

**PREP:** 20 minutes plus overnight to marinate
**COOK:** 5 minutes ★ **MAKES** 24 appetizer servings

**¼ cup dry sherry**

**3 teaspoons salt**

**¼ teaspoon whole black peppercorns**

**1 bay leaf**

**3 pounds large shrimp, shelled and deveined, leaving tail part of shell on, if desired**

**⅔ cup fresh lemon juice (about 4 large lemons)**

**½ cup distilled white vinegar**

**½ cup vegetable oil**

**3 tablespoons pickling spices, tied in cheesecloth bag**

**2 teaspoons sugar**

**2 dill sprigs**

**1.** In 4-quart saucepan, combine 6 *cups water*, sherry, 2 teaspoons salt, peppercorns, and bay leaf; heat to boiling over high heat. Add shrimp; heat to boiling. Shrimp should be opaque throughout when water returns to boil; if needed, cook about 1 minute longer. Drain.

**2.** In large bowl, combine lemon juice, vinegar, oil, pickling spices, sugar, dill, and remaining 1 teaspoon salt. Add shrimp and toss well to coat. Spoon into ziptight plastic bags, press out air, and seal. Refrigerate shrimp overnight to marinate, turning bags occasionally.

**3.** Remove shrimp from marinade and arrange in chilled bowl. Serve with cocktail picks.

**EACH SERVING:** About 69 calories, 9g protein, 1g carbohydrate, 2g total fat (0g saturated), 70mg cholesterol, 166mg sodium.

# Shrimp Cocktail

The outfitting of shrimp boats with refrigeration in the early twentieth century made it possible to transport fresh shrimp to more American cities. The original Rémoulade Sauce, based on mayonnaise and subtly spiced with mustard and horseradish, comes from France.

**PREP:** 25 minutes plus chilling ★ **COOK:** 25 minutes
**MAKES** 8 appetizer servings

1 lemon, thinly sliced

4 bay leaves

20 whole black peppercorns

10 whole allspice berries

2 teaspoons salt

24 extra-large shrimp (1 pound),
   shelled and deveined

Red Cocktail Sauce (opposite)

Rémoulade Verte (opposite)

12 small romaine lettuce leaves

24 (7-inch) bamboo skewers

**1.** In 5-quart Dutch oven, combine *2 quarts water*, lemon, bay leaves, peppercorns, allspice berries, and salt; heat to boiling. Cover and boil 15 minutes.

**2.** Add shrimp; cook just until opaque throughout, 1 to 2 minutes. Drain and rinse with cold running water to stop cooking. Cover and refrigerate shrimp up to 24 hours.

**3.** Prepare Red Cocktail Sauce and/or Rémoulade Verte.

**4.** Just before serving, place bowls of sauces in center of platter; arrange romaine leaves around bowls, leaf tips facing out. Thread each shrimp on a bamboo skewer and arrange skewers on romaine.

**EACH SERVING WITHOUT SAUCE:** About 51 calories, 10g protein, 1g carbohydrate, 1g total fat (0g saturated), 70mg cholesterol, 141mg sodium.

# Red Cocktail Sauce

**PREP:** 15 minutes ★ **MAKES** about 1 cup

1 cup bottled cocktail sauce

2 tablespoons chopped fresh cilantro

2 tablespoons minced jalapeño chile

2 teaspoons fresh lime juice

In small bowl, combine cocktail sauce, cilantro, jalapeño, and lime juice until well blended. Cover and refrigerate up to 24 hours.

**EACH TABLESPOON:** About 18 calories, 0g protein, 4g carbohydrate, 0g total fat (0g saturated), 0mg cholesterol, 191mg sodium.

# Rémoulade Verte

**PREP:** 20 minutes ★ **MAKES** about ²/₃ cup

¹/₃ cup mayonnaise

2 tablespoons sour cream

3 tablespoons finely chopped dill pickle

1 tablespoon chopped fresh parsley

¾ teaspoon chopped fresh tarragon or
   ¹/₄ teaspoon dried tarragon

¹/₂ teaspoon chopped fresh chives

1 anchovy fillet, finely chopped

1 teaspoon capers, drained and chopped

1 teaspoon Dijon mustard

In small bowl, combine mayonnaise, sour cream, pickle, parsley, tarragon, chives, anchovy, capers, and mustard; stir until well blended. Cover and refrigerate up to 24 hours.

**EACH TABLESPOON:** About 61 calories, 0g protein, 0g carbohydrate, 6g total fat (1g saturated), 6mg cholesterol, 143mg sodium.

# Buffalo Chicken Wings

On an otherwise rather typical day in 1964, Teressa Bellissimo, owner of the Anchor Bar in Buffalo, New York, accidentally received too many chicken wings from one of her suppliers. She fried them, swished them in butter, spiced them up with hot sauce, and served the wings with her cooling blue-cheese dressing on the side. This recipe saves on some calories by broiling the wings instead of frying them.

**PREP:** 15 minutes ★ **BROIL:** 20 minutes
**MAKES** 18 appetizers

**4 ounces blue cheese, crumbled (1 cup)**

**½ cup sour cream**

**¼ cup mayonnaise**

**¼ cup milk**

**¼ cup chopped fresh parsley**

**1 tablespoon fresh lemon juice**

**½ teaspoon salt**

**3 pounds chicken wings (18 wings), tips discarded, if desired**

**3 tablespoons butter or margarine**

**¼ cup hot pepper sauce**

**1 medium bunch celery, cut into sticks**

1. Preheat broiler. In medium bowl, combine blue cheese, sour cream, mayonnaise, milk, parsley, lemon juice, and ¼ teaspoon salt. Cover and refrigerate.

2. Arrange chicken wings on rack in broiling pan; sprinkle with remaining ¼ teaspoon salt. Broil 5 inches from heat source 10 minutes. Turn wings; broil until golden, 10 to 15 minutes longer.

3. Meanwhile, in 1-quart saucepan, melt butter with hot pepper sauce over low heat, stirring occasionally; keep sauce warm.

4. In large bowl, toss wings with seasoned butter to coat well. Arrange chicken wings and celery on platter along with blue-cheese sauce and serve.

**EACH APPETIZER (WITHOUT WINGTIP):** About 169 calories, 10g protein, 3g carbohydrate, 13g total fat (5g saturated), 39mg cholesterol, 349mg sodium.

# Swiss Fondue

The name of this ever-popular hot cheese dish from Switzerland comes from the French word *fondre* (to melt). This classic version uses Swiss cheese, Gruyère cheese, and white wine to create the perfect balance of flavors.

**PREP** 15 minutes ★ **COOK** 15 minutes
**MAKES** 6 first-course servings

1 garlic clove, cut in half

1½ cups dry white wine

1 tablespoon kirsch or brandy

8 ounces Swiss or Emmental cheese, shredded (2 cups)

8 ounces Gruyère cheese, shredded (2 cups)

3 tablespoons all-purpose flour

⅛ teaspoon ground black pepper

pinch ground nutmeg

1 loaf (16 ounces) French bread, cut into 1-inch cubes

1. Rub inside of fondue pot or heavy nonreactive 2-quart saucepan with garlic; discard garlic. Pour wine into fondue pot. Heat over medium-low heat until very hot but not boiling; stir in kirsch.

2. Meanwhile, in medium bowl, toss Swiss cheese, Gruyère, and flour until mixed. Add cheese mixture, one handful at a time, to wine, stirring constantly and vigorously until cheese has melted and mixture is thick and smooth. If mixture separates, increase heat to medium, stirring just until smooth. Stir in pepper and nutmeg.

3. Transfer fondue to table; place over tabletop heater to keep hot, if you like. To eat, spear cubes of French bread onto long-handled fondue forks and dip into cheese mixture.

**EACH SERVING:** About 567 calories, 29g protein, 45g carbohydrate, 25g total fat (14g saturated), 76mg cholesterol, 689mg sodium.

# Deviled Eggs

Church suppers and picnics were extremely popular in the mid-twentieth century. At least one platter of deviled eggs was usually served.

**PREP:** 40 minutes ★ **MAKES** 24 deviled eggs

12 large eggs

¼ cup sliced pimientos, chopped

¼ cup low-fat mayonnaise dressing

1 tablespoon plus 1 teaspoon Dijon mustard

½ teaspoon ground red pepper (cayenne)

¼ teaspoon salt

1. In 3-quart saucepan, place eggs and enough *cold water* to cover by at least 1 inch; heat to boiling over high heat. Immediately remove saucepan from heat and cover tightly; let stand 15 minutes. Pour off hot water and run cold water over eggs to cool. Peel eggs.

2. Cut eggs lengthwise in half. Gently remove yolks and place in small bowl; with fork, finely mash yolks. Stir in pimientos, mayonnaise dressing, mustard, ground red pepper, and salt until well mixed.

3. Place egg-white halves in jelly-roll pan lined with paper towels (to prevent eggs from rolling). Spoon egg-yolk mixture into egg halves. Cover and refrigerate up to 4 hours.

**EACH DEVILED EGG:** About 45 calories, 3g protein, 1g carbohydrate, 3g total fat (1g saturated), 0g fiber, 106mg cholesterol, 100mg sodium.

# Chafing-Dish Meatballs

*(pictured on page 4)*

These mini meatballs, flavored with typical Mexican spices, make great party fare, especially when served from an elegant chafing dish.

**PREP:** 30 minutes ★ **COOK:** 40 minutes
**MAKES** 20 appetizer servings

1½ **pounds ground beef chuck**

¾ **cup plain dried bread crumbs**

1 **large egg**

3 **garlic cloves, minced**

1¼ **teaspoons salt**

½ **teaspoon ground black pepper**

¼ **cup water**

1 **can (28 ounces) plum tomatoes**

1 **chipotle chile in adobo**\*

2 **teaspoons vegetable oil**

1 **small onion, finely chopped**

1 **teaspoon ground cumin**

1 **cup canned chicken broth**

¼ **cup coarsely chopped fresh cilantro**

**1.** In large bowl, combine ground beef, bread crumbs, egg, one-third of garlic, 1 teaspoon salt, pepper, and water just until well blended but not overmixed. Shape mixture into ¾-inch meatballs, handling meat as little as possible.

**2.** In blender, at low speed, puree tomatoes with their juice and chipotle chile until smooth.

**3.** In nonreactive 5-quart Dutch oven, heat oil over medium heat. Add onion; cook, stirring often, until tender, about 5 minutes. Stir in cumin and remaining garlic; cook 30 seconds. Stir in tomato mixture, broth, and remaining ¼ teaspoon salt; heat to boiling over high heat.

**4.** Add meatballs; heat to boiling. Reduce heat and simmer, uncovered, 30 minutes. Transfer mixture to chafing dish and sprinkle with cilantro. Serve with cocktail picks.

\*Canned chipotle chiles in adobo (smoked jalapeño chiles in a vinegary marinade) are available in Hispanic markets and in the ethnic section of some supermarkets.

**EACH SERVING:** About 125 calories, 8g protein, 5g carbohydrate, 8g total fat (3g saturated), 31mg cholesterol, 310mg sodium.

## The Chafing Dish

Culinary historian Evan Jones cites the chafing dish as "an important part of American dining room paraphernalia as early as the mid-1800s." Delmonico's in New York City was one of the first restaurants to serve food in a sterling-silver covered dish set over a low flame. Other restaurants quickly followed suit. Chafing dishes often featured foods such as turkey tetrazzini: diced cooked turkey dressed up with a rich cream sauce. By the mid-1900s, chafing dishes started appearing on buffet tables everywhere to keep such popular foods as chicken à la king hot until guests helped themselves.

# Chapter 2

# Poultry

Americans have always craved chicken. The settlers quickly learned from the Native Americans how to slowly spit-roast chicken on greenwood sticks until "smoked to a turn." They also knew that a great stew pot was something to be cherished (the luckiest brides were given one) and that even the toughest fowl would become succulent after a few hours of simmering. They soon discovered that the broth was delicious and the pot even better when they added dumplings and cooked them until plump and tender.

Pit-barbecued chickens "arrived" in New York society when they made their debut at political rallies in the 1700s. As the economy cycled over the years, the poor became poorer and chickens became harder to come by. But that didn't stop folks from carving up this versatile, juicy bird whenever possible.

Nineteenth-century cookbooks offered few poultry recipes because of the greater availability of game and wild fowl. Eliza Leslie in her 1848 book *Directions for Cookery in Its Various Branches,* provides only ten poultry recipes. Her Baked Chicken Pie recipe advises: "It will be much improved by the addition of a quarter of a hundred oysters; or by interspersing the pieces of chicken with slices of cold boiled ham. You may add also some yolks of eggs boiled hard."

In the 1930s, Louisiana Senator Huey P. Long rallied the vote of the poor by promising them "a chicken in every pot." He used the example of Henri IV, who attempted to attract the support of the hungry by promising them a "chicken in [their] pot every Sunday."

Today almost everyone has a favorite way of preparing chicken. Southerners batter and fry it, smoke it, barbecue it, and turn it into fricassée, while Midwesterners love to roast it. Californians stir-fry their chicken, and Cajuns toss it into the gumbo pot. However you choose to serve the bird, you can count on chicken being on the menu—not just on Sunday but any day of the week.

# Sunday Roast Chicken

*(pictured on page 22)*

The Pilgrims brought domesticated chickens to our shores. Ever since then, roast chicken has been America's favorite Sunday dinner. This one is stuffed the simplest way, with just a couple of sprigs of fresh thyme tucked beneath the skin.

**PREP:** 20 minutes ★ **ROAST:** 1 hour
**MAKES** 4 main-dish servings

1 chicken (3½ pounds)
2 sprigs plus 1 tablespoon chopped
    fresh thyme
¾ teaspoon salt
¼ teaspoon coarsely ground black pepper
⅛ teaspoon ground allspice
1 jumbo onion (1 pound), cut into 12 wedges
¼ cup water
2 teaspoons olive oil
2 large Granny Smith apples, each cored
    and cut into quarters
2 tablespoons applejack brandy or Calvados
½ cup canned chicken broth

1. Preheat oven to 450°F. Remove giblets and neck from chicken; reserve for another use. Rinse chicken inside and out with cold running water; drain. Pat chicken dry with paper towels.

2. With fingertips, gently separate skin from meat on chicken breast. Place 1 thyme sprig under skin of each breast half. In cup, combine chopped thyme, salt, pepper, and allspice.

3. With chicken breast side up, lift wings up toward neck, then fold wing tips under back of chicken so wings stay in place. Tie legs together with string.

4. In medium roasting pan (14" by 10"), toss onion, chopped thyme mixture, water, and oil. Push onion mixture to sides of pan. Place chicken, breast side up, on small rack in the center of the roasting pan.

5. Roast chicken and onion mixture 40 minutes. Add apples to pan; roast about 20 minutes longer. Chicken is done when temperature on meat thermometer inserted in thickest part of thigh, next to body, reaches 175° to 180°F and juices run clear when thigh is pierced with tip of knife.

6. Transfer chicken to warm platter; let stand for 10 minutes to set juices for easier carving.

7. Meanwhile, remove rack from roasting pan. With slotted spoon, place onion mixture around chicken on platter. Skim and discard fat from drippings in pan. Add applejack to pan drippings; cook 1 minute over medium heat, stirring constantly. Add broth; heat to boiling. Serve pan-juice mixture with chicken. Remove skin from chicken before eating, if desired.

**EACH SERVING WITH SKIN:** About 589 calories, 49g protein, 22g carbohydrate, 33g total fat (9g saturated), 159mg cholesterol, 708mg sodium.

**EACH SERVING WITHOUT SKIN:** About 441 calories, 43g protein, 22g carbohydrate, 20g total fat (5g saturated), 132mg cholesterol, 686mg sodium.

# Herb-Roasted Chicken with Moist Bread Stuffing

One of the simplest (and best) ways to stuff a chicken is to mix up a bowl of old-fashioned bread stuffing. Many of the stuffings in the earliest cookbooks were bread stuffings, including two in the 1796 cookbook, *American Cookery*. All are listed under the heading "To Stuff and Roast a Turkey, or Fowl." Our stuffing recipe is rather straightforward: simple to mix up and very delicious. If you bake the stuffing outside the bird, tightly covering the dish with foil will keep it moist. This allows the stuffing to steam, somewhat imitating the way it cooks when inside a bird.

**PREP:** 10 minutes ★ **ROAST:** 1 hour
**MAKES** 4 main-dish servings

**1 chicken (3½ pounds)**
**3 tablespoons butter or margarine, softened**
**2 tablespoons chopped fresh chives**
**1 tablespoon chopped fresh parsley**
**¼ teaspoon salt**
**¼ teaspoon coarsely ground black pepper**
**Moist Bread Stuffing (at right)**

**1.** Preheat oven to 450°F. Remove giblets and neck from chicken; reserve for another use. Rinse chicken inside and out with cold running water; drain. Pat chicken dry with paper towels.

**2.** In cup, combine butter, chives, and parsley until very well blended. With fingertips, gently separate skin from meat on chicken breast and thighs. Rub herb mixture on meat under skin. Sprinkle salt and pepper on outside of chicken. With chicken breast side up, lift wings up toward neck, then fold wing tips under back of chicken so wings stay in place. Tie legs together with string.

**3.** Place chicken, breast side up, on rack in small roasting pan (13" by 9"). Roast chicken about 1 hour. Chicken is done when temperature on meat thermometer inserted in thickest part of chicken thigh, next to body, reaches 175° to 180°F and juices run clear when thigh is pierced with tip of knife.

**4.** Transfer chicken to warm platter; let stand 10 minutes to set juices for easier carving. Remove skin from chicken before eating, if desired. Serve with Moist Bread Stuffing.

**EACH SERVING WITH SKIN AND WITHOUT STUFFING:** About 469 calories, 48g protein, 0g carbohydrate, 30g total fat (10g saturated), 169mg cholesterol, 275mg sodium.

**EACH SERVING WITHOUT SKIN OR STUFFING:** About 321 calories, 41g protein, 0g carbohydrate, 16g total fat (6g saturated), 142 mg cholesterol, 254 mg sodium.

## Moist Bread Stuffing

In 4-quart saucepan, melt *4 tablespoons butter or margarine* over medium heat. Add *3 stalks celery*, coarsely chopped, and *1 small onion*, finely chopped; cook, stirring occasionally, until tender, about 12 minutes.

Remove saucepan from heat. Add *1 loaf (16 ounces) sliced firm white bread*, cut into ¾-inch cubes, *1 can (14½ ounces) chicken broth or 1¾ cups Old-Fashioned Chicken Broth* (page 49), *¼ cup chopped fresh parsley, ½ teaspoon dried thyme, ½ teaspoon salt, ¼ teaspoon dried sage,* and *¼ teaspoon coarsely ground black pepper*; toss to combine well.

Use to stuff chicken or serve in baking dish alongside chicken. Spoon stuffing into greased 9" by 9" baking dish; cover with foil. Bake in preheated 325°F oven until heated through, about 30 minutes. Makes about 5 cups stuffing.

**EACH ½ CUP STUFFING:** About 170 calories, 4g protein, 24g carbohydrate, 6g total fat (3g saturated), 13mg cholesterol, 473 mg sodium.

## Chicken, Baltimore Style

*Split a young chicken down the back as for broiling; take out the breastbone and cut off the tips of the wings. Cut into four pieces, dredge with salt and pepper, dip them in egg and crumbs and put in a pan with enough melted butter poured over each piece to moisten it. Roast in a hot oven about twenty minutes. Make a rich cream sauce or Bechamel sauce, pour on a dish and place the chicken on it. Garnish with slices of fried bacon.*

**—Good Housekeeping Everyday Cook Book**, 1903

# Barbecued Chicken, North Carolina Style

**B**arbecue is serious business in North Carolina. In the southern part of the state, cooks make a vinegar and mustard sauce; in the northeastern part, vinegar and pepper flakes are used. Only in the western part of the state will you find a barbecue sauce made with tomatoes, such as this one.

**PREP:** 15 minutes ★ **GRILL:** 25 minutes
**MAKES** 4 main-dish servings

1 can (15 ounces) tomato sauce

⅓ cup cider vinegar

3 tablespoons honey

2 tablespoons olive oil

1 teaspoon dry mustard

¾ teaspoon salt

¾ teaspoon ground black pepper

¼ teaspoon liquid smoke

1 chicken (3½ pounds), cut into 8 pieces and skin removed from all but wings

1. Prepare grill. In nonreactive 2-quart saucepan, combine tomato sauce, vinegar, honey, oil, dry mustard, ½ teaspoon salt, ½ teaspoon pepper, and liquid smoke; heat to boiling over medium heat. Boil 2 minutes; remove from heat. (Makes about
2 cups sauce.) Reserve 1 cup sauce to serve with the chicken.

2. Sprinkle chicken with remaining ¼ teaspoon each salt and pepper. Arrange chicken on grill over medium heat and grill, turning occasionally, 15 minutes. Continue to grill, turning and brushing chicken every 2 minutes with barbecue sauce, until juices run clear when thickest part of chicken is pierced with tip of knife, 10 to 15 minutes longer. Serve with reserved barbecue sauce.

**EACH SERVING WITHOUT EXTRA SAUCE:** About 491 calories, 49g protein, 11g carbohydrate, 27g total fat (7g saturated), 154mg cholesterol, 685mg sodium.

**EACH ¼ CUP SAUCE:** About 73 calories, 1g protein, 11g carbohydrate, 4g total fat (0g saturated), 0mg cholesterol, 540mg sodium.

# Chicken Fricassée

Chicken Fricassée, chicken that is fried and then stewed with chopped vegetables in a creamy white sauce, is a traditional Southern dish that is served in many homes. Enjoy it over hot buttery egg noodles.

**PREP:** 20 minutes ★ **COOK:** 1 hour
**MAKES** 6 main-dish servings

- 1 chicken (3½ pounds), cut into 8 pieces and excess fat removed
- ½ teaspoon salt
- 2 tablespoons butter or margarine
- 1 medium onion, coarsely chopped
- 2 stalks celery, sliced
- 2 carrots, peeled and sliced
- 2 tablespoons all-purpose flour
- 1 can (14½ ounces) chicken broth
- ½ cup heavy cream
- ⅛ teaspoon ground black pepper
- 1 tablespoon fresh lemon juice
- 2 tablespoons chopped fresh parsley
- 4 cups wide egg noodles, cooked as label directs

1. Sprinkle chicken with salt. In 12-inch skillet, melt butter over medium-high heat. Add chicken to skillet, in batches if necessary, and cook until browned, about 4 minutes per side. With slotted spoon, transfer chicken pieces to plate as they are browned. Pour off all but 3 tablespoons drippings from skillet.

2. Reduce heat to medium; add onion, celery, and carrots to skillet. Cook, stirring, until vegetables begin to soften, about 5 minutes.

3. Add flour and cook, stirring, 1 minute. Add chicken broth and cook, stirring until browned bits are loosened from bottom of pan. Return chicken and vegetables to skillet along with any juices on plate; heat to boiling. Reduce heat; cover and simmer, turning pieces occasionally, until chicken is tender, 40 to 45 minutes.

4. Transfer chicken to large, deep platter and cover with foil to keep warm. Add cream and pepper to sauce in skillet and whisk until blended; heat to boiling. Reduce heat and simmer until sauce thickens slightly, about 5 minutes. Stir in lemon juice. Pour sauce over chicken; sprinkle with parsley. Serve over hot noodles.

**EACH SERVING:** About 542 calories, 37g protein, 26g carbohydrate, 31g total fat (12g saturated), 163mg cholesterol, 628mg sodium.

# Country Captain

**N**ineteenth-century cookbook author Eliza Leslie attributes Country Captain to a British army captain who brought the recipe back to England after his tour of duty in India. Proud Georgians, however, disagree with this story. They claim the mysterious captain sailed into the famous port city of Savannah during the lucrative spice-trading period and entrusted his recipe to friends. Whatever its true origin, curried chicken in a tomato-based sauce has a blend of spices and flavors typical of East Indian cooking.

---

**PREP:** 30 minutes ★ **BAKE:** 1 hour
**MAKES** 8 main-dish servings

---

2 tablespoons plus 1 teaspoon vegetable oil

2 chickens (3½ pounds each), each cut into 8 pieces and skin removed from all but wings

2 medium onions, chopped

1 large Granny Smith apple, peeled, cored, and chopped

1 large green pepper, chopped

3 large garlic cloves, finely chopped

1 tablespoon grated, peeled fresh ginger

3 tablespoons curry powder

½ teaspoon coarsely ground black pepper

¼ teaspoon ground cumin

1 can (28 ounces) plum tomatoes in puree

1 can (14½ ounces) chicken broth or 1¾ cups Old-Fashioned Chicken Broth (page 49)

½ cup dark seedless raisins

1 teaspoon salt

¼ cup chopped fresh parsley

**1.** In nonreactive 8-quart Dutch oven, heat 2 tablespoons oil over medium-high heat until very hot. Add chicken, in batches, and cook until golden brown, about 5 minutes per side. With slotted spoon, transfer the chicken pieces to bowl as they are browned.

**2.** Preheat oven to 350°F. In same Dutch oven, heat remaining 1 teaspoon oil over medium-high heat. Add onions, apple, green pepper, garlic, and ginger; cook, stirring frequently, 2 minutes. Reduce heat to medium; cover and cook 5 minutes longer.

**3.** Stir in curry powder, black pepper, and cumin; cook 1 minute. Add tomatoes with their puree, broth, raisins, salt, and chicken. Heat to boiling over high heat; boil 1 minute. Cover and place in oven. Bake 1 hour. Sprinkle with parsley.

---

**EACH SERVING:** About 347 calories, 43g protein, 19g carbohydrate, 11g total fat (2g saturated), 133mg cholesterol, 825mg sodium.

# Chicken Cacciatore

Chicken cacciatore (hunter's style) is found on the menu of nearly every Italian-American restaurant. In Italy the dish was often prepared with freshly shot guinea fowl or pheasant, but in the States it is usually prepared with chicken. Use white mushrooms or other favorite varieties. Soft polenta or white rice makes a fine accompaniment to this dish.

**PREP:** 15 minutes ★ **COOK:** 45 minutes
**MAKES** 4 main-dish servings

2 tablespoons olive oil

1 chicken (3½ pounds), cut into 8 pieces and skin removed from all but wings

3 tablespoons all-purpose flour

1 medium onion, finely chopped

4 garlic cloves, crushed with garlic press

8 ounces mushrooms, trimmed and thickly sliced

1 can (14 to 16 ounces) tomatoes

½ teaspoon dried oregano, crumbled

½ teaspoon salt

¼ teaspoon dried sage

⅛ teaspoon ground red pepper (cayenne)

**1.** In nonstick 12-inch skillet, heat oil over medium-high heat until very hot. On waxed paper, coat chicken with flour, shaking off excess. Add chicken to skillet and cook until golden brown, about 3 minutes per side. With slotted spoon, transfer the chicken pieces to bowl or plate as they are browned.

**2.** Add onion and garlic to skillet. Reduce heat to medium-low and cook, stirring occasionally, until onion is tender, about 5 minutes. Add mushrooms; cook, stirring frequently, until just tender, about 3 minutes.

**3.** Add tomatoes with their juice, breaking them up with side of spoon. Add oregano, salt, sage, ground red pepper, and chicken; heat to boiling over high heat. Reduce heat; cover skillet and simmer until juices run clear when thickest part of chicken is pierced with tip of knife, about 25 minutes.

**4.** Transfer chicken to warm serving bowl. Spoon sauce over chicken.

**EACH SERVING:** About 371 calories, 44g protein, 18g carbohydrate, 13g total fat (3g saturated), 133mg cholesterol, 608mg sodium.

# Fried Chicken

Almost every Southerner has a special recipe for fried chicken. Some shake it to coat before frying, others batter it and a few crumb and bake it. Even cooks who agree that frying chicken is the best way to cook it disagree on the amount of oil that should be used. Some immerse their chicken completely in oil, while others fry it in just enough oil to reach halfway up the sides of the chicken. But all southern cooks agree on one thing: the best frying pan is a very well-seasoned cast-iron skillet, preferably one that has been handed down for generations.

**PREP:** 15 minutes
**COOK:** 20 minutes per batch plus 8 minutes
**MAKES** 8 main-dish servings

4 cups vegetable oil

1½ cups milk

2 cups all-purpose flour

1¾ teaspoons salt

1 teaspoon baking powder

¾ teaspoon ground black pepper

2 chickens (3 pounds each), each cut into 8 pieces

1 can (14½ ounces) chicken broth

1. In deep 12-inch skillet, heat oil over medium heat to 360°F on deep-fat thermometer. Meanwhile, pour ½ cup milk into pie plate. On waxed paper, combine 1¾ cups flour, 1 teaspoon salt, baking powder, and ½ teaspoon pepper. Dip chicken in milk, then coat well with flour mixture. Repeat, dipping and coating chicken twice.

2. Carefully place one-third of chicken pieces, skin side down, in hot oil. Cover and cook until underside of chicken is golden brown, about 5 minutes. Turn chicken, skin side up. Reduce heat to medium-low to maintain 300°F temperature. Cook 8 to 10 minutes longer for white meat; 13 to 15 minutes longer for dark meat, turning pieces every 4 to 5 minutes, until well browned on all sides and juices run clear when thickest part of chicken is pierced with tip of knife. With spatula or tongs, loosen chicken from skillet bottom. Transfer chicken pieces, skin side up, to paper towels to drain; keep warm. Repeat with remaining chicken.

3. Prepare gravy: Spoon 2 tablespoons oil from skillet into 2-quart saucepan. Over medium heat, with wooden spoon, stir remaining ¼ cup flour into oil until blended. Cook, stirring constantly, until flour is light brown. With wire whisk, gradually stir in remaining 1 cup milk, broth, remaining ¾ teaspoon salt, and remaining ¼ teaspoon pepper. Cook, stirring constantly, until gravy has thickened and boils. (Makes 2⅔ cups gravy). Serve gravy with chicken.

**EACH SERVING**: About 657calories, 46g protein, 26g carbohydrate, 40g total fat (9g saturated), 138mg cholesterol, 942mg sodium.

# Fried Chicken

Our thanks go to the Spaniards for bringing the first chickens to Florida by way of the West Indies. The English colonists also brought chickens to the New World, as they were easy to bring onboard ship and could be killed for food, if necessary. The English preferred baking and boiling chickens. It was the Scottish who enjoyed frying chickens and who likely shared this custom when they settled in the South. And just as likely, the African-American plantation cooks who were allowed to raise chickens observed this efficient cooking method and tried it out for themselves with great success.

In 1872, Annabella P. Hill offered a recipe for frying chicken in batter, instructing to first half-fry the chicken in boiling oil "then dip it in a thin fritter batter and finish the frying." She then recommended a water-based pan gravy to be served alongside. The Maryland custom of serving fried chicken with a creamy white gravy was recorded by B. C. Howard in *Fifty Years in a Maryland Kitchen*. In true Maryland fashion, the sauce is served in its own gravy dish alongside the chicken—not spooned on top.

More than one hundred years later, all agree that fried chicken is one of the South's most famous and beloved dishes.

# Creole Chicken and Sausage Gumbo

**S**ince the first pots of gumbo in the late eighteenth century, this Cajun stew was known for being a melting pot of flavors. *Gumbo* is derived from the African word *gombo* ("okra" in Bantu), which is fitting since okra is often used to thicken the pot. An authentic gumbo gets its rich flavor from a roux that is made in a skillet—usually black iron—by slowly browning flour in fat until it's deep brown.

**PREP:** 1 hour 10 minutes plus cooling
**COOK:** 1 hour 30 minutes
**MAKES** 18 cups or 12 main-dish servings

²⁄₃ cup all-purpose flour

1 chicken (3¹⁄₂ pounds), cut into 8 pieces

12 ounces fully cooked andouille or kielbasa sausage, cut into ¹⁄₂-inch-thick slices

6 cups canned chicken broth

1 can (6 ounces) tomato paste

2 cups water

2 medium onions, thinly sliced

12 ounces okra, sliced, or 1 package (10 ounces) frozen cut okra, thawed

1 large yellow pepper, chopped

4 stalks celery with leaves, cut into ¹⁄₄-inch-thick slices

³⁄₄ cup chopped fresh parsley

4 garlic cloves, thinly sliced

2 bay leaves

1¹⁄₂ teaspoons salt

1 teaspoon dried thyme

1 teaspoon ground red pepper (cayenne)

1 teaspoon ground black pepper

¹⁄₂ teaspoon ground allspice

1 can (14 to 16 ounces) tomatoes, drained and chopped

¹⁄₂ cup finely chopped green-onion tops

2 tablespoons distilled white vinegar

3 cups regular long-grain rice, cooked as label directs

**1.** Preheat oven to 375°F. Place flour in oven-safe 12-inch skillet (if skillet is not oven-safe, wrap handle with double layer of foil). Bake until flour begins to brown, about 25 minutes. Stir with wooden spoon, breaking up any lumps. Bake, stirring flour every 10 minutes, until it turns nut brown, about 35 minutes longer. Remove flour from oven and cool. Press flour through sieve to remove any lumps.

**2.** Heat nonreactive 8-quart Dutch oven over medium-high heat until very hot. Cook chicken, skin side down first, in batches, until golden brown, about 5 minutes per side. Transfer chicken pieces to large bowl as they are browned. Add sausage to Dutch oven and cook over medium heat, stirring constantly, until lightly browned, about 5 minutes. With slotted spoon, transfer sausage to chicken in bowl.

**3.** Reduce heat to medium-low. Gradually stir in browned flour, about 3 tablespoons at a time; cook, stirring constantly, 2 minutes.

**4.** Immediately add broth, stirring until browned bits are loosened from bottom of pan. Blend tomato paste with water; add to Dutch oven. Stir in onions, okra, yellow pepper, celery, ¹⁄₄ cup parsley, garlic, bay leaves, salt, thyme, ground red pepper, black pepper, and allspice. Add sausage, chicken, and tomatoes; heat to boiling over high heat. Reduce heat; simmer until liquid has thickened, about 1 hour.

**5.** Add remaining ¹⁄₂ cup parsley, green onions, and vinegar; heat through. Remove from heat; cover and let stand 10 minutes. Discard bay leaves. Serve gumbo in bowls over rice.

**EACH SERVING:** About 447 calories, 27g protein, 28g carbohydrate, 25g total fat (8g saturated), 107mg cholesterol, 1,357mg sodium.

# Plantation Chicken 'n' Dumplings

Fricassée a chicken, add homemade dumplings, and you have many a Southerner's favorite dish. Before baking powder was invented in the 1850s, Southerners rolled out dumpling dough, cut it into strips, and cooked it up flat, slippery, and chewy. Today dumplings are usually lowered into simmering broth by the spoonful and cooked until light and puffy.

**PREP:** 15 minutes ★ **COOK:** 1 hour
**MAKES** 6 main-dish servings

2 tablespoons vegetable oil

6 large bone-in chicken breast halves (3¼ pounds), skin removed

4 large carrots, peeled and cut into 1-inch pieces

2 large stalks celery, cut into ¼-inch-thick slices

1 medium onion, finely chopped

1 cup plus 2 tablespoons all-purpose flour

2 teaspoons baking powder

1 teaspoon salt

½ teaspoon dried thyme

1 large egg

1½ cups milk

2 cups water

1 can (14½ ounces) low-sodium chicken broth

¼ teaspoon ground black pepper

1 package (10 ounces) frozen peas

**1.** In 8-quart Dutch oven, heat 1 tablespoon oil over medium-high heat. Add 3 chicken breast halves and cook until golden brown, about 5 minutes per side. With slotted spoon, transfer chicken pieces to bowl as they are browned. Repeat with remaining chicken.

**2.** Add remaining 1 tablespoon oil to drippings in Dutch oven. Add carrots, celery, and onion; cook, stirring frequently, until vegetables are golden brown and tender, about 10 minutes.

**3.** Meanwhile, prepare dumplings: In small bowl, combine 1 cup flour, baking powder, ½ teaspoon salt, and thyme. In cup, with fork, beat the egg with ½ cup milk. Stir egg mixture into flour mixture until just blended.

**4.** Return chicken to Dutch oven; add water, broth, pepper, and remaining ½ teaspoon salt. Heat to boiling over high heat. Drop dumpling mixture by rounded tablespoons on top of chicken and vegetables to make 12 dumplings. Reduce heat; cover and simmer 15 minutes.

**5.** With slotted spoon, transfer dumplings, chicken, and vegetables to serving bowl; keep warm. Reserve broth in Dutch oven.

**6.** In cup, blend remaining 2 tablespoons flour with remaining 1 cup milk until smooth; stir into broth in Dutch oven. Heat to boiling over high heat; boil 1 minute to thicken slightly. Add peas and heat through. Pour sauce over the chicken and dumplings.

**EACH SERVING:** About 437 calories, 46g protein, 38g carbohydrate, 10g total fat (3g saturated), 137mg cholesterol, 951mg sodium.

# San Francisco Stir-Fry Chicken

During the Gold Rush, many Chinese immigrants cooked for the well-to-do, incorporating recipes and techniques from their homeland into the dishes they prepared. Stir-fries soon became a part of America's food melting pot.

**PREP:** 20 minutes ★ **COOK:** 10 minutes
**MAKES** 4 main-dish servings

- 1 pound skinless, boneless chicken breast halves
- 2 tablespoons soy sauce
- 2 tablespoons dry sherry
- 2 teaspoons cornstarch
- 2 teaspoons grated, peeled fresh ginger
- 1/4 teaspoon sugar
- 1/4 teaspoon crushed red pepper
- 2 tablespoons vegetable oil
- 6 green onions, cut into 2-inch pieces
- 1 green pepper, cut into 1/2-inch pieces
- 1 red pepper, cut into 1/2-inch pieces
- 1/4 cup dry-roasted unsalted peanuts

**1.** With knife held in position almost parallel to work surface, cut each chicken breast half crosswise into 1/8-inch-thick slices. In medium bowl, combine soy sauce, sherry, cornstarch, ginger, sugar, and crushed red pepper; add chicken, tossing to coat.

**2.** In 12-inch skillet, heat 1 tablespoon oil over medium-high heat until very hot. Add green onions and red and green peppers. Cook, stirring frequently (stir-frying), until vegetables are tender-crisp, 2 to 3 minutes. With slotted spoon, transfer vegetables to bowl.

**3.** Increase heat to high and add remaining 1 tablespoon oil to skillet; heat until very hot. Add chicken mixture and stir-fry until chicken loses its pink color throughout, 2 to 3 minutes. Return vegetables to skillet; heat through. To serve, transfer chicken and vegetables to warm platter and sprinkle with peanuts.

**EACH SERVING:** About 277 calories, 30g protein, 9g carbohydrate, 13g total fat (2g saturated), 66mg cholesterol, 594mg sodium.

## "All Aboard... Dinner is now being served!"

On November 3, 1842, the Baltimore & Ohio Railroad pulled out of Baltimore with company executives on board for a 178-mile ride. No stop was planned, so guests were served an elegant cold repast—the first meal to be served on a train. From then, dining cars rapidly caught on. By the year 1930 1,700 dining cars on 63 different railroads served over 80 million meals!

Each line had its specialties: fresh crab cakes on the Baltimore & Ohio, fresh trout on the Santa Fe, prime beefsteak on the Union Pacific, and big baked, stuffed potatoes on the Northern Pacific. There was traditional chicken pie on the Great Northern, lobster Newburg on the New York Central, sugar-cured ham on the Southern Pacific, and luscious fresh strawberry shortcake on the Pullman Company Line.

# Arroz con Pollo

In early-twentieth-century America, the increasing influence of Spanish culture gave rise to dishes such as arroz con pollo (chicken with rice). In true Spanish tradition, our skillet dish contains chicken, rice, peas, and tomatoes.

**PREP:** 15 minutes ★ **COOK:** 40 minutes
**MAKES** 4 main-dish servings

1 tablespoon vegetable oil

1 chicken (3½ pounds), cut into 8 pieces and skin removed from all but wings

1 medium onion, finely chopped

1 red pepper, chopped

1 garlic clove, finely chopped

⅛ teaspoon ground red pepper (cayenne)

1 cup regular long-grain rice

1 can (14½ ounces) chicken broth or 1¾ cups Old-Fashioned Chicken Broth (page 49)

¼ cup water

1 strip (3" by ½") lemon peel

¼ teaspoon dried oregano

¼ teaspoon salt

1 cup frozen peas

¼ cup chopped pimiento-stuffed olives (salad olives)

¼ cup chopped fresh cilantro

lemon wedges

1. In 5-quart Dutch oven, heat oil over medium-high heat until very hot. Add chicken and cook until golden brown, about 5 minutes per side. With slotted spoon, transfer chicken pieces to bowl as they are browned.

2. Reduce heat to medium. Add onion and red pepper to Dutch oven and cook until tender, about 5 minutes. Stir in garlic and ground red pepper; cook 30 seconds. Add rice; cook, stirring, 1 minute. Stir in broth, water, lemon peel, oregano,

salt, and chicken; heat to boiling. Reduce heat; cover and simmer until juices run clear when thickest part of chicken is pierced with tip of knife, about 20 minutes longer.

3. Stir in peas; cover and heat through. Remove from heat and let stand 5 minutes.

4. Transfer chicken to serving bowl. Sprinkle with olives and cilantro; serve with lemon wedges.

**EACH SERVING:** About 387 calories, 26g protein, 48g carbohydrate, 9g total fat (2g saturated), 81mg cholesterol, 927mg sodium.

# Chicken Enchiladas

The word *enchilada,* Spanish for "filled with chile," first appeared here in print in 1885. By the mid-twentieth century, enchiladas were a popular dish in Mexican-American restaurants. And hostesses discovered that it was the perfect buffet dish for casual at-home supper parties.

**PREP:** 15 minutes ★ **BAKE:** 20 minutes
**MAKES** 4 main-dish servings

1 can (4 to 4½ ounces) chopped mild green chiles, undrained

¾ cup loosely packed fresh cilantro leaves and stems

3 green onions, sliced

2 tablespoons sliced pickled jalapeño chiles

2 tablespoons fresh lime juice

¼ teaspoon salt

⅓ cup water

4 (8-inch) flour tortillas

8 ounces cooked chicken or turkey, shredded (2 cups)

¼ cup heavy or whipping cream

3 ounces Monterey Jack cheese, shredded (¾ cup)

**1.** Preheat the oven to 350°F. Grease an 11" by 7" baking dish.

**2.** In blender, combine chiles, cilantro, green onions, pickled jalapeños, lime juice, salt, and water; puree until smooth. Transfer to 8-inch skillet and heat to boiling over medium heat; boil 2 minutes. Dip one side of each tortilla in sauce; spread 1 tablespoon sauce over other (dry) side of tortillas; top with chicken. Roll up tortillas and place, seam side down, in prepared baking dish.

**3.** Stir cream into remaining sauce in skillet; spoon over filled tortillas. Cover with foil and bake 15 minutes. Remove foil; sprinkle with cheese and bake until cheese melts, about 5 minutes longer.

**EACH SERVING:** About 402 calories, 30g protein, 23g carbohydrate, 21g total fat (9g saturated), 106mg cholesterol, 713mg sodium.

# Chicken à la King

It's fitting that a dish as elegant as chicken à la king would have many wanting to claim it as their own. Some credit Foxhall Keene, son of Wall Street broker James R. Keene, for coming up with the idea, then asking Delmonico's to prepare it for him. He called it chicken à la Keene. Another tale credits Chef George Greenwald of New York's Brighton Beach Hotel with making it for the proprietors, Mr. and Mrs. E. Clark King III. And still another story suggests that Claridge's restaurant in London made the first chicken à la king for James R. Keene, when his horse won the 1881 Grand Prix. This famous dish was—and often still is—ladled from a silver chafing dish onto toast points, over rice, or into flaky patty shells.

**PREP:** 15 minutes ★ **COOK:** 20 minutes
**MAKES** 8 servings

6 tablespoons butter or margarine

8 ounces mushrooms, trimmed and sliced

¼ cup chopped green pepper

6 tablespoons all-purpose flour

3 cups half-and-half

4 cups cubed, cooked chicken or turkey

1 jar (4 ounces) chopped pimientos, drained

2 egg yolks

2 tablespoons medium-dry sherry

1 teaspoon salt

8 frozen patty shells, warmed as package directs

**1.** In 10-inch skillet, melt butter over medium heat. Add mushrooms and green pepper; cook, stirring, until tender, about 5 minutes.

**2.** Add flour and cook, stirring, 1 minute. Gradually stir in half-and-half. Cook, stirring constantly with wooden spoon, until sauce has thickened. Add chicken and pimientos. Heat to boiling, stirring often. Reduce heat to low; cover and simmer 5 minutes.

**3.** In cup, with fork, stir yolks until mixed; stir in ¼ cup sauce. Gradually pour yolk mixture into sauce, stirring vigorously until well blended and smooth. Cook, stirring, until sauce has thickened.

**4.** Stir in sherry and salt. Spoon chicken mixture into patty shells.

**EACH SERVING:** About 589 calories, 28g protein, 27g carbohydrate, 41g total fat (14g saturated), 172mg cholesterol, 662mg sodium.

# Brunswick Stew

Brunswick Counties in both North Carolina and Virginia lay claim to creating this famous southern stew. Most historians document 1828 as the year when Dr. Creed Haskins of the Virginia State Legislature asked Jimmy Matthews to stir up a batch of squirrel stew for a political rally. Over time, the squirrel has disappeared from the pot and been replaced by chicken or rabbit.

**PREP:** 30 minutes  ★  **COOK:** 40 minutes
**MAKES** 6 servings

3 slices bacon

1 chicken (3½ pounds), cut into 8 pieces

½ teaspoon dried thyme

½ teaspoon salt

1 medium onion, chopped

½ cup chopped carrot

½ cup chopped celery

1 tablespoon minced garlic

2 cans (14½ ounces each) stewed tomatoes

1 cup canned chicken broth

1 cup frozen baby lima beans

1 cup frozen cut okra

1 cup fresh or frozen corn kernels

dash Worcestershire sauce

dash hot pepper sauce

1. In nonreactive 6-quart Dutch oven, cook bacon over medium-high heat until crisp. With slotted spoon, transfer bacon to paper towels to drain. Crumble and set aside.

2. Sprinkle chicken with thyme and salt. Add chicken to drippings in Dutch oven, in batches if necessary; cook over medium-high heat until golden brown, about 3 minutes per side. With slotted spoon, transfer chicken pieces to bowl as they are browned.

3. Discard all but 1 tablespoon drippings from pan; reduce heat to medium. Add onion, carrot, and celery to Dutch oven; cook, stirring, 3 minutes. Stir in garlic; cook 30 seconds. Return chicken to pan. Stir in tomatoes and broth; heat to boiling. Reduce heat; cover and simmer until juices run clear when thickest part of chicken is pierced with tip of knife, about 30 minutes. Stir in lima beans, okra, and corn; cover and simmer 10 minutes. Stir in the bacon, Worcestershire, and the hot pepper sauce.

**EACH SERVING:** About 447 calories, 38g protein, 28g carbohydrate, 21g total fat (6g saturated), 107mg cholesterol, 843mg sodium.

# Chicken Curry

**I**n *The Virginia House-Wife,* Mary Randolph tells her readers how to make a dish of curry in the East Indian manner. In *Direction for Cookery,* Eliza Leslie includes a recipe for chicken curry that contains many of the spices used to make curry powder: "two table-spoonfuls of powdered ginger, one table-spoonful of fresh turmeric, a teaspoonful of ground black pepper; some mace, a few cloves, some cardamom seeds, and a little cayenne pepper with a small portion of salt."

**PREP:** 15 minutes plus cooling
**COOK:** 1 hour 15 minutes
**MAKES** 6 main-dish servings

1 chicken (3½ pounds), cut into 8 pieces

4 medium onions, finely chopped

2 carrots, peeled and finely chopped

2 stalks celery with leaves, finely chopped

8 parsley sprigs

1 lime

4 tablespoons butter or margarine

2 Granny Smith apples, peeled, cored, and chopped

3 garlic cloves, finely chopped

1 tablespoon curry powder

3 tablespoons all-purpose flour

½ cup half-and-half or light cream

⅓ cup golden raisins

2 tablespoons mango chutney, chopped

2 teaspoons minced, peeled fresh ginger

½ teaspoon salt

pinch ground red pepper (cayenne)

**1.** In 5-quart Dutch oven, combine chicken, one-fourth of onions, carrots, celery, and parsley sprigs with just enough *water* to cover. Heat to boiling over high heat. Reduce heat; partially cover and simmer, turning once, until chicken loses its pink color throughout, 25 to 30 minutes. With slotted spoon, transfer chicken to bowl. When cool enough to handle, remove and discard skin and bones; with hands, shred chicken.

**2.** Meanwhile, strain broth through sieve into bowl; discard vegetables. Return broth to Dutch oven. Heat to boiling; boil broth until reduced to 2 cups. Skim and discard fat from broth; reserve broth.

**3.** From lime, grate ½ teaspoon peel and squeeze 5 teaspoons juice; reserve.

**4.** In 12-inch skillet, melt butter over medium heat. Add remaining three-fourths of onions, apples, garlic, and curry powder; cook, stirring, until apples are tender, about 10 minutes. Sprinkle with flour, stirring to blend. Gradually add 2 cups reserved broth, stirring constantly until broth has thickened and boils. Stir in reserved lime peel and juice, half-and-half, raisins, chutney, ginger, salt, and ground red pepper. Reduce heat; simmer, stirring occasionally, 5 minutes. Add chicken and heat through.

**EACH SERVING:** About 379 calories, 30g protein, 33g carbohydrate, 14g total fat (7g saturated), 117mg cholesterol, 449mg sodium.

# Old-Time Turkey with Giblet Gravy

Colonial America had an affinity for turkey. Some Native Americans caught wild turkey; others domesticated it. The name appears to be a corruption of the word *furkee,* which is Native American for "turkey." For a moist bird, we prefer to bake the stuffing separately.

**PREP:** I hour ★ **ROAST:** 3 hours 45 minutes
**MAKES** I4 main-dish servings

**Country Sausage and Corn Bread Stuffing (page 42)**

**I turkey (I4 pounds)**

**I½ teaspoons salt**

**½ teaspoon coarsely ground black pepper**

**Giblet Gravy (page 42)**

**I.** Prepare Country Sausage and Corn Bread Stuffing and set aside.

**2.** Preheat oven to 325°F. Remove giblets and neck from turkey; reserve for making Giblet Gravy. Rinse turkey inside and out with cold running water and drain well; pat dry with paper towels.

**3.** Loosely spoon some stuffing into neck cavity. Fold neck skin over stuffing; fasten neck skin to turkey back with one or two skewers.

**4.** Loosely spoon remaining corn bread stuffing into body cavity (bake any leftover stuffing in small covered casserole during last 30 minutes of roasting time). Fold skin over cavity opening; skewer closed, if necessary. Tie legs and tail together with string; push drumsticks under band of skin, or use stuffing clamp. Secure wings to body with string, if desired.

**5.** Place turkey, breast side up, on rack in large roasting pan (17" by 11½"). Sprinkle salt and pepper on outside of turkey. Cover with loose tent of foil.

**6.** Roast about 3 hours 45 minutes. Start checking for doneness during last hour of roasting. Place stuffing (in casserole) in oven after turkey has roasted 3 hours. Bake until heated through, about 30 minutes.

**7.** To brown turkey, remove foil during last hour of roasting; baste occasionally with pan drippings. Turkey is done when temperature on meat thermometer inserted in thickest part of thigh, next to body, reaches 180°F and juices run clear when thickest part of thigh is pierced with tip of knife. (Breast temperature should be 170°F; stuffing temperature 160° to 165°F.)

**8.** While turkey is roasting, prepare giblets and neck for Giblet Gravy.

**9.** Transfer turkey to large platter; keep warm. Let stand at least 15 minutes to set juices for easier carving. Prepare Giblet Gravy.

**I0.** Serve turkey with stuffing and gravy.

**EACH SERVING WITHOUT SKIN, STUFFING, OR GRAVY:** About I43 calories, 25g protein, 0g carbohydrate, 4g total fat (Ig saturated), 65mg cholesterol, I45mg sodium.

## Country Sausage and Corn Bread Stuffing

Heat 12-inch skillet over medium-high heat until very hot. Add *1 pound pork sausage meat* and cook, breaking up sausage with side of spoon, until browned, about 10 minutes. With slotted spoon, transfer sausage to large bowl. Discard all but 2 tablespoons sausage drippings.

Add *4 tablespoons butter or margarine, 3 stalks celery*, coarsely chopped, *1 large onion (12 ounces)*, coarsely chopped, and *1 red pepper*, coarsely chopped, to skillet. Cook, stirring occasionally, until vegetables are golden brown and tender, about 10 minutes. Stir in *1 can (14½ ounces) chicken broth or 1¾ cups Old-Fashioned Chicken Broth* (page 49), *½ teaspoon coarsely ground black pepper,* and *¾ cup water*. Heat to boiling, stirring until browned bits are loosened from bottom of skillet.

Add vegetable mixture, *1 package (14 to 16 ounces) corn bread stuffing mix*, and *¼ cup chopped fresh parsley* to sausage in bowl; stir to combine well. Use to stuff turkey or serve in baking dish. Spoon stuffing into greased 13" by 9" baking dish. Cover with foil. Makes about 12 cups stuffing.

---

**EACH ½ CUP STUFFING:** About 137 calories, 4g protein, 15g carbohydrate, 7g total fat (2g saturated), 13mg cholesterol, 414mg sodium.

## Giblet Gravy

In 3-quart saucepan, combine *gizzard, heart, neck,* and *4 cups water;* heat to boiling over high heat. Reduce heat; cover and simmer 45 minutes. Add *liver* and cook 15 minutes longer. Strain giblet broth through sieve into large bowl. Pull meat from neck; discard bones. Cover and refrigerate meat and broth separately.

## Giving Thanks since 1621

In 1621, in Plymouth, Massachusetts, the colonists had survived their first year in the New World, so Governor William Bradford decided it was "time to feast." He invited Chief Massasoit and ninety-two braves of the Wampanoag tribe to join them "to give thanks to God." They feasted on venison (supplied by their guests), roast duck and goose, clams, oysters, eel, leeks, watercress, corn bread, popcorn, wild plums, and homemade sweet wine. Historians believe that wild turkey may have been served at this first Thanksgiving, as "the governor sent four men on fowling" to bring back food for the feast. Some say the celebration lasted as long as three days. On the next recorded Day of Thanks at the Plymouth Colony on July 30, 1623, turkey was definitely served, along with cranberries and pumpkin pie.

On November 26, 1789, George Washington proclaimed the first national Thanksgiving observance. And in the nineteenth century, Sarah Josepha Hale, forty years the editor of Godey's Lady's Book, lobbied president Lincoln to make Thanksgiving a national holiday. Centuries later, the tradition continues.

To make gravy, remove rack from roasting pan. Strain *pan drippings* through sieve into 4-cup glass measuring cup or medium bowl. Add *1 cup giblet broth* to hot roasting pan and heat to boiling, stirring until browned bits are loosened from bottom of pan; add to drippings in measuring cup. Let stand until fat separates from meat juice, about 1 minute. Spoon *2 tablespoons fat* from drippings into 2-quart saucepan; skim and discard any remaining fat. Add *remaining giblet broth* and enough *water* to drippings in cup to equal 3 cups.

Heat fat in saucepan over medium heat; stir in *2 tablespoons all-purpose flour* and *½ teaspoon salt*. Cook, stirring, until flour turns golden brown. With wire whisk, gradually whisk in *meat-juice mixture* and cook, whisking, until gravy has thickened slightly and boils; boil 1 minute. Stir in reserved giblets and neck meat; heat through. Pour gravy into gravy boat. Makes about 3½ cups gravy.

**EACH ¼ CUP GRAVY:** About 70 calories, 7g protein, 2g carbohydrate, 3g total fat (1g saturated), 0g fiber, 63mg cholesterol, 140mg sodium.

# Turkey Tetrazzini

In the early 1900s, chicken Tetrazzini was created and named after the Italian opera singer Luisa Tetrazzini, who was extremely popular at that time. By 1923 (and perhaps in an even earlier edition), *The Original Boston Cooking-School Cook Book* contained a recipe for a turkey, mushroom, and spaghetti dish baked in a rich cream sauce. With the rising popularity of ethnic food during the twentieth century, this dish became a frequent offering on Italian-American restaurant menus.

**PREP:** 30 minutes  ★  **BAKE:** 30 minutes
**MAKES** 6 main-dish servings

4 tablespoons butter or margarine

¼ cup all-purpose flour

2¾ cups canned chicken broth

¼ cup dry white wine

¼ teaspoon dried thyme

pinch ground nutmeg

½ cup heavy or whipping cream

1 small onion, chopped

10 ounces mushrooms, trimmed and cut into quarters

8 ounces linguine, cooked as label directs

12 ounces cooked turkey, coarsely chopped (3 cups)

3 tablespoons freshly grated Parmesan cheese

**1.** Preheat oven to 400°F. In 2-quart saucepan, melt 3 tablespoons butter over medium heat. Stir in flour and cook, stirring occasionally, 3 minutes. With wire whisk, whisk in broth, wine, thyme, and nutmeg until smooth. Heat to boiling, whisking constantly. Reduce heat and simmer, whisking frequently, 5 minutes. Stir in cream; set sauce aside.

**2.** In 10-inch skillet, melt remaining 1 tablespoon butter over medium heat. Add onion and cook until tender, about 5 minutes. Add mushrooms and cook, stirring occasionally, 10 minutes longer.

**3.** In 2- to 2½-quart baking dish, combine linguine, mushroom mixture, and turkey. Stir in sauce; sprinkle with Parmesan. Bake until bubbly, about 30 minutes.

**EACH SERVING:** About 458 calories, 30g protein, 37g carbohydrate, 21g total fat (11g saturated), 104mg cholesterol, 648mg sodium.

# Turkey Potpie with Cornmeal Crust

**A** chicken pie recipe appears in the 1796 book *American Cookery* by Amelia Simmons, the first cookbook written by an American and printed here. Her recipe begins with: "Roll one inch thick pastry No. 8 and cover a deep dish." The chicken pieces and butter are layered and covered with another layer of thick pastry. It is then baked for one and a half hours. Our recipe uses turkey instead of chicken because we love the richer taste of turkey. You could substitute an equal amount of chicken, if you prefer.

**PREP:** 30 minutes ★ **BAKE:** 35 minutes
**MAKES** 10 main-dish servings

- 1 tablespoon vegetable oil
- 1 medium rutabaga (1 pound), peeled and cut into ½-inch pieces
- 3 carrots, peeled and cut into ½-inch pieces
- 1 large onion (12 ounces), chopped
- 1 pound all-purpose potatoes (3 medium), peeled and cut into ½-inch pieces
- 2 large stalks celery, chopped
- ¾ teaspoon salt
- 1 pound cooked turkey or chicken, cut into ½-inch pieces (4 cups)
- 1 package (10 ounces) frozen peas
- 1 can (14½ ounces) chicken broth
- 1 cup milk
- ¼ cup all-purpose flour
- ¼ teaspoon ground black pepper
- ⅛ teaspoon dried thyme
- Cornmeal Crust (at right)
- 1 large egg, beaten

**1.** Prepare potpie filling: In nonstick 12-inch skillet, heat oil over medium-high heat. Add rutabaga, carrots, and onion; cook, stirring, 10 minutes.

Stir in potatoes, celery, and ½ teaspoon salt; cook, stirring frequently, until rutabaga is tender-crisp, about 10 minutes longer. Spoon into 13" by 9" baking dish; add turkey and peas.

**2.** In 2-quart saucepan, heat broth to boiling. In small bowl, blend milk and flour until smooth. Stir milk-flour mixture into broth; add pepper, thyme, and remaining ¼ teaspoon salt. Heat to boiling over high heat, stirring. Stir sauce into chicken-vegetable mixture in baking dish.

**3.** Prepare Cornmeal Crust. Preheat oven to 425°F.

**4.** On lightly floured surface, with floured rolling pin, roll dough into rectangle about 4 inches larger than top of baking dish. Place dough rectangle over filling. Trim edge, leaving 1-inch overhang. Fold overhang under and flute edge. Brush crust with some beaten egg. If desired, reroll trimmings; cut into decorative shapes to garnish top of pie. Brush dough cutouts with egg. Cut several slits in crust to allow steam to escape during baking.

**5.** Place potpie on foil-lined cookie sheet to catch any overflow during baking. Bake potpie until crust is golden brown and filling is hot and bubbling, 35 to 40 minutes. During last 10 minutes of baking, cover edges of crust with foil to prevent overbrowning.

**EACH SERVING:** About 416 calories, 21g protein, 42g carbohydrate, 18g total fat (5g saturated), 60mg cholesterol, 644mg sodium.

## Cornmeal Crust

In large bowl, combine *1½ cups all purpose-flour, ¼ cup cornmeal,* and *¾ teaspoon salt.* With pastry blender or two knives used scissor-fashion, cut in *⅔ cup vegetable shortening* until flour mixture resembles coarse crumbs. Sprinkle *6 to 7 tablespoons cold water,* 1 tablespoon at a time, over flour mixture, mixing with fork after each addition until dough is just moist enough to hold together.

# Rock Cornish Hens with Wild Rice Stuffing

**B**y the mid-nineteenth century, poultry was so readily available that the "only on Sundays" chicken became plentiful enough to eat every day. In 1965, Donald John Tyson crossed the White Rock with a Cornish game cock, creating a juicy, tasty little bird that weighed between one and two pounds. His specialty item commanded a higher price than regular chickens and was ready for market in thirty days instead of the forty-two days chicken took.

**PREP:** 1 hour ★ **ROAST:** 50 minutes
**MAKES** 8 main-dish servings

**Wild Rice and Mushroom Stuffing (at right)**

**4 Cornish hens (1½ pounds each)**

**¼ cup honey**

**2 tablespoons fresh lemon juice**

**2 tablespoons dry vermouth**

**½ teaspoon salt**

**¼ teaspoon dried thyme**

**1.** Prepare Wild Rice and Mushroom Stuffing; set aside.

**2.** Preheat oven to 400°F. Remove giblets and necks from hens; reserve for another use. With poultry shears, cut each hen lengthwise in half. Rinse hen halves with cold running water; pat dry with paper towels.

**3.** With fingertips, carefully separate skin from meat on each hen half to form pocket; spoon some stuffing into each pocket. Place hens, skin side up, in two large roasting pans (17" by 11½").

**4.** In small bowl, combine honey, lemon juice, vermouth, salt, and thyme. Brush hens with some honey mixture. Roast hens, basting occasionally with remaining honey mixture and drippings in pan, until juices run clear when thickest part of thigh is pierced with tip of knife, about 50 minutes, rotating pans between upper and lower oven racks halfway through roasting.

**EACH SERVING:** About 521 calories, 37g protein, 30g carbohydrate, 28g total fat (8g saturated), 191mg cholesterol, 554mg sodium.

## Wild Rice and Mushroom Stuffing

In 3-quart saucepan, melt *1 tablespoon butter or margarine* over medium heat. Add *1 small onion, finely chopped,* and cook until tender, about 5 minutes. Add *1 pound mushrooms,* trimmed and chopped, and cook, stirring occasionally, until tender, about 10 minutes.

Meanwhile, rinse *1 cup (6 ounces) wild rice;* drain. To mixture in saucepan, add wild rice, *1 can (14½ ounces) chicken broth or 1¾ cups Old-Fashioned Chicken Broth* (page 49), and *¼ teaspoon salt;* heat to boiling over high heat. Reduce heat; cover and simmer until rice is tender and all liquid has been absorbed, 45 to 50 minutes. Stir in *¼ cup chopped fresh parsley.* Makes 4 cups stuffing.

# Holiday Goose
# à l'Orange

In the early days in the South, many a bride received a pair of down geese as a special gift. They provided stuffing for heirloom feather beds and pillows and quills for writing. Popular, too, were recipes for roasted goose for special occasions, such as one from the 1870s that begins: "On the day before Christmas, kill a fat goose and dress it."

**PREP:** 30 minutes ★ **ROAST:** 4 hours 30 minutes
**MAKES** 10 main-dish servings

---

**1 fresh or frozen (thawed) goose
(about 12 pounds)**

**5 medium oranges, each cut in half**

**1 bunch fresh thyme**

**4 bay leaves**

**½ teaspoon dried thyme**

**1¼ teaspoons salt**

**½ teaspoon coarsely ground black pepper**

**3 tablespoons orange-flavored liqueur**

**2 tablespoons cornstarch**

**½ cup orange marmalade**

**1.** Preheat oven to 400°F. Remove giblets and neck from goose; reserve for another use. Trim and discard fat from body cavity and any excess skin. Rinse goose inside and out with cold running water and drain well; pat dry with paper towels. With goose, breast side up, lift wings up toward neck, then fold wing tips under back of goose so wings stay in place. Place 6 orange halves, thyme sprigs, and bay leaves in body cavity. Tie legs and tail together with kitchen string. Fold neck skin over back. With two-tine fork, prick goose skin in several places to drain fat during roasting.

**2.** Place goose, breast side up, on rack in large roasting pan (17" by 11½"). In cup, combine dried thyme, 1 teaspoon salt, and pepper; rub mixture over goose. Cover goose and roasting pan with foil. Roast 1 hour 30 minutes. Turn oven control to 325°F; roast 2 hours longer.

**3.** Meanwhile, in small bowl, from remaining 4 orange halves, squeeze ¾ cup juice. Stir in 1 tablespoon liqueur, cornstarch, and remaining ¼ teaspoon salt; set aside. In cup, mix orange marmalade with remaining 2 tablespoons liqueur. Remove foil and roast goose 45 minutes. Remove goose from oven and turn oven control to 450°F. Brush marmalade mixture over goose. Roast goose until skin is golden brown and crisp, about 10 minutes longer. Transfer goose to warm platter; let stand 15 minutes to set juices for easier carving.

**4.** Prepare sauce: Remove rack from roasting pan. Strain pan drippings through sieve into 8-cup measuring cup or large bowl. Let stand until fat separates from meat juice; skim and reserve fat for another use (there should be about 5 cups fat). Measure meat juice; if necessary, add enough *water* to meat juice to equal 1 cup. Return meat juice to pan and add reserved orange-juice mixture. Heat sauce to boiling over medium heat, stirring; boil 1 minute. Serve sauce with goose. Remove skin before eating, if desired.

---

**EACH SERVING OF GOOSE WITHOUT SKIN OR SAUCE:** About 460 calories, 50g protein, 12g carbohydrate, 25g total fat (8g saturated), 170mg cholesterol, 345mg sodium.

**EACH TABLESPOON ORANGE SAUCE:** About 5 calories, 0g protein, 1g carbohydrate, 0g total fat, 0mg cholesterol, 20mg sodium.

# Chapter 3

# Meat

Meat has always been a major part of the American diet. Early on, wild game was plentiful, and the settlers, took full advantage. When supplies began to dwindle, the colonists began raising pork, mutton, and beef, with pork the most plentiful and popular of the three. The smokehouse supplied succulent smoked hams and slabs of bacon. Meat was served at least once a day: rib-sticking stews, New England boiled-beef-and-vegetables, wursts and sauerkraut in German settlements in New York and Pennsylvania, and hog and hominy suppers in the South.

During the nineteenth century, known as the "bountiful harvest" century, Americans moved West, built ranches, and raised cattle on the open range. Beef and other meats were packed into railroad cars and transported to cities and towns nationwide.

Simple, straightforward preparations, such as frying, braising, stewing, and roasting, remained popular. But with the greater availability of meat in the early twentieth century, homemakers became more creative, inspired by women's magazines and food manufacturers who provided hostesses with never-fail and elegant ways to prepare and present dishes, such as crown roast of pork stuffed with a savory sausage dressing.

During the depression, meat was often stretched into meat-and-potato pies, ground-meat casseroles, and vegetable-meat stews. After World War II, however, meat dishes with European, Middle Eastern, and Southeast Asian influences were enjoyed.

In the 1960s, meats went gourmet. This was due in large part to Julia Child and her entertaining, instructive television series *The French Chef*. With her help, housewives across America wowed guests with specialties such as Beef Wellington and Beef Bourguignon. But by the end of the century, health concerns brought leaner beef and pork, with hardly a trace of visible fat, to the market. As the century came to a close, celebrity chefs taught us how to bring back the flavor by blackening, marinating, brining, and dry rubbing almost every type of meat, thereby continuing America's love of meat.

◄ *Roasted Prime Ribs of Beef*

# Roasted Prime Ribs of Beef

*(pictured on page 48)*

In the late nineteenth century, beef was often on the menu—and it still is. In our recipe, roast beef is served the most impressive way, as roasted prime ribs of beef with Yorkshire Pudding. The English colonists loved pudding and often served Yorkshire Pudding with their beef roast. The recipe for this savory pan pudding hasn't changed much. The key is the delectable pan drippings that are stirred into the custard mixture. James Beard advises in *American Cookery:* "The first three ribs are considered the best, although in my opinion, a larger roast is preferable—the first five ribs, well trimmed, so that carving will be easy."

**PREP:** 15 minutes ★ **ROAST:** 2 hours 30 minutes
**MAKES** 8 main-dish servings

1 (3-rib) beef rib roast from small end
  (5½ pounds), trimmed and chine bone
  removed

1 teaspoon salt

½ teaspoon dried rosemary, crumbled

¼ teaspoon ground black pepper

1 lemon

1½ cups fresh bread crumbs
  (about 3 slices bread)

½ cup chopped fresh parsley

2 garlic cloves, finely chopped

1 tablespoon olive oil

2 tablespoons Dijon mustard

Creamy Horseradish Sauce (at right)

Yorkshire Pudding (opposite)

1. Preheat oven to 325°F. In medium roasting pan (14" by 10"), place rib roast, fat side up. In small bowl, combine salt, rosemary, and pepper. Use to rub on roast.

2. Roast until meat thermometer inserted in thickest part of meat (not touching bone) reaches 140°F, about 2 hours 30 minutes. Internal temperature of meat will rise to 145°F (medium) upon standing. Or roast until desired degree of doneness.

3. About 1 hour before roast is done, prepare bread coating: From lemon, grate ½ teaspoon peel and squeeze 1 tablespoon juice. In small bowl, combine lemon peel and juice, bread crumbs, parsley, garlic, and oil. Remove roast from oven; evenly spread mustard on top of roast. Press bread-crumb mixture onto mustard-coated roast. Roast 1 hour longer or until desired doneness.

4. Meanwhile, prepare Creamy Horseradish Sauce.

5. When roast is done, transfer to warm large platter and let stand 15 minutes to set the juices for easier carving.

6. Meanwhile, prepare Yorkshire Pudding. Serve alongside roast and Creamy Horseradish Sauce.

**EACH SERVING:** About 352 calories, 39g protein, 5g carbohydrate, 18g total fat (7g saturated), 112mg cholesterol, 508mg sodium.

## Creamy Horseradish Sauce

In small bowl, combine *1 bottle (6 ounces) white horseradish,* drained, *½ cup mayonnaise, 1 teaspoon sugar,* and *½ teaspoon salt.* Whip *½ cup heavy or whipping cream;* fold into horseradish mixture. Makes about 1⅔ cups.

**EACH TABLESPOON:** About 49 calories, 0g protein, 1g carbohydrate, 5g total fat (2g saturated), 9mg cholesterol, 74mg sodium.

## Yorkshire Pudding

Turn oven control to 450°F. In medium bowl, with wire whisk, combine *1½ cups all-purpose flour* and *¾ teaspoon salt*. Add *1½ cups milk* and *3 large eggs,* beaten. Beat until smooth. Pour *3 tablespoons drippings* from roast beef pan into 13" by 9" baking pan; bake 2 minutes. Remove pan from oven; pour batter over drippings. Bake until puffed and lightly browned, about 25 minutes. Cut into squares. Makes 8 accompaniment servings.

**EACH SERVING:** About 183 calories, 6g protein, 20g carbohydrate, 8g total fat (4g saturated), 90mg cholesterol, 246mg sodium.

# Roasted Beef Tenderloin

The most tender of all cuts of beef—the tenderloin—has very little fat. Until the 1900s, the traditional way to prepare beef tenderloin was to marinate and then roast it. It was often larded (filled with strips of pork fat) to keep it moist.

**PREP:** 20 minutes plus marinating
**ROAST:** 40 minutes
**MAKES** 10 main-dish servings

## MARINADE & BEEF

2 cups dry red wine

2 tablespoons olive oil

1 medium onion, sliced

1 tablespoon chopped fresh rosemary leaves

2 garlic cloves, crushed with garlic press

2 bay leaves

1 whole beef tenderloin (about 4 pounds),*
   trimmed

¼ cup cracked black peppercorns

## HORSERADISH-TARRAGON SAUCE

⅔ cup mayonnaise

½ cup sour cream

2 to 3 tablespoons chopped fresh
   tarragon leaves

2 tablespoons bottled white horseradish,
   drained

1 tablespoon Dijon mustard

**1.** Prepare marinade: In jumbo (2-gallon) ziptight plastic bag, combine red wine, oil, onion, rosemary, garlic, and bay leaves. Add tenderloin, turning to coat. Seal bag, pressing out as much air as possible. Place bag in shallow baking dish; refrigerate at least 4 hours or overnight, turning bag occasionally.

**2.** Preheat oven to 425°F. Remove meat from marinade; turn thinner end of meat under to make meat an even thickness. With string, tie tenderloin at 2-inch intervals to help hold its shape. Place peppercorns on waxed paper. Press tenderloin into peppercorns, turning to coat.

**3.** Place tenderloin on rack in large roasting pan (17" by 11½"); roast until meat thermometer inserted in center of meat reaches 140°F, 40 to 45 minutes. Internal temperature of meat will rise to 145°F (medium) upon standing. Or roast until desired doneness. Transfer tenderloin to warm large platter; let stand 10 minutes to set juices for easier slicing.

**4.** Meanwhile, prepare horseradish-tarragon sauce: In small bowl, combine mayonnaise, sour cream, tarragon, horseradish, and mustard; stir until well blended. Cover beef and refrigerate if not serving right away.

**5.** To serve, remove string and cut tenderloin into slices. Serve with horseradish-tarragon sauce.

*If you buy an untrimmed tenderloin, it should weigh 6 to 6½ pounds to yield about 4 pounds trimmed.

**EACH SERVING WITH SAUCE:** About 495 calories, 44g protein, 3g carbohydrate, 34g total fat (10g saturated), 137mg cholesterol, 250mg sodium.

# Steak Diane

If you were lucky enough to dine at New York City's '21' Club in the late 1940s, (known as the '21' back then) you would likely have seen this steak (with its flaming brandy sauce) being served from a gleaming copper chafing dish.

**PREP:** 10 minutes ★ **COOK:** 20 minutes
**MAKES** 4 main-dish servings

2 beef rib-eye steaks, ¾ inch thick
   (about 12 ounces each), trimmed

salt

ground black pepper

4 tablespoons butter or margarine

¼ cup brandy

2 small shallots, minced

3 tablespoons chopped fresh chives

½ cup dry sherry

1. With meat mallet or with rolling pin, between two sheets of plastic wrap or waxed paper, pound steaks to ¼-inch thickness. Sprinkle both sides of steaks with salt and pepper.

2. In chafing dish or 12-inch skillet, melt 2 table-spoons butter over high heat. Add 1 steak; cook until browned, 3 to 4 minutes per side.

3. Pour 2 tablespoons brandy over steak and carefully ignite with match. When flaming stops, stir in half of shallots and half of chives. Cook, stirring constantly, until shallots are tender, about 1 minute. Add ¼ cup sherry; heat through.

4. Place steak on warm dinner plate and pour one-fourth of sherry mixture over. Keep warm. Repeat with remaining rib-eye steak.

**EACH SERVING:** About 377 calories, 27g protein, 2g carbohydrate, 23g total fat (11g saturated), 110mg cholesterol, 205mg sodium.

# Filet Mignon with Béarnaise Sauce

Filet mignon made its debut at New York's Architectural League in 1899. In this recipe, the filet is accompanied by a traditional béarnaise sauce: a thick hollandaise made with tarragon vinegar and white wine instead of lemon juice.

**PREP:** 5 minutes ★ **COOK:** 25 minutes
**MAKES** 4 main-dish servings

Béarnaise Sauce (below)

4 beef tenderloin steaks (filet mignon), 1½
   inches thick (6 ounces each), trimmed

½ teaspoon salt

¼ teaspoon coarsely ground black pepper

1 tablespoon olive oil

1. Prepare Béarnaise Sauce; keep warm.

2. Sprinkle steaks with salt and pepper. In nonstick 12-inch skillet, heat oil over high heat until very hot. Add steaks and cook, without turning, until browned, about 7 minutes. Turn steaks and cook 7 minutes longer for medium-rare or until desired doneness. Transfer to plates; keep warm.

3. To serve, spoon Béarnaise Sauce over meat.

**EACH SERVING:** About 302 calories, 35g protein, 0g carbohydrate, 17g total fat (5g saturated), 105mg cholesterol, 381mg sodium.

## Béarnaise Sauce

In nonreactive 1-quart saucepan, combine *½ cup tarragon vinegar, ⅓ cup dry white wine,* and *2 finely chopped shallots;* heat to boiling over high heat. Boil until liquid has reduced to ¼ cup, about 7 minutes. With back of spoon, press mixture through fine sieve into medium bowl.

With wire whisk, beat in *3 large egg yolks, ¼ cup water,* and *pinch of ground black pepper.* Set bowl over saucepan of simmering water. Heat, whisking constantly, until egg-yolk mixture bubbles around edge and has thickened, about 10 minutes. Reduce heat to very low. With wire whisk, whisk in *½ cup cold butter (1 stick),* cut into 8 pieces (do not use margarine), one piece at a time, whisking to incorporate each piece of butter completely before adding more. Stir in *1 tablespoon chopped fresh tarragon.* Makes 1 cup.

**EACH TABLESPOON:** About 68 calories, 1g protein, 1g carbohydrate, 7g total fat (4g saturated), 55mg cholesterol, 60mg sodium.

# Mom's Pot Roast

To braise beef, Fannie Farmer advised in *The Boston Cooking-School Cook Book* of 1896: "[Begin] with 3 Lbs. beef from lower part of round or face of rump. Wipe meat, sprinkle with salt and pepper, dredge with flour, and brown entire surface in pork fat. When turning meat, avoid piercing with fork or skewer, which allows the inner juices to escape. Place on trivet in deep granite pan or in earthen pudding-dish, and surround with vegetables, peppercorns, and three cups boiling water; cover closely, and bake four hours in very slow oven, basting every half-hour, and turn after second hour. Throughout the cooking, the liquid should be kept below the boiling point. Serve with Horseradish Sauce or with brown sauce made from the liquor in pan." Today we call it pot roast.

**PREP:** 25 minutes ★ **BAKE:** 3 hours
**MAKES** 8 main-dish servings

1 tablespoon vegetable oil
1 boneless beef chuck cross-rib pot roast or
    boneless chuck eye roast (4 pounds),
    trimmed

1 large onion (12 ounces), coarsely chopped
1 carrot, peeled and coarsely chopped
1 stalk celery, coarsely chopped
2 garlic cloves, finely chopped
1 can (15 ounces) crushed tomatoes
½ cup canned chicken broth
1 teaspoon salt
½ teaspoon dried thyme, crumbled
¼ teaspoon ground black pepper
1 bay leaf

1. Preheat oven to 350°F. In nonreactive 5-quart Dutch oven, heat oil over high heat until very hot. Add roast and cook until browned on all sides, about 8 minutes. Transfer roast to plate.

2. Add onion, carrot, and celery to Dutch oven; cook, stirring, over medium-high heat until lightly browned, about 3 minutes. Add garlic; cook, stirring, until fragrant, about 20 seconds. Return roast to Dutch oven; add tomatoes, broth, salt, thyme, pepper, and bay leaf; heat to boiling. Cover and place in oven. Bake, turning roast once, until roast is tender, about 3 hours.

3. When roast is done, transfer to large platter and keep warm. Discard bay leaf. Skim and discard fat from liquid in Dutch oven. Transfer half of vegetables and liquid to blender; cover, with center part of cover removed to let steam escape, and puree until smooth. Pour pureed mixture back into Dutch oven and stir until combined; heat to boiling. Cut meat into thin slices and serve with the vegetables and sauce.

**EACH SERVING:** About 304 calories, 35g protein, 6g carbohydrate, 15g total fat (5g saturated), 114mg cholesterol, 573mg sodium.

# New York Strip with Maître d'Hôtel Butter

Whether you know this steak as Kansas City strip, New York strip, or shell steak, it's guaranteed to be flavorful.

**PREP:** 10 minutes plus chilling ★ **COOK:** 10 minutes
**MAKES** 4 servings

¼ cup butter or margarine, softened

1 tablespoon chopped fresh parsley

¼ teaspoon freshly grated lemon peel

1½ teaspoons fresh lemon juice

4 boneless beef strip (shell) steaks, 1 inch thick (about 8 ounces each), trimmed

½ teaspoon salt

¼ teaspoon ground black pepper

**1.** In small bowl, beat butter, parsley, and lemon peel and juice with wooden spoon until well blended. Transfer butter mixture to waxed paper and shape into log about 3 inches long. Wrap, twisting ends of waxed paper to seal. Refrigerate until firm, about 2 hours.

**2.** For grilling: Prepare grill. Sprinkle steaks with salt and pepper. Place steaks on grill over medium-high heat; grill steaks 5 to 6 minutes per side for medium-rare or until desired doneness.

**3.** For cast-iron skillet: Heat 12-inch cast-iron skillet over medium-high heat until very hot. Sprinkle steaks with salt and pepper. Add steaks; cook 5 to 6 minutes per side for medium-rare or until desired doneness.

**4.** Cut chilled butter into ½-inch-thick slices. Top each steak with pat of butter and serve.

**EACH SERVING:** About 383 calories, 43g protein, 0g carbohydrate, 22g total fat (11g saturated), 147mg cholesterol, 523mg sodium.

# Shaker Flank Steak

The Shakers formed communities throughout New England in the nineteenth century. Our recipe for flank steak simmered in a fresh vegetable sauce illustrates the Shakers' love of straightforward cooking using homegrown foods.

**PREP:** 20 minutes ★ **COOK:** 1 hour 45 minutes
**MAKES** 4 servings

1 beef flank steak (1¼ pounds)

½ teaspoon salt

½ teaspoon ground black pepper

2 tablespoons all-purpose flour

2 tablespoons vegetable oil

1 medium onion, chopped

1 carrot, peeled and chopped

1 stalk celery, chopped

1 cup water

⅓ cup ketchup

1 to 2 tablespoons fresh lemon juice

**1.** Sprinkle flank steak with ¼ teaspoon salt and ¼ teaspoon pepper. Coat steak lightly with flour, shaking off excess flour.

**2.** In 12-inch skillet, heat oil over medium-high heat until very hot. Add steak and cook until browned, about 4 minutes per side. Transfer steak to plate.

**3.** Reduce heat to medium-low. To drippings in skillet, add onion, carrot, and celery. Cook, stirring, until vegetables have lightly browned, about 2 minutes. Stir in water and ketchup. Return steak to skillet; heat to boiling. Reduce heat; cover and simmer, turning once, until meat is tender, about 1 hour 30 minutes.

**4.** Transfer steak to cutting board. Turn off heat; stir lemon juice, remaining ¼ teaspoon salt, and remaining ¼ teaspoon pepper into sauce in skillet. Slice steak thinly across grain. Transfer to warm platter. Spoon some sauce over meat; serve remaining sauce alongside.

EACH SERVING: About 378 calories, 29g protein, 15g carbohydrate, 22g total fat (7g saturated), 74mg cholesterol, 642mg sodium.

# Chicken-Fried Steak with Milk Gravy

**N**ot chicken at all, but beef steak pounded thin, then battered and fried until crispy and golden, just like fried chicken. It's been a staple on menus in the Deep South for decades and is almost always served with a creamy milk pan gravy.

PREP: 10 minutes ★ COOK: 20 minutes
MAKES 6 main-dish servings

¾ cup all-purpose flour

1½ teaspoons salt

1 teaspoon paprika

1 teaspoon coarsely ground black pepper

⅛ teaspoon ground red pepper (cayenne)

6 beef cubed steaks (6 ounces each)

½ cup vegetable oil

½ cup beef broth

2 cups milk

**1.** Preheat oven to 200°F. Line jelly-roll pan with paper towels. On waxed paper, combine flour, salt, paprika, black pepper, and ground red pepper. Reserve 3 tablespoons seasoned-flour mixture. Coat cubed steaks with remaining flour mixture, shaking off excess.

**2.** In 12-inch skillet, heat oil to 375°F. Cook steaks, two at a time, 2 minutes; turn and cook 1 minute longer. Transfer steaks to paper towel–lined jelly-roll pan to drain; place in oven. Repeat with remaining steaks, transferring each batch to jelly-roll pan in oven when done.

**3.** Discard all but 2 tablespoons oil from skillet. Reduce heat to medium-high. Stir in reserved flour mixture; cook, stirring, 1 minute. With wire whisk, whisk in broth until browned bits are loosened from bottom of skillet; boil 1 minute. Whisk in milk and heat to boiling; boil 2 minutes. Makes 2 cups.

**4.** Place steaks on platter and serve with gravy.

EACH SERVING WITH GRAVY: About 385 calories, 38g protein, 16g carbohydrate, 18g total fat (5g saturated), 103mg cholesterol, 757mg sodium.

# Swiss Steak

"**S**wissing" is a technique of smoothing cloth by running it between rollers, much the same as round steak is processed to make Swiss Steak.

**PREP:** 25 minutes ★ **COOK:** 1 hour 30 minutes
**MAKES** 6 servings

1 boneless round steak, ½ inch thick (1½ pounds), trimmed and cut into 6 pieces

¾ teaspoon salt

½ teaspoon ground black pepper

¼ cup all-purpose flour

¼ cup olive oil

1 medium onion, halved and sliced

½ pound mushrooms, trimmed and sliced

1 green pepper, sliced

2 garlic cloves, minced

½ teaspoon dried thyme

¾ cup dry red wine or beef broth

1 can (14½ ounces) stewed tomatoes

**1.** Sprinkle steaks with ½ teaspoon salt and pepper. Coat lightly with flour, shaking off excess.

**2.** In 12-inch skillet, heat oil over medium-high heat until hot. Cook steaks, in batches, until browned, about 4 minutes per batch. Transfer to a plate.

**3.** Reduce heat to medium. Add onion, mushrooms, green pepper, garlic, thyme, and remaining ¼ teaspoon salt. Cook, stirring, until vegetables are tender, about 6 minutes. Add wine; cook, stirring until browned bits are loosened from bottom of pan, about 1 minute. Stir in stewed tomatoes.

**4.** Return steaks to skillet, pressing them down into the liquid and vegetables; heat to boiling. Reduce heat; cover and simmer until steaks are fork-tender, 1 hour to 1 hour 15 minutes, stirring occasionally.

**EACH SERVING:** About 290 calories, 26g protein, 15g carbohydrate, 14g total fat (3g saturated), 61mg cholesterol, 506mg sodium.

# Deviled Short Ribs

**I**n eighteenth century England, "Deviled Bones" were popular dinner fare. Craig Claiborne elaborates in *The New York Times Food Encyclopedia:* "The bones were generally those of cold poultry, game, or beef. The pieces of meat were covered with one of three kinds of devil sauces: mustard, curry or white." Our deviled ribs are marinated in a mustard-based sauce.

**PREP:** 10 minutes plus marinating
**ROAST:** 2 hours 45 minutes
**MAKES** 6 main-dish servings

6 tablespoons spicy brown mustard

2 tablespoons cider vinegar

2 tablespoons green jalapeño chile sauce

2 teaspoons Worcestershire sauce

4 pounds beef chuck short ribs

¾ teaspoon ground black pepper

1½ cups fresh bread crumbs (about 3 slices bread)

**1.** In small bowl, combine 3 tablespoons mustard, vinegar, 1 tablespoon jalapeño sauce, and Worcestershire; with wire whisk, whisk until blended. Transfer to ziptight plastic bag; add short ribs, turning to coat. Seal bag, pressing out as much air as possible. Refrigerate at least 1 hour or up to 24 hours to marinate.

**2.** Preheat oven to 425°F. Arrange ribs on rack in medium roasting pan (14" by 10"); brush with remaining marinade. Roast 40 minutes. Turn oven control to 325°F; roast 1 hour 20 minutes longer.

**3.** In small bowl, combine remaining 3 tablespoons mustard, remaining 1 tablespoon jalapeño sauce, and pepper. Brush on tops of ribs. Press bread crumbs onto coated ribs; roast until crumbs are crisp and lightly browned, 45 minutes longer.

**EACH SERVING:** About 762 calories, 34g protein, 6g carbohydrate, 64g total fat (27g saturated), 143mg cholesterol, 400mg sodium.

# Blackened Steaks

French Canadians exiled in the 1750s for refusing to swear allegiance to the British crown settled in the low bayou country near New Orleans. Soon known as Cajuns, their cooking was highly spiced and quite distinctive.

**PREP:** 5 minutes ★ **COOK:** 10 minutes
**MAKES** 4 main-dish servings

1 teaspoon dried thyme, crumbled
1 teaspoon onion powder (not onion salt)
$\frac{1}{2}$ teaspoon salt
$\frac{1}{2}$ teaspoon ground black pepper
$\frac{1}{4}$ teaspoon ground red pepper (cayenne)
$\frac{1}{4}$ teaspoon sugar
4 boneless beef strip (shell) steaks, 1 inch thick (8 ounces each), trimmed
2 teaspoons olive oil

**1.** In bowl, combine thyme, onion powder, salt, black pepper, ground red pepper, and sugar. Use to rub on both sides of steaks.

**2.** In 12-inch cast-iron skillet, heat oil over medium-high heat until very hot. Add steaks; cook 5 to 6 minutes per side for medium-rare or until desired doneness.

**EACH SERVING:** About 293 calories, 37g protein, 1g carbohydrate, 14g total fat (5g saturated), 98mg cholesterol, 362mg sodium.

# Beef Pizzaiolo

Beef pizzaiolo shares its topping's main ingredients of tomatoes, peppers, and onions with that of its "cousin," pizza.

**PREP:** 15 minutes ★ **COOK:** 25 minutes
**MAKES** 4 main-dish servings

2 boneless beef top loin steaks, $\frac{3}{4}$ inch thick (10 ounces each), trimmed
$\frac{1}{2}$ teaspoon salt
$\frac{1}{4}$ teaspoon coarsely ground black pepper
1 tablespoon olive oil
1 large onion (12 ounces), cut in half and sliced
1 small red pepper, cut into 1-inch pieces
1 small green pepper, cut into 1-inch pieces
2 garlic cloves, crushed with garlic press
$\frac{1}{2}$ cup canned chicken broth
2 tablespoons red wine vinegar
1 teaspoon sugar
8 cherry tomatoes, each cut in half
$\frac{1}{2}$ cup loosely packed fresh basil leaves, chopped, plus additional sprigs

**1.** Pat steaks dry with paper towels. Sprinkle steaks with $\frac{1}{4}$ teaspoon salt and black pepper.

**2.** Heat nonstick 12-inch skillet over medium-high heat until hot. Add steaks; cook 4 minutes. Turn steaks over; cook 4 to 5 minutes longer for medium-rare or until desired doneness. Transfer steaks to platter; cover with foil to keep warm.

**3.** In same skillet, heat oil over medium heat until hot. Add onion, red and green peppers, garlic, and remaining $\frac{1}{4}$ teaspoon salt; cook, stirring often, until vegetables are tender and golden, about 10 minutes.

**4.** Increase heat to medium-high. Stir in broth, vinegar, sugar, and cherry tomatoes; heat to boiling. Cook 1 minute. Remove skillet from heat and stir in chopped fresh basil.

**5.** To serve, slice steaks and arrange on 4 dinner plates; top with pepper mixture. Garnish with the basil sprigs.

**EACH SERVING:** About 315 calories, 32g protein, 16g carbohydrate, 13g total fat (4g saturated), 88mg cholesterol, 450mg sodium.

# Grillades and Grits

Sunday brunch is a weekly ritual in Louisiana, where grillades and grits is almost always on the menu. The only variable is the meat: Cajuns often use pork, Creole restaurants in New Orleans serve white veal, and the Afro-Americans use baby beef. All, however, serve it on top of a mound of grits with a ladleful of brown tomato sauce over all.

**PREP:** 15 minutes ★ **COOK:** 1 hour
**MAKES** 4 main-dish servings

**4 beef minute steaks (6 ounces each)**
**½ teaspoon salt**
**¼ teaspoon ground black pepper**
**3 teaspoons vegetable oil**
**1 medium onion, chopped**
**1 green pepper, chopped**
**1 stalk celery, chopped**
**2 garlic cloves, finely chopped**
**1 can (14 to 16 ounces) tomatoes in puree**
**1 cup beef broth**
**1 teaspoon Worcestershire sauce**
**2 bay leaves**
**1 tablespoon red wine vinegar**
**hot cooked old-fashioned or quick hominy grits**

1. Sprinkle beef with salt and black pepper. In non-stick 12-inch skillet, heat 1 teaspoon oil over medium-high heat until very hot. Add steaks and cook until browned, about 2 minutes per side, transferring steaks to plate as they are browned.

2. Add remaining 2 teaspoons oil to skillet; reduce heat to medium. Add onion; cook, stirring, 5 minutes. Add green pepper, celery, and garlic; cook, stirring, 3 minutes. Add tomatoes with their puree, breaking them up with side of spoon. Stir in broth, Worcestershire, and bay leaves. Increase heat to high; heat to boiling.

3. Return steaks to skillet; reduce heat. Cover and simmer 40 minutes. Transfer steaks to platter; keep warm. Increase heat to high; stir in vinegar and heat to boiling. Boil until sauce has thickened, about 5 minutes. Discard bay leaves. To serve, spoon sauce over steaks and pass grits separately.

**EACH SERVING:** About 437 calories, 37g protein, 13g carbohydrate, 26g total fat (9g saturated), 107mg cholesterol, 772mg sodium.

# Salisbury Steak

Civil War soldiers who suffered stomach problems were served chopped beef patties by Dr. James Henry Salisbury. A recipe carrying Salisbury's name appeared in print around 1888.

**PREP:** 25 minutes ★ **COOK:** 35 minutes
**MAKES** 4 main-dish servings

**1 large onion (12 ounces), halved**
**1¼ pounds ground beef chuck**
**¼ cup finely crushed saltine crackers (about 6 crackers)**
**¼ cup milk**
**1 large egg, lightly beaten**
**½ teaspoon salt**
**¼ teaspoon ground black pepper**
**1 tablespoon vegetable oil**
**10 ounces mushrooms, trimmed and sliced**
**1 can (14½ ounces) beef broth**
**3 tablespoons all-purpose flour**
**1 teaspoon Worcestershire sauce**

1. Mince enough onion to equal ¼ cup. Thinly slice remaining onion. In large bowl, combine minced onion, ground beef, crushed crackers, milk, egg, ¼ teaspoon salt, and ⅛ teaspoon pepper just until well blended but not overmixed. Shape mixture into 4 oval patties, about ¾ inch thick, handling meat as little as possible.

2. In nonstick 12-inch skillet, heat oil over medium-high heat. Add beef patties; cook until browned, about 4 minutes per side, reducing heat if necessary. With spatula, transfer patties to plate. Discard all but 2 tablespoons drippings from skillet. Add sliced onion, mushrooms, remaining ¼ teaspoon salt, and remaining ⅛ teaspoon pepper to skillet. Cover; cook over medium-low heat, stirring occasionally, until onion is tender, about 10 minutes.

3. In small bowl, blend broth and flour until smooth; add to skillet. Heat to boiling, stirring constantly. Return patties to skillet, pressing them down into sauce. Reduce heat to low; simmer, turning once, until patties are cooked through, about 10 minutes.

**EACH SERVING:** About 408 calories, 35g protein, 20g carbohydrate, 21g total fat (7g saturated), 149mg cholesterol, 835mg sodium.

# Nana's Meat Loaf

According to James Beard, the meat loaf we know today did not become a mainstay of our diet until the twentieth century. Properly prepared, meat loaf resembles a good pâté: highly seasoned, firm and moist, and equally delicious hot or cold. What's the secret to a tender and tasty loaf? Always, always use ground chuck. Our recipe comes from the "Susan, Our Teenage Cook" series, which ran in *Good Housekeeping* magazine for decades.

**PREP:** 15 minutes ★ **BAKE:** 1 hour
**MAKES** 8 main-dish servings

**2 pounds ground beef chuck**

**2 large eggs**

**2 cups fresh bread crumbs (about
    4 slices bread)**

**2 green onions, finely chopped**

**1 medium onion, finely chopped**

**¾ cup ketchup**

**¼ cup milk**

**2 tablespoons bottled white horseradish**

**1½ teaspoons salt**

**1 teaspoon dry mustard**

1. Preheat oven to 400°F. In large bowl, combine ground beef, eggs, bread crumbs, green onions, onion, ¼ cup ketchup, milk, horseradish, salt, and dry mustard just until well blended but not over-mixed.

2. Spoon mixture into 9" by 5" metal loaf pan, pressing firmly. Spread remaining ½ cup ketchup on top of loaf. Bake 1 hour. Let meat loaf stand 10 minutes to set juices for easier slicing.

**EACH SERVING:** About 283 calories, 27g protein, 15g carbohydrate, 13g total fat (5g saturated), 125mg cholesterol, 845mg sodium.

# Meat Loaf Surprise

"**S**urprise" variations of favorite recipes became very popular in the mid-1900s. Sometimes mashed potatoes were piped on top of ground-meat pies, while other times potatoes were rolled up inside a meat loaf jelly-roll fashion. Our Meat Loaf Surprise contains not only potatoes but a layer of spinach too.

**PREP:** 30 minutes ★ **BAKE:** 1 hour 15 minutes
**MAKES** 8 main-dish servings

---

1½ **pounds all-purpose potatoes (about 3 large), peeled and cut into 2-inch pieces**

¼ **cup milk**

2 **tablespoons butter or margarine**

1¼ **teaspoons salt**

¼ **teaspoon ground black pepper**

1 **can (14½ ounces) diced tomatoes**

½ **cup water**

2 **pounds ground beef chuck**

2 **large eggs**

¾ **cup seasoned dried bread crumbs**

¼ **cup freshly grated Parmesan cheese**

1 **garlic clove, minced**

1 **package (10 ounces) frozen chopped spinach, thawed and squeezed dry**

**1.** In 3-quart saucepan, combine potatoes and enough *water* to cover; heat to boiling over high heat. Reduce heat to low; cover and simmer until potatoes are fork-tender, 10 to 15 minutes. Drain potatoes and return to saucepan. Add milk, butter, ½ teaspoon salt, and ⅛ teaspoon pepper. With potato masher, mash potatoes until mixture is smooth; set aside.

**2.** Preheat oven to 350°F. In blender or in food processor with knife blade attached, puree tomatoes with their juice and water until smooth.

**3.** In large bowl, mix ground beef, eggs, bread crumbs, Parmesan, garlic, ½ teaspoon salt, remaining ⅛ teaspoon pepper, and ½ cup tomato mixture until well combined but not overmixed.

**4.** On 14" by 12" sheet of waxed paper, pat meat mixture into 11" by 9" rectangle. Spread mashed potatoes over meat rectangle leaving 1-inch border all around. Spoon spinach over potatoes; sprinkle with remaining ¼ teaspoon salt.

**5.** Starting at a narrow end, roll up layered meat mixture jelly-roll fashion, lifting waxed paper and using long metal spatula to help loosen meat from waxed paper. Carefully place rolled meat loaf, seam side down, in 13" by 9" baking dish.

**6.** Pour remaining tomato mixture over and around meat loaf. Bake 1 hour 15 minutes. Let stand 10 minutes to set juices for easier slicing.

---

**EACH SERVING:** About 374 calories, 30g protein, 24g carbohydrate, 17g total fat (8g saturated), 138mg cholesterol, 955mg sodium.

# Barbecued Beef Brisket

Texas has always been known for its grand barbecues, many times with beef brisket slow-roasting over a pit for hours until meltingly tender.

**PREP:** 15 minutes
**COOK/GRILL:** 3 hours 35 minutes
**MAKES** 12 main-dish servings

## BRISKET

1 fresh beef brisket (4½ pounds), trimmed

1 medium onion, cut into quarters

1 large carrot, peeled and cut into 1½-inch pieces

1 bay leaf

1 teaspoon whole black peppercorns

¼ teaspoon whole allspice

## CHUNKY BBQ SAUCE

1 tablespoon vegetable oil

1 large onion (12 ounces), finely chopped

3 garlic cloves, finely chopped

2 tablespoons minced, peeled fresh ginger

1 teaspoon ground cumin

1 can (14½ ounces) tomatoes in puree, chopped

1 bottle (12 ounces) chili sauce

⅓ cup cider vinegar

2 tablespoons light (mild) molasses

2 tablespoons brown sugar

2 teaspoons dry mustard

1 tablespoon cornstarch

2 tablespoons water

**1.** Prepare brisket: In 8-quart Dutch oven, place brisket, onion, carrot, bay leaf, peppercorns, allspice, and enough *water* to cover; heat to boiling over high heat. Reduce heat; cover and simmer until meat is tender, about 3 hours.

**2.** Meanwhile, prepare chunky BBQ sauce: In nonstick 12-inch skillet, heat oil over medium heat. Add onion and cook, stirring occasionally, until tender, about 10 minutes. Add garlic and ginger; cook, stirring, 1 minute. Stir in cumin; cook 1 minute. Stir in tomatoes with their puree, chili sauce, vinegar, molasses, brown sugar, and dry mustard; heat to boiling over high heat. Reduce heat; simmer, stirring occasionally, 5 minutes.

**3.** Meanwhile, in cup, blend cornstarch and water until smooth. Stir cornstarch mixture into sauce. Heat to boiling, stirring; boil 1 minute. Cover and refrigerate sauce if not using right away. Makes about 4 cups.

**4.** When brisket is done, transfer to platter. If not serving right away, cover and refrigerate until ready to serve.

**5.** Prepare grill. Place brisket on grill (preferably one with a cover). Cover and cook over medium heat 10 minutes. Turn brisket and cook 5 minutes longer. Spoon 1 cup barbecue sauce on top of brisket; cook until brisket is heated through, about 5 minutes. (Do not turn brisket after topping with sauce.) Reheat remaining sauce in small saucepan on grill. Slice brisket thinly across the grain and serve with sauce.

**EACH SERVING:** About 241 calories, 26g protein, 6g carbohydrate, 11g total fat (4g saturated), 81mg cholesterol, 174mg sodium.

**EACH 1/4 CUP SAUCE:** About 61 calories, 1g protein, 13g carbohydrate, 1g total fat (0g saturated), 0mg cholesterol, 328mg sodium.

# Beef Stroganoff

This dish was named in honor of a member of the Stroganov family, who were affluent Russian merchants. Stroganoff usually begins with the finest beef tenderloin, which is quickly cooked in a hot skillet and covered with sour cream sauce that is flavored with fresh or dried tarragon and paprika. Sometimes a splash of brandy is added, as in our classic rendition.

**PREP:** 15 minutes ★ **COOK:** 30 minutes
**MAKES** 4 main-dish servings

1 pound beef tenderloin, trimmed

2 tablespoons butter or margarine

1 medium onion, thinly sliced

¾ cup canned chicken broth

1 teaspoon Hungarian sweet paprika

4 ounces mushrooms, trimmed and sliced

1 tablespoon fresh lemon juice

1 tablespoon brandy

½ teaspoon dried tarragon, crumbled

½ teaspoon salt

⅛ teaspoon ground black pepper

½ cup sour cream

3 teaspoons chopped fresh dill or
   flat-leaf parsley

1. Cut tenderloin into ⅜-inch-thick slices, then cut into 1½" by ⅜" strips.

2. In 12-inch skillet, melt butter over medium heat. Add half of beef (do not crowd); cook until browned on both sides, about 4 minutes, using slotted spoon to transfer meat to bowl as it is browned. Repeat with remaining beef strips.

3. Reduce heat to medium-low. Stir in onion and cook until tender, about 5 minutes. Add ¼ cup broth and paprika; cook, stirring, until onion is very tender, about 5 minutes longer.

4. Add mushrooms, lemon juice, brandy, tarragon, salt, and pepper. Cook, stirring, until mushrooms are tender and almost all liquid has evaporated, about 8 minutes.

5. Stir in beef, remaining ½ cup broth, sour cream, and 2 teaspoons dill. Cook until heated through (do not boil), about 2 minutes. To serve, sprinkle with remaining 1 teaspoon dill.

**EACH SERVING:** About 336 calories, 26g protein, 7g carbohydrate, 21g total fat (11g saturated), 99mg cholesterol, 599mg sodium.

## Spiced Beef (or Beef a la Mode)

*One piece of the round of beef (known as the "pot roast"), weighing from three to five pounds. Put two tablespoons of butter in stewing kettle over a hot fire; when butter melts, brown the meat on both sides. Remove the meat temporarily and add flour to the butter; let it brown and thicken, then add three pints of boiling water, one bay leaf, one sprig of celery, some parsley, and one large onion with a clove stuck in it, two carrots, one turnip, one tablespoon of salt and one shake of pepper. Replace the meat in this liquid at once and let it simmer for at least six hours. Turn the meat over and stir it occasionally. The secret of the success with this dish is slow cooking. When finished it should be as tender as bread. Place the meat on a hot platter, strain the gravy over it and serve garnished with sliced boiled carrots and sprigs of parsley. The gravy should be thick and of a dark brown color.*

—**Good Housekeeping Everyday Cook Book**, 1903

## Cottage Pie

This recipe is similar to one of Ireland's most favorite dishes, shepherd's pie, which is made with a savory lamb filling and topped with puffs of mashed potatoes. Cottage pie is usually made with ground beef. In Fannie Farmer's original cookbook, it is made with chopped roasted beef that is sandwiched between two layers of mashed potatoes: one layer is the crust and the other's the topping.

**PREP:** 40 minutes ★ **BAKE:** 20 minutes
**MAKES** 4 main-dish servings

**2 pounds all-purpose potatoes (6 medium), peeled and cut into quarters**

¹⁄₂ **cup milk**

**3 tablespoons butter or margarine**

¹⁄₄ **cup plus 1 tablespoon freshly grated Parmesan cheese**

**1 teaspoon salt**

¹⁄₄ **plus** ¹⁄₈ **teaspoon ground black pepper**

**1 medium onion, chopped**

**2 carrots, peeled and chopped**

**1 pound ground beef chuck**

**2 tablespoons tomato paste**

**2 tablespoons all-purpose flour**

¹⁄₄ **cup dry red wine**

**1 cup canned chicken broth**

¹⁄₄ **teaspoon dried thyme**

**1 cup frozen peas**

1. Preheat oven to 425°F. In 4-quart saucepan, combine potatoes and enough *water* to cover; heat to boiling. Boil until potatoes are tender, about 20 minutes; drain and return to saucepan. With potato masher, mash potatoes with milk and 2 tablespoons butter. Stir in ¹⁄₄ cup Parmesan, ¹⁄₂ teaspoon salt, and ¹⁄₄ teaspoon pepper; set mashed potatoes aside.

**2.** Meanwhile, in nonstick 10-inch skillet, melt remaining 1 tablespoon butter over medium heat. Add onion and carrots; cook until vegetables are tender, about 5 minutes. Add ground beef and cook over medium-high heat, breaking up meat with side of spoon, until beef is no longer pink, about 5 minutes. Skim and discard fat. Add tomato paste and cook, stirring, 1 minute. Add flour and cook, stirring, 1 minute longer. Stir in wine and cook until wine has evaporated. Add broth, thyme, remaining ½ teaspoon salt, and remaining ⅛ teaspoon pepper, stirring until browned bits are loosened from bottom of skillet. Heat to boiling; stir in peas.

**3.** Transfer beef mixture to 9-inch deep-dish pie plate. Spoon mashed potatoes on top; spread evenly. Sprinkle with remaining 1 tablespoon Parmesan. Place pie on foil-lined cookie sheet and bake until slightly browned, about 20 minutes.

EACH SERVING: About 554 calories, 34g protein, 50gcarbohydrate, 24g total fat (12g saturated), 107mg cholesterol, 1,282mg sodium.

# Oven Beef Stew

Our forefathers served a one-pot stew called beef with dumplings. They simmered cubes of beef with a simple bouquet of vegetables in a large pot and added a layer of dumplings for the last fifteen minutes of cooking. It wasn't until the late 1800s that the technique of browning the beef, then finishing the stew in the oven became popular.

PREP: 30 minutes ★ BAKE: 2 hours
MAKES 6 main-dish servings

2½ **pounds beef chuck, trimmed and cut into 2-inch pieces**

1 **teaspoon salt**

¼ **teaspoon ground black pepper**

4 **teaspoons vegetable oil**

1 **tablespoon butter or margarine**

1 **large onion (12 ounces), chopped**

1 **stalk celery, chopped**

2 **garlic cloves, finely chopped**

½ **teaspoon dried thyme**

2 **tablespoons all-purpose flour**

2 **cups canned chicken broth**

1 **tablespoon tomato paste**

1 **bay leaf**

4 **large carrots, peeled and cut into 2-inch pieces**

1 **pound all-purpose potatoes, peeled and cut into 2-inch pieces**

1 **tablespoon chopped fresh parsley**

**1.** Preheat oven to 375°F. Pat beef dry with paper towels. In bowl, toss beef with ½ teaspoon salt and the pepper.

**2.** In nonreactive 5-quart Dutch oven, heat 2 teaspoons oil over medium-high heat. Add half of beef; cook until well browned, about 5 minutes, using slotted spoon to transfer meat to bowl as it is browned. Repeat with remaining beef, adding 2 teaspoons oil if necessary.

**3.** Reduce heat to medium; add butter and heat until melted. Add onion, celery, garlic, thyme, and remaining ½ teaspoon salt. Cook until onions and celery are tender, about 5 minutes. Stir in flour; cook 1 minute. Stir in broth, tomato paste, and bay leaf; cook, stirring until browned bits are loosened from bottom of pot.

**4.** Return beef to Dutch oven; heat to boiling. Cover tightly and bake 1 hour. Stir in carrots and potatoes; cover and bake until meat and vegetables are fork-tender, about 1 hour. Sprinkle with parsley.

EACH SERVING: About 375 calories, 32g protein, 26g carbohydrate, 16g total fat (6g saturated), 100mg cholesterol, 910mg sodium.

# Tamale Pie

The roots of this pie date back to the Aztecs in Tenochtitlán (Mexico City), who served Cortés *tamalli,* meat that is coated with cornmeal dough and steamed inside a softened cornhusk. Recipes for tamale pies differ: some have only a bottom layer of cornmeal batter, while others have cornmeal on top also.

**PREP:** 25 minutes ★ **BAKE:** 45 minutes
**MAKES** 6 main-dish servings

2 teaspoons vegetable oil

I medium onion, chopped

I pound ground beef chuck

I tablespoon chili powder

I teaspoon ground cumin

I cup medium-hot salsa

I can (15¼ to 16 ounces) whole-kernel corn, drained

4 cups water

I cup cornmeal

I teaspoon salt

½ cup shredded Cheddar cheese

1. Preheat oven to 350°F. In nonstick 12-inch skillet, heat oil over medium-high heat. Add onion and cook until tender and golden, about 5 minutes. Stir in ground beef and cook, breaking up meat with side of spoon, until meat has browned, about 5 minutes. Skim and discard any fat. Stir in chili powder and cumin; cook 2 minutes longer. Remove from heat; stir in salsa and corn.

2. In 2-quart saucepan, heat water to boiling. With wire whisk, gradually whisk in cornmeal and salt. Cook over medium heat, whisking frequently, 5 minutes.

3. Pour half of cornmeal mixture into shallow 2-quart casserole. Spoon beef mixture over cornmeal, spoon remaining cornmeal over beef, and sprinkle Cheddar on top. Bake 45 minutes. Remove casserole from oven and let stand about 15 minutes for easier serving.

**EACH SERVING:** About 334 calories, 21g protein, 33g carbohydrate, 13g total fat (5g saturated), 57mg cholesterol, 1,026mg sodium.

# Chili con Carne

Chili con carne gained popularity at an authentic San Antonio chilley [*sic*] stand at the 1893 Chicago World's Fair. Texans usually prefer cubed or shredded meat in their chili, but midwesterners often choose ground meat, as in our recipe.

**PREP:** 20 minutes ★ **COOK:** 35 minutes
**MAKES** 6 main-dish servings

I tablespoon olive oil

I medium onion, chopped

2 garlic cloves, finely chopped

2 green peppers, chopped

2 pounds ground beef chuck

3 pickled jalapeño chiles, seeded and finely chopped (2 tablespoons)

3 tablespoons chili powder

2 teaspoons unsweetened cocoa

1¼ teaspoons salt

¾ teaspoon ground coriander

½ teaspoon dried oregano

¼ teaspoon ground red pepper (cayenne)

I can (14 to 16 ounces) tomatoes, chopped

1. In nonstick 12-inch skillet, heat oil over medium heat. Add onion and garlic; cook, stirring occasionally, until onion is tender, about 5 minutes. Add green peppers and cook, stirring, until tender-crisp, about 5 minutes longer.

2. Add ground beef and cook, breaking up meat with side of spoon, until meat is no longer pink.

Stir in pickled jalapeños, chili powder, cocoa, salt, coriander, oregano, and ground red pepper; cook 1 minute. Add tomatoes with their juice; heat to boiling. Reduce heat; simmer, stirring occasionally, until slightly thickened, 15 to 20 minutes.

**EACH SERVING:** About 326 calories, 33g protein, 10g carbohydrate, 18g total fat (6g saturated), 94mg cholesterol, 758mg sodium.

# Mustard and Herb Racks of Lamb

The classic—ask your butcher to loosen the backbone from the ribs for easier carving.

**PREP:** 10 minutes ★ **ROAST:** 1 hour 5 minutes
**MAKES** 8 main-dish servings

**2 lamb rib roasts (racks of lamb), 8 ribs each (2½ pounds each), trimmed**

**½ teaspoon salt**

**3 tablespoons butter or margarine**

**2 cups fine fresh bread crumbs (about 4 slices firm white bread)**

**2 teaspoons dried rosemary, crumbled**

**¼ teaspoon ground black pepper**

**2 tablespoons chopped fresh parsley**

**2 tablespoons Dijon mustard**

**1.** Preheat oven to 375°F. In large roasting pan (17" by 11½"), place roasts, rib side down; sprinkle with salt. Roast lamb 50 minutes.

**2.** Meanwhile, in 10-inch skillet, melt butter over medium heat. Add bread crumbs, rosemary, and pepper; cook, stirring frequently, until crumbs are golden brown, about 4 minutes. Stir in parsley.

**3.** Spread mustard on tops of roasts. Press breadcrumb mixture onto mustard, patting so it adheres. Roast lamb until meat thermometer inserted in center of lamb (not touching bone) reaches 140°F,

15 to 20 minutes longer. Internal temperature of meat will rise to 145°F (medium) upon standing. Or roast to desired doneness.

**4.** When roasts are done, transfer to cutting board and let stand 10 minutes to set juices for easier carving. Cut off backbone from ribs. Transfer roasts to warm platter. To serve, cut lamb with sharp knife between bones to separate chops.

**EACH SERVING:** About 311 calories, 27g protein, 7g carbohydrate, 18g total fat (8g saturated), 99mg cholesterol, 436mg sodium.

## The Progressive Dinner Party

During the boom years of the 1950s, having a home in suburbia was a must, and so was entertaining one's neighbors. Progressive dinner parties, a dinner that's held in three or four homes, with a different course served in each home were all the rage. Each hostess prepared one course (instead of the whole dinner), so it saved both time and money.

Going from home to home or backyard to backyard makes a progressive dinner party fun. So why not throw one? As the party organizer, you get to choose the hostesses, the theme of the dinner, and usually the menu. Select foods that not only go together but that can be made ahead. Here's the key to a smooth-flowing party: Suggest that the hostess for the subsequent course leave a little early, so she has plenty of time to have the food hot and waiting when everyone arrives at her home.

# New England Boiled Dinner

Nineteenth century cooks would often serve this dish with a sprinkling of cider vinegar. Today the most common condiments are homemade horseradish sauce or spicy mustard.

**PREP:** 15 minutes ★ **COOK:** 3 hours 30 minutes
**MAKES** 8 main-dish servings

1 corned beef brisket (4 to 4½ pounds)

1 medium onion studded with 4 whole cloves

2 quarts water

8 medium all-purpose potatoes (2½ pounds), each peeled and cut in half

8 carrots, each peeled and cut in half

1 small rutabaga (2 pounds), peeled, cut in half, and each half cut into 8 wedges

1 small green cabbage (2 pounds), cut into 8 wedges

2 tablespoons chopped fresh parsley

Dijon mustard

bottled white horseradish

1. In 8-quart Dutch oven, place brisket, clove-studded onion, and water; heat to boiling over high heat. With slotted spoon, skim foam from surface. Reduce heat; cover and simmer until brisket is tender, 2 hours 30 minutes to 3 hours.

2. Add potatoes, carrots, and rutabaga to Dutch oven; heat to boiling over high heat. Reduce heat; cover and simmer until vegetables are tender, about 30 minutes. With slotted spoon, transfer brisket and vegetables to deep large platter; keep warm.

3. Heat liquid remaining in Dutch oven to boiling over high heat. Add cabbage; heat to boiling. Cover and cook until cabbage is tender, about 5 minutes.

4. Slice brisket very thinly across the grain. Transfer sliced meat to platter with vegetables. Place cabbage wedges on platter, sprinkle parsley on vegetables, and serve mustard and horseradish alongside.

**EACH SERVING:** About 587 calories, 35g protein, 43g carbohydrate, 31g total fat (10g saturated), 157mg cholesterol, 1,887mg sodium.

# Red Flannel Hash

Red flannel hash has always been a popular way to use up New England boiled dinner leftovers. It is the beets, of course, that contribute the authentic red hue to the dish.

**PREP:** 15 minutes ★ **COOK:** 30 minutes
**MAKES** 4 main-dish servings

3 tablespoons butter or margarine

1 large onion (12 ounces), chopped

2 cups chopped cooked lean corned beef

2 cups chopped cooked all-purpose potatoes

1 cup finely chopped cooked beets

¼ teaspoon coarsely ground black pepper

1 tablespoon chopped fresh parsley

1. In 10-inch skillet, melt butter over medium heat. Add onion and cook, stirring often, until tender, about 5 minutes. Stir in corned beef, potatoes, beets, and pepper until well combined. Cook, pressing hash down firmly with spatula, until bottom of hash has browned, about 15 minutes.

2. With spatula, turn hash over, one small section at a time. Press down with spatula; cook until second side has browned, 5 to 10 minutes longer. Sprinkle with parsley.

**EACH SERVING:** About 337 calories, 23g protein, 21g carbohydrate, 18g total fat (9g saturated), 89mg cholesterol, 947mg sodium.

# Crown Roast of Pork

From the time the settlers arrived in the New World, pork has been a mainstay in the American diet. History has recorded many menus centered around the pork barrel (sides of pork in salt brine), which helped the colonists survive the long, blustery winters. Eating "high on the hog" is a well-worn expression that denotes comfort and plenty. This spectacular roast pays homage to our love of pork.

**PREP:** 20 minutes ★ **ROAST:** 3 hours 30 minutes
**MAKES** 14 main-dish servings

- 1 pork rib crown roast (7 pounds)
- 2½ teaspoons salt
- ½ plus ⅛ teaspoon ground black pepper
- 6 tablespoons butter or margarine
- 4 stalks celery, chopped
- 1 large onion (12 ounces), chopped
- 1 pound Golden Delicious apples (3 medium), peeled, cored, and chopped
- 8 cups fresh bread cubes (about 12 slices firm white bread)
- ½ cup apple juice
- 1 large egg, lightly beaten
- 1 teaspoon poultry seasoning
- ¼ cup Calvados, applejack brandy, or water
- 3 tablespoons all-purpose flour
- 1 can (14½ ounces) chicken broth

1. Preheat oven to 325°F. Rub roast with 1 teaspoon salt and ¼ teaspoon pepper. Place roast, rib ends down, in large roasting pan (17" by 11½"). Roast 1 hour.

2. Meanwhile, in 5-quart Dutch oven, melt butter over medium heat. Add celery and onion; cook, stirring, until tender, about 5 minutes. Add apples and cook until tender, 6 to 8 minutes longer. Remove Dutch oven from heat. Stir in bread cubes, apple juice, egg, poultry seasoning, 1 teaspoon salt, and ¼ teaspoon pepper. Toss until well combined.

3. Remove roast from oven and turn, rib ends up. Fill cavity of roast with stuffing. (Place any leftover stuffing into greased 1½-quart casserole. Bake leftover stuffing, uncovered, during last 30 minutes of roasting time.)

4. Return pork to oven; roast until meat thermometer inserted in thickest part of roast (not touching bone) reaches 155°F, about 2 hours 30 minutes. Internal temperature of pork will rise to 160°F upon standing. If stuffing browns too quickly, cover with foil.

5. When roast is done, transfer to warm platter. Let stand 15 minutes to set juices for easier carving.

6. Meanwhile, prepare gravy: Pour pan drippings into 2-cup measuring cup or medium bowl (set roasting pan aside); let stand until fat separates from meat juice. Skim off 3 tablespoons fat from drippings. If necessary, add enough melted butter to fat to equal 3 tablespoons. Pour into 2-quart saucepan. Skim and discard any remaining fat from meat juice. Add Calvados to roasting pan. Heat over medium heat, stirring until browned bits are loosened from bottom of pan. Add to meat juice in cup.

7. Into fat in saucepan, with wire whisk, whisk flour, remaining ½ teaspoon salt, and remaining ⅛ teaspoon pepper until blended; cook, stirring, over medium heat 1 minute. Gradually whisk in meat-juice mixture and broth. Heat to boiling, stirring constantly; boil 1 minute. Serve roast with gravy and stuffing.

**EACH SERVING:** About 406 calories, 32g protein, 19g carbohydrate, 21g total fat (9g saturated), 104mg cholesterol, 716mg sodium.

# Stuffed Pork Chops

The word *stuffing* first appeared in print in 1538. It replaced the word *forcemeat,* which comes from the French word *farcir* (to stuff). In the Midwest, where pork has always been plentiful and suppers are hearty and generous, stuffing is frequently used to "overstuff" thick pork chops (at least 1 inch thick, please!).

**PREP:** 20 minutes  ★  **COOK:** 30 minutes
**MAKES** 4 main-dish servings

4 teaspoons vegetable oil

1 small onion, chopped

1 Golden Delicious apple, peeled, cored, and chopped

pinch dried thyme

2 slices white bread, toasted and cut into $1/4$-inch pieces

2 tablespoons plus $1/2$ cup canned chicken broth

1 tablespoon spicy brown mustard

4 pork loin chops, 1 inch thick (8 ounces each)

$1/4$ teaspoon salt

**1.** In 12-inch skillet, heat 2 teaspoons oil over medium heat. Add onion and cook until tender, about 5 minutes. Add apple and thyme; cook 3 minutes longer. Transfer apple mixture to medium bowl. Wipe skillet clean.

**2.** Stir bread pieces, 2 tablespoons broth, and mustard into apple mixture. Pat pork dry with paper towels. Holding knife parallel to surface, cut a horizontal pocket in each chop. Stuff apple mixture into pocket of each chop and secure with toothpicks. Sprinkle with salt.

**3.** In same skillet, heat remaining 2 teaspoons oil over medium heat until hot. Cook chops until they just lose their pink color throughout, about 7 minutes per side.

**4.** Transfer chops to platter. Keep warm. Increase heat to high. Add remaining $1/2$ cup broth to skillet; heat to boiling. Boil broth until reduced to $1/4$ cup, 3 to 5 minutes. Pour sauce over chops.

**EACH SERVING:** About 367 calories, 39g protein, 15g carbohydrate, 15g total fat (4g saturated), 102mg cholesterol, 540mg sodium.

# Smothered Pork Chops

"Smothering" foods is common in soul-food cookery. It refers to the technique of simmering meat or poultry in a thickened gravy until the meat is falling off the bone. True Southerners insist that a seasoned black-iron skillet is essential. According to Craig Claiborne, the term *smothered* may have come from the method of weighting down food with a heavy plate topped with at least five pounds to make sure it stays smothered as it cooks.

**PREP:** 10 minutes ★ **COOK:** 20 minutes
**MAKES** 4 main-dish servings

3/4 cup all-purpose flour

1 teaspoon salt

1/4 teaspoon ground black pepper

1/4 teaspoon ground nutmeg

4 pork rib or loin chops, 3/4 inch thick
   (6 to 8 ounces each)

2 tablespoons butter or margarine

1/2 cup chopped onion

1 cup canned chicken broth

1/4 cup buttermilk

2 tablespoons chopped fresh parsley

1. In large bowl, combine flour, salt, pepper, and nutmeg. Coat each pork chop with flour mixture, shaking off excess. Reserve the 2 tablespoons seasoned flour.

2. Meanwhile, in 12-inch skillet, melt butter over me- dium-high heat. Add pork chops and cook until golden brown, 3 to 5 minutes per side. Transfer chops to plate; keep warm.

3. Reduce heat to medium. Add onion to skillet; cook, stirring, until tender, about 5 minutes. Sprinkle onion with reserved seasoned flour; cook, stirring, 1 minute. Add broth, stirring to loosen any browned bits from bottom of skillet; simmer 1 minute. Stir in buttermilk. Return pork chops to pan. Simmer 6 minutes, turning once, until cooked through. Sprinkle with parsley.

**EACH SERVING:** About 319 calories, 28g protein, 16g carbohydrate, 15g total fat (7g saturated), 78mg cholesterol, 813mg sodium.

# Ham and Grits with Red-Eye Gravy

As the story goes, Andrew Jackson had a cook who sipped whiskey. He once asked his "tipsy" cook to make some ham and gravy "as red as your eyes." Others contend that the gravy got its name from the "red eye" that seems to appear in the middle of the reduced gravy. In the Deep South, sliced ham or ham steak is quickly fried in a cast-iron skillet (usually a black one), then the gravy is made right in the skillet from the ham drippings and a little strong coffee for extra flavor. It is served with a hefty portion of grits alongside for a true plantation breakfast.

**PREP:** 5 minutes ★ **COOK:** 30 minutes
**MAKES** 6 main-dish servings

4 1/2 cups water

1 cup old-fashioned hominy grits

1/2 teaspoon salt

3 tablespoons butter or margarine

1 tablespoon vegetable oil

6 slices country ham, 1/4 inch thick
   (about 2 ounces each)

1/2 cup strong brewed coffee

1/4 teaspoon sugar

1. In 2-quart saucepan, heat 4 cups water to boiling over medium-high heat; slowly stir in grits and salt. Reduce heat to low; cover and cook, stirring occasionally, until thickened, 15 to 20 minutes. Remove from heat. Stir in butter and keep warm.

**2.** Meanwhile, in 12-inch skillet, heat oil over medium heat until very hot. Cook ham, 3 slices at a time, turning once, until browned; transfer to platter and keep warm.

**3.** Add coffee, remaining ½ cup water, and sugar to drippings in skillet. Heat to boiling over medium heat, stirring until browned bits are loosened from bottom of skillet. Cook, stirring occasionally, 5 minutes. Serve gravy over ham and grits.

**EACH SERVING:** About 279 calories, 18g protein, 21g carbohydrate, 13g total fat (5g saturated), 55mg cholesterol, 1,780mg sodium.

# Honey-Glazed Ham

In the South, hams are available two ways: country-cured and sugar-cured. Country hams are salt-cured the old-fashioned way. Smithfield hams go through a series of saltings, chillings, and washings, ten days of smoking, and at least six months of aging in a smokehouse. To warrant the coveted Smithfield label, a ham must be prepared in the town of Smithfield, Virginia, although the ham itself may come from the surrounding area. These hams are usually soaked before being cooked to remove some of their salt. Our recipe uses a sugar-cured ham. It comes precooked and ready to heat, glaze, and eat.

**PREP:** 45 minutes ★ **ROAST:** 3 hours
**MAKES** 24 main-dish servings

## HAM & GLAZE

**1 fully cooked smoked whole ham
   (about 14 pounds)**

**½ cup packed brown sugar**

**½ cup honey**

**1 teaspoon ground ginger**

## MUSTARD SAUCE

**1 cup sour cream**

**¾ cup mayonnaise**

**1 jar (8 ounces) Dijon mustard with seeds**

**1 teaspoon Worcestershire sauce**

**½ teaspoon coarsely ground black pepper**

**1.** Preheat oven to 325°F. With sharp knife, remove skin and trim fat from ham, leaving ¼-inch-thick layer of fat. Place ham, fat side up, on rack in large roasting pan (17" by 11½"). Bake ham 2 hours 30 minutes.

**2.** Meanwhile, prepare glaze: In 1-quart saucepan, combine brown sugar, honey, and ginger; heat to boiling over medium-high heat. Boil 1 minute. When bubbling subsides, brush ham with some glaze. Bake ham, brushing occasionally with remaining glaze, until meat thermometer inserted into thickest part of ham (not touching bone) reaches 140°F, 30 minutes to 1 hour longer.

**3.** Meanwhile, prepare mustard sauce: In medium bowl, stir sour cream, mayonnaise, mustard, Worcestershire, and pepper until combined. Cover and refrigerate until ready to serve. Makes about 2½ cups.

**4.** Serve ham with mustard sauce.

**EACH SERVING WITHOUT SAUCE:**
About 325 calories, 36g protein, 10g carbohydrate, 15g total fat (5g saturated), 95mg cholesterol, 2400mg sodium.

**EACH TABLESPOON MUSTARD SAUCE:**
About 50 calories, 1g protein, 1g carbohydrate, 5g total fat (1g saturated), 4mg cholesterol, 170mg sodium.

# Best Barbecued Ribs

**A**mericans love their barbecue, but *barbecue* means different things to different people. In the Lone Star State, almost everywhere you go beef brisket and pork spareribs dripping with thick, spicy sauce are often on the menu. The tomato-based Texas sauce is spiked with vinegar, molasses, tinged with smoke, and laced with plenty of chiles and spice. In the Carolina back country, neighbors slather whole hogs with spicy, vinegary concoctions that don't contain any tomato at all. They then slowly roast the hogs, pull the meat off with a large fork, and pile it onto freshly baked buns. Around the Great Lakes, barbecue aficionados add fruitwood to the fire and use a sweeter, less spicy sauce. In Kansas City, they season racks of ribs with a spicy dry rub similar to the one in our recipe. No matter which region it comes from, American barbecue can be counted on to be delicious and satisfying.

**PREP:** 40 minutes plus standing
**GRILL:** 1 hour 10 minutes
**MAKES** 8 main-dish servings

## BARBECUE SAUCE

2 cups ketchup

1 cup apple cider or juice

2 tablespoons Worcestershire sauce

2 tablespoons light (mild) molasses

2 tablespoons cider vinegar

2 tablespoons brown sugar

2 tablespoons yellow mustard

½ teaspoon ground black pepper

¼ teaspoon ground red pepper (cayenne)

## RIBS

2 tablespoons paprika

1 tablespoon brown sugar

2 teaspoons chili powder

2 teaspoons salt

1½ teaspoons ground black pepper

1 teaspoon ground cumin

½ teaspoon ground red pepper (cayenne)

4 racks pork baby back ribs (1 pound each)*

1. Prepare barbecue sauce: In 4-quart saucepan, combine ketchup, cider, Worcestershire, molasses, vinegar, brown sugar, mustard, black pepper, and red pepper. Heat to boiling; reduce heat and simmer, stirring occasionally, until sauce thickens slightly, about 30 minutes.

2. Prepare ribs: In small bowl, combine paprika, brown sugar, chili powder, salt, black pepper, cumin, and ground red pepper. Pat ribs dry with paper towels. Sprinkle on both sides with spice mixture. Let stand 30 minutes.

3. Meanwhile, prepare grill.

4. Place 28" by 12" sheet of heavy-duty foil on surface. Place 1 rack of ribs in center of foil. Place 2 ice cubes under ribs. Bring long sides of foil up and fold several times to seal well. Fold in ends to seal tightly. Repeat with three more sheets of foil, 6 ice cubes, and remaining 3 racks of ribs.

5. Place foil packets on grill rack over medium heat. Cover and cook ribs over medium heat 1 hour, carefully turning packets over once with tongs. With kitchen scissors, cut an X in top of each foil packet to release steam; carefully peel back foil. Remove ribs and place directly on grill. Brush ribs with some sauce; cook, brushing and turning frequently, 10 minutes longer. Serve with remaining sauce on the side.

*If available, use St. Louis-cut baby back ribs because they are meatier.

**EACH SERVING:** About 532 calories, 28g protein, 32g carbohydrate, 33g total fat (12g saturated), 129mg cholesterol, 1,507mg sodium.

# Chapter 4

# Side Dishes

Not knowing what they would find in their new homeland, the Pilgrims brought vegetable seeds for cabbage, string beans (called French beans), peas, onion, and parsnip to the New World. In time, the Virginia colonists planted asparagus, beets, broccoli, cauliflower, cucumbers, and various greens. To minimize their dependency on English imports, the Jamestown settlers learned how to cultivate corn, white and sweet potatoes, winter squash (including pumpkin), tomatoes, and wild greens, such as ramps and fiddlehead ferns.

The colonists learned how to store vegetables in root cellars, pickle and salt-preserve them, and turn cabbage into sauerkraut. Fruit was often turned into preserves, and by the early nineteenth century, fresh vegetables were canned. The popularity of domestic (home) gardening soared by the nineteenth century. In her 1824 regional cookbook, *The Virginia Housewife*, Mary Randolph devoted an entire section to produce. By the end of the century, commercial canneries made it easy to enjoy vegetables effortlessly year-round.

In the 1920s, Clarence Birdseye, a young scientist on assignment in Labrador with the U.S. Fish and Wildlife Service, discovered that his daily catch froze quickly in the Arctic temperatures yet tasted very fresh when thawed. He seized upon this concept and launched the frozen-food industry in 1924.

By the 1960s, the way Americans viewed food began to change. We came to appreciate the Chinese technique of stir-frying, which produced tender-crisp vegetables that were nutritious as well as delicious. Julia Child also influenced our appreciation for vegetables cooked in the French manner: until tender instead of soft and tasteless. In 1971, Alice Waters opened Chez Panisse, where the menu was based on fresh, local ingredients very simply prepared. Farmers' markets sprung up across the country by the mid-1970s as more and more consumers demanded fresh, regional produce of uncompromising quality.

Over the last several hundred years we have come full circle: like the colonists, we have gained an appreciation for high-quality fresh vegetables that can be appreciated on a daily basis.

◀ *Asparagus with Hollandaise Sauce*

## To Cook Asparagus

**To Steam:** In asparagus steamer or 3-quart saucepan fitted with rack, heat *½ inch water* to boiling over medium-high heat; add *1 pound asparagus,* trimmed. Cover and steam until tender-crisp, 8 to 10 minutes (depending on thickness of asparagus).

**To Boil:** In 12-inch skillet, heat *1 inch water* to boiling over high heat. Add *1 pound asparagus,* trimmed, and *½ teaspoon salt;* heat to boiling. Reduce heat to medium-high; cook, uncovered, until tender-crisp, 5 to 10 minutes (depending on thickness of asparagus). Drain.

# Asparagus with Hollandaise Sauce

*(pictured on page 76)*

Fannie Farmer offers four simple ways to prepare asparagus in her 1896 cookbook: on toast, in white sauce, with hollandaise sauce, and in fried bread shells with white sauce spooned over. Asparagus with hollandaise sauce remains a favorite way to enjoy this vegetable. For the best flavor, use good-quality butter—never margarine. For an easy variation, steam or boil asparagus and serve it with melted butter and lemon wedges.

**PREP:** 10 minutes ★ **COOK:** 10 minutes
**MAKES** 4 accompaniment servings

1 pound asparagus, tough ends trimmed
¼ teaspoon salt
Hollandaise Sauce (below)

1. Boil or steam asparagus as directed in box (opposite). Sprinkle with salt; transfer to serving dish. Keep warm.

2. Meanwhile, prepare Hollandaise Sauce. Serve sauce alongside asparagus.

**EACH SERVING WITHOUT SAUCE:** About 20 calories, 3g protein, 3g carbohydrate, 0g total fat (0g saturated), 0mg cholesterol, 145mg sodium.

# Hollandaise Sauce

**PREP:** 5 minutes ★ **COOK:** 10 minutes
**MAKES** scant 1 cup

3 large egg yolks
¼ cup water
2 tablespoons fresh lemon juice
½ cup butter (1 stick), cut into 8 pieces (do not use margarine)
¼ teaspoon salt

1. In heavy nonreactive 1-quart saucepan, with wire whisk, whisk egg yolks, water, and lemon juice until well blended. Cook over medium-low heat, stirring constantly with wooden spoon or heat-safe rubber spatula, until egg-yolk mixture just begins to bubble at edge, 6 to 8 minutes.

2. Reduce heat to low. With wire whisk, whisk in butter one piece at a time, until each addition is incorporated and sauce has thickened. Remove from heat and stir in salt. Strain through sieve, if you like.

**EACH TABLESPOON:** About 62 calories, 1g protein, 0g carbohydrate, 7g total fat (4g saturated), 55mg cholesterol, 96mg sodium.

# Brussels Sprouts with Bacon

**B**russels sprouts are a member of the cabbage family. They grow on a stalk, completely covering it with their round heads. Botanical texts date Brussels sprouts back to the sixteenth century. In 1812, Thomas Jefferson planted some and made a notation about it in his garden book. Mrs. Sarah Rorer in *Mrs. Rorer's Philadelphia Cook Book,* advises readers to add ¼ teaspoon of bicarbonate of soda (baking soda) to the cooking water "to render [sprouts] soft."

**PREP:** 15 minutes ★ **COOK:** 25 minutes
**MAKES** 10 accompaniment servings

**3 containers (10 ounces each) Brussels sprouts, trimmed and cut lengthwise in half**

**6 slices bacon**

**1 tablespoon olive oil**

**2 garlic cloves, finely chopped**

**½ teaspoon salt**

**¼ teaspoon coarsely ground black pepper**

1. In 4-quart saucepan, heat *2 quarts water* to boiling over high heat. Add Brussels sprouts; heat to boiling. Cook until tender-crisp, about 5 minutes; drain.

2. In 12-inch skillet, cook bacon over medium heat until browned. With slotted spoon, transfer bacon to paper towels to drain; crumble.

3. Discard all but 1 tablespoon bacon drippings from skillet. Add oil and heat over medium-high heat. Add Brussels sprouts, garlic, salt, and pepper. Cook, stirring frequently, until Brussels sprouts are lightly browned, about 5 minutes. Sprinkle with the bacon.

**EACH SERVING:** About 96 calories, 5g protein, 8g carbohydrate, 6g total fat (1g saturated), 4mg cholesterol, 202mg sodium.

# Harvard Beets

**T**he origin of the first recipe for Harvard beets is debatable. One tale links it to a seventeenth-century English tavern named Harwood, where this beet dish was on the menu. A Russian émigré who was a customer moved to America and opened a restaurant in Boston in 1846 that he named Harwood. Just as in the English tavern, he served Harwood beets, but due to his Russian accent it sounded like "Harvard." Another tale relates the name to Harvard's crimson team color, which is similar to the bright red of beets.

**PREP:** 20 minutes ★ **COOK:** 10 minutes
**MAKES** 6 accompaniment servings

**¼ cup sugar**

**1 tablespoon cornstarch**

**½ teaspoon salt**

**⅓ cup cider vinegar**

**1 tablespoon butter or margarine**

**1 teaspoon minced onion**

**3 cups cooked, sliced beets or 2 cans (16 ounces each) sliced beets, drained**

In 1-quart saucepan, combine sugar, cornstarch, and salt. Add vinegar in slow, steady stream, stirring until well blended. Add butter and onion. Cook, stirring constantly over medium heat, until sauce has thickened and boils. Reduce heat and simmer 1 minute. Add beets and cook, stirring occasionally, just until heated through.

**EACH SERVING:** About 82 calories, 1g protein, 16g carbohydrate, 2g total fat (1g saturated), 5mg cholesterol, 255mg sodium.

## Yale Beets

Prepare as directed but substitute *½ cup orange juice* for vinegar and substitute *1 teaspoon freshly grated orange peel* for onion.

# Pennsylvania-Dutch Hot Slaw

Europeans were eating cabbage as far back as the Middle Ages. The New England colonists stayed close to their British roots and always boiled it. The Amish and Mennonites who settled in the Pennsylvania countryside loved cabbage. They prepared sauerkraut as well as creamy, hot wilted slaw from recipes brought from Germany. It is interesting to note that Pennsylvania- Dutch hot slaw closely resembles the Alsatian dish *émincé de choux verts aux lardons chauds* (hot cabbage and bacon salad). It features a warm bacon dressing, which slightly wilts the shredded cabbage while leaving just a bit of pleasant crunch.

**PREP:** 10 minutes ★ **COOK:** 10 minutes
**MAKES** 4 accompaniment servings

3 slices bacon, finely chopped

$\frac{1}{2}$ small head green cabbage (16 ounces), cored and thinly sliced

1 small onion, chopped

2 tablespoons cider vinegar

$\frac{1}{4}$ cup sugar

$\frac{1}{2}$ teaspoon celery seeds

$\frac{1}{4}$ teaspoon salt

1. In 5-quart Dutch oven, cook bacon over medium heat until browned. With slotted spoon, transfer bacon to paper towels to drain.

2. To drippings in pot, add cabbage and onion. Cook, stirring frequently, until cabbage is tender-crisp, about 5 minutes. Stir in vinegar, sugar, celery seeds, salt, and bacon. Cook 1 minute longer.

**EACH SERVING:** About 178 calories, 3g protein, 20g carbohydrate, 10g total fat (4g saturated), 11mg cholesterol, 277mg sodium.

# Cajun Maquechou

The ingredients in this Cajun dish are rather basic: corn, onions, bell pepper, and cream. Some believe the dish was brought to Louisiana by the Spaniards and that its name originates from the Spanish word *machica*, a dish of toasted corn-meal that's sweetened with sugar and spices. Others believe the word comes from *maigrichou*, meaning "thin child," for the dish is like a (thin) soup.

**PREP:** 20 minutes ★ **COOK:** 45 minutes
**MAKES** 8 accompaniment servings

4 slices bacon, chopped

1 large onion (12 ounces), chopped

1 large red pepper, chopped

5 cups corn kernels cut from cobs (about 8 ears) or 3 packages (10 ounces each) frozen whole-kernel corn

1 can (14$\frac{1}{2}$ ounces) diced tomatoes, drained

$\frac{1}{4}$ cup heavy cream

$\frac{3}{4}$ teaspoon salt

$\frac{1}{2}$ teaspoon sugar

$\frac{1}{8}$ to $\frac{1}{4}$ teaspoon ground red pepper (cayenne)

chopped fresh parsley (optional)

1. In nonstick 12-inch skillet, cook bacon over medium heat until crisp. With slotted spoon, transfer bacon to paper towels to drain.

2. To drippings in skillet, add onion and red pepper. Cook, stirring frequently, until vegetables are lightly browned, about 12 minutes.

3. Stir in corn, tomatoes, cream, salt, sugar, and ground red pepper; heat to boiling over high heat. Reduce heat; cover and simmer, stirring occasionally, until corn is tender, about 15 minutes. Stir in bacon and sprinkle with parsley, if using.

**EACH SERVING:** About 202 calories, 5g protein, 25g carbohydrate, 11g total fat (4g saturated), 18mg cholesterol, 398mg sodium.

# Corn Pudding

Corn pudding dates back to the plantations in the Deep South, where corn was freshly picked from the fields. The secret to the creamiest corn pudding is the way the corn is cut off the cob. According to Evan Jones in *American Food*: "In the smoothest, most luscious corn pudding I know, much depends on the amount of liquid in the corn pulp. Some Kentuckians say this delicacy must be made with young field corn, and served as a vegetable. Mixed with eggs, milk or cream, butter, salt, pepper, and a hint of sugar. 'When it doesn't shake', say some Southern cooks, 'it is ready.' "

**PREP:** 25 minutes ★ **BAKE:** 45 minutes
**MAKES** 8 accompaniment servings

1¼ **teaspoons salt**

2 **cups corn kernels cut from cobs (3 to 4 ears)**

2 **tablespoons all-purpose flour**

2 **tablespoons sugar**

⅛ **teaspoon ground black pepper**

1¾ **cups milk**

¼ **cup heavy or whipping cream**

2 **tablespoons butter or margarine, melted**

3 **large eggs**

**1.** Preheat oven to 325°F. Lightly grease 8-inch square baking dish.

**2.** In 2-quart saucepan, heat *1½ cups water* and ½ teaspoon salt to boiling over high heat. Add corn kernels and heat to boiling; boil 2 minutes. Drain; pat corn dry with paper towels.

**3.** In medium bowl, with wire whisk, combine flour, sugar, remaining ¾ teaspoon salt, and pepper. Gradually whisk in milk, cream, butter, and eggs until smooth. Stir in corn. Pour mixture into prepared baking dish.

**4.** Place baking dish in medium roasting pan (14" by 10"); place pan on oven rack. Pour enough *boiling water* into roasting pan to come halfway up sides of baking dish. Bake until top is lightly browned and knife inserted in center comes out clean, about 45 minutes.

**EACH SERVING:** About 170 calories, 6g protein, 15g carbohydrate, 10g total fat (5g saturated), 105mg cholesterol, 451mg sodium.

## Corn Custard with Basil

Prepare recipe as above, but substitute basil-flavored milk for the plain milk in Step 3. To prepare basil-flavored milk, in 1-quart saucepan, heat *1¾ cups milk* and *1 cup loosely packed fresh basil sprigs* over medium-high heat until bubbles form around edge. Remove from heat; cover and let steep about 10 minutes. Discard basil.

## Liberty and Victory Gardens

With the declaration of World War I in 1917, President Woodrow Wilson named Herbert Hoover as head of the U.S. Food Administration. The task at hand was enormous—the United States had to feed not only the armed forces and its citizens at home, but also its allies. Public relations campaigns announced that "Food Will Win the War." Families were urged to plant vegetables in their backyards, and these plots soon became known as liberty gardens.

The success of the liberty garden campaign prompted the government once again to encourage citizens to plant gardens during World War II wherever there was a flower bed, a plowable backyard, or some available land. The newly named victory gardens popped up in some rather unlikely spots, such as the Portland Zoo and Chicago's Arlington Racetrack. About 20 million gardens were planted, which produced about 1 million tons of vegetables that were worth at least $85 million. Not surprisingly, home canning soared during this time: over three-quarters of American families preserved over 165 jars a year. Not only were they able to grow much-needed food, but Americans were also awakened to the glories of enjoying fresh produce, which has been appreciated ever since.

# Smothered Greens

The tradition of eating "a mess of greens" dates back to the Virginia colonists, who planted mustard, collard, and other greens and cooked them up in a large pot along with a ham hock for flavor. The potlikker (the broth left in the pot), which was rich in vitamins, was enjoyed by the field hands working the plantations.

**PREP:** 30 minutes ★ **COOK:** 1 hour 15 minutes
**MAKES** 10 accompaniment servings

---

5 pounds assorted greens, such as kale, collard greens, or mustard greens

2 smoked ham hocks (1½ pounds)

1 medium onion

2 quarts water

1 teaspoon salt

hot pepper sauce

1. Remove stems and tough ribs from greens; rinse well with cool running water. Cut into ½-inch pieces.

2. In 8-quart saucepot, combine ham hocks, onion, water, and salt; heat to boiling over high heat. Add greens to pot in batches, stirring to wilt. Heat to boiling. Reduce heat; cover and simmer until very tender, about 1 hour. Discard ham hocks. Serve with hot pepper sauce.

---

**EACH SERVING:** About 82 calories, 5g protein, 13g carbohydrate, 3g total fat (1g saturated), 2mg cholesterol, 560mg sodium.

# Creamed Spinach

Spinach was brought here by the Spanish settlers. In our recipe the spinach is creamed by folding it into a luscious white sauce enriched with cream cheese and sour cream.

**PREP:** 20 minutes ★ **COOK:** 15 minutes
**MAKES** 6 accompaniment servings

**2 tablespoons butter or margarine**

**3 large shallots, finely chopped (about ¾ cup)**

**2 tablespoons all-purpose flour**

**½ cup milk**

**¾ teaspoon salt**

**¼ teaspoon coarsely ground black pepper**

**⅛ teaspoon ground nutmeg**

**1 package (3 ounces) cream cheese, softened and cut into pieces**

**3 packages (10 ounces each) frozen chopped spinach, thawed and squeezed dry**

**1 cup loosely packed fresh parsley leaves**

**¼ cup sour cream**

**1.** In 4-quart saucepan, melt butter over medium-low heat. Add shallots and cook, stirring frequently, until tender, about 3 minutes. Add flour and cook, stirring, 1 minute. With wire whisk, gradually whisk in milk; heat to boiling, whisking constantly. Reduce heat and simmer, stirring occasionally, until sauce has thickened and boils, about 2 minutes. Stir in salt, pepper, and nutmeg.

**2.** Remove from heat; stir in cream cheese until smooth. Stir in spinach, parsley, and sour cream; heat through (do not boil).

**EACH SERVING:** About 180 calories, 7g protein, 14g carbohydrate, 12g total fat (7g saturated), 33mg cholesterol, 500mg sodium.

# Minted Sugar Snaps

Green peas were one of the first vegetables that the Pilgrims planted in their gardens. American cookbook author Amelia Simmons advised: "All Peas should be picked *carefully* from the vines as soon as dew is off, shelled and cleaned without water, and boiled immediately; they are thus the richest flavored." Our recipe uses tender sugar snap peas, which don't require shelling.

**PREP:** 15 minutes ★ **COOK:** 5 minutes
**MAKES** 4 accompaniment servings

**1 tablespoon butter or margarine**

**¼ teaspoon salt**

**⅛ teaspoon coarsely ground black pepper**

**1 pound snap peas, strings removed**

**1 garlic clove, minced**

**⅓ cup loosely packed fresh mint leaves, finely chopped**

**½ teaspoon freshly grated lemon peel**

**¼ teaspoon freshly grated lime peel**

In nonstick 12-inch skillet, heat butter, salt, and pepper over medium heat until butter has melted. Add snap peas and cook, stirring, until tender-crisp, about 5 minutes. Remove from heat. Add garlic, mint, and lemon and lime peels; toss well.

**EACH SERVING:** About 77 calories, 3g protein, 9g carbohydrate, 3g total fat (2g saturated), 8mg cholesterol, 175mg sodium.

# Butter Beans with Bacon

**N**ative Americans combined lima beans with corn, creating the Narrangansett dish *misickquatash* (succotash, also known as *sukquttahash* and *msakwitash*), a recipe they shared with the colonists. Nowadays, lima beans (known in the South as butter beans) are skillet-fried in bacon drippings, then simmered until nice and tender.

**PREP:** 5 minutes ★ **COOK:** 20 minutes
**MAKES** 4 accompaniment servings

4 slices bacon

1 package (10 ounces) frozen baby lima beans

2 stalks celery, thinly sliced

$\frac{1}{4}$ teaspoon salt

$\frac{1}{8}$ teaspoon ground black pepper

$\frac{1}{3}$ cup water

**1.** In 10-inch skillet, cook bacon over medium heat until browned. With slotted spoon, transfer bacon to paper towels to drain; crumble. Discard all but 1 tablespoon bacon drippings from skillet.

**2.** To drippings in skillet, add frozen lima beans, celery, salt, and pepper. Cook over medium heat, stirring frequently, until vegetables are tender, about 5 minutes.

**3.** Add water to skillet; heat to boiling over high heat. Reduce heat and simmer 5 minutes. Spoon bean mixture into serving bowl; sprinkle with crumbled bacon.

**EACH SERVING:** About 156 calories, 7g protein, 19g carbohydrate, 6g total fat (2g saturated), 8mg cholesterol, 314mg sodium.

# Creamed Onions and Peas

**I**n 1896, Fannie Farmer offered Onions in Cream: "Prepare and cook as Boiled Onions...cover with Cream or Thin White Sauce." Our recipe includes a double amount of green peas. If you prefer, use half the amount.

**PREP:** 30 minutes ★ **COOK:** 25 minutes
**MAKES** 12 accompaniment servings

1 container or bag (10 ounces) pearl onions

2 tablespoons butter or margarine

2 tablespoons all-purpose flour

$\frac{1}{2}$ teaspoon salt

$\frac{1}{4}$ teaspoon dried thyme

$\frac{1}{8}$ teaspoon ground nutmeg

$\frac{1}{8}$ teaspoon ground black pepper

$2\frac{1}{4}$ cups milk

2 bags (16 ounces each) frozen peas, thawed

**1.** In 12-inch skillet, heat *1 inch water* to boiling over high heat. Add onions; heat to boiling. Reduce heat to low; cover and simmer until tender, 10 to 15 minutes. Drain.

**2.** When cool enough to handle, peel onions, leaving a bit of root end attached to help onions hold their shape.

**3.** Meanwhile, in 2-quart saucepan, melt butter over medium heat. Stir in flour, salt, thyme, nutmeg, and pepper until blended; cook, stirring constantly, 1 minute. With wire whisk, gradually stir in milk; cook, stirring, until sauce has thickened slightly and boils.

**4.** Return onions to skillet. Add sauce and peas; cover and cook, stirring often, over medium-high heat until sauce boils and peas are heated through.

**EACH SERVING:** About 116 calories, 6g protein, 15g carbohydrate, 4g total fat (2g saturated), 12mg cholesterol, 225mg sodium.

# Green Bean Casserole with Frizzled Onions

In the mid-twentieth century, the Campbell Soup Company created a simple green-bean bake made with a can of condensed cream of mushroom soup, green beans (either frozen or canned), some milk, canned french fried onions, a little soy sauce, and black pepper. It was then baked and topped with more onions. Our delicious homemade version uses freshly fried onions, fresh green beans, and sautéed mushrooms.

**PREP:** 50 minutes ★ **BAKE:** 21 minutes
**MAKES** 6 accompaniment servings

---

1 medium onion, very thinly sliced

6 tablespoons all-purpose flour

½ cup vegetable oil

⅛ plus ¼ teaspoon salt

1 pound green beans, trimmed and cut in half

2 tablespoons butter or margarine

8 ounces mushrooms, trimmed and sliced

1 large garlic clove, minced

1 cup milk

⅛ teaspoon ground black pepper

**1.** In large bowl, separate onion slices into rings. Add 4 tablespoons flour to onions; toss to coat, shaking off excess.

**2.** In 10-inch skillet, heat oil over medium-high heat until hot. Add onions, leaving excess flour in bowl. Cook onions, stirring frequently, until onions are browned, 3 to 5 minutes. With slotted spoon, transfer onions to paper towels to drain. Sprinkle with ⅛ teaspoon salt. Discard oil from the skillet.

**3.** In same skillet, heat *1 inch water* to boiling over high heat. Add beans; heat to boiling. Cook beans, uncovered, until tender-crisp, 4 to 5 minutes. Drain. Rinse with cold running water to stop cooking; drain well and pat dry with paper towels.

**4.** Preheat oven to 400°F. Lightly grease a shallow 2-quart casserole.

**5.** In same skillet, melt butter over medium heat. Add mushrooms, garlic, and remaining ¼ teaspoon salt. Cook, stirring, until liquid has evaporated and mushrooms begin to brown, about 5 minutes.

**6.** In small bowl, with wire whisk, blend remaining 2 tablespoons flour and milk until smooth. Stir into mushroom mixture; heat to boiling. Reduce heat to low and simmer, stirring, 5 minutes. Stir in green beans. Turn mixture into prepared casserole. Cover loosely with foil. Bake until bubbling, about 20 minutes. Top with onions; bake until onions are heated through, about 1 minute.

---

**EACH SERVING:** About 289 calories, 5g protein, 17g carbohydrate, 24g total fat (6g saturated), 16mg cholesterol, 212mg sodium.

# Narraganset Succotash

The oldest succotash recipe (on record) calls for boiling two fowls and includes four pounds of brisket, a turnip, five or six sliced potatoes, two quarts of dried white beans, and four quarts of cooked dried corn. Today, recipes use bacon drippings and toss in lima beans instead of the traditional kidney beans.

PREP: 15 minutes ★ COOK: 30 minutes
MAKES 10 accompaniment servings

5 slices bacon

3 stalks celery, cut into 1/4-inch-thick slices

1 medium onion, chopped

2 cans (15 1/4 to 16 ounces each) whole-kernel corn, drained

2 packages (10 ounces each) frozen baby lima beans

1/2 cup canned chicken broth or Old-Fashioned Chicken Broth (page 49)

3/4 teaspoon salt

1/4 teaspoon coarsely ground black pepper

2 tablespoons chopped fresh parsley

1. In 12-inch skillet, cook bacon over medium heat until browned. With slotted spoon, transfer to paper towels to drain; crumble.

2. Discard all but 2 tablespoons drippings from skillet. Add celery and onion; cook over medium heat, stirring occasionally, until vegetables are tender and golden, about 15 minutes. Stir in corn, frozen lima beans, broth, salt, and pepper; heat to boiling over high heat. Reduce heat; cover and simmer, until heated through, 5 to 10 minutes longer. Stir in parsley and sprinkle with bacon.

EACH SERVING: About 155 calories, 7g protein, 24g carbohydrate, 5g total fat (2g saturated), 5mg cholesterol, 490mg sodium.

# French-Fried Onion Rings

It wasn't until the 1906 edition of *The Boston Cooking-School Cook Book* that a recipe for french-fried onions appeared: "Peel onions, cut in one-fourth-inch slices, and separate into rings. Dip in milk, drain, and dip in flour. Fry in deep fat, drain on brown paper, and sprinkle with salt." The recipe is still a favorite today.

PREP: 15 minutes ★ COOK: 5 minutes per batch
MAKES 4 accompaniment servings

1 jumbo onion (1 pound), cut into 1/4-inch-thick slices

vegetable oil for frying

1/4 cup milk

1 cup all-purpose flour

1/2 teaspoon salt

1. Separate onion slices into rings. In 4-quart saucepan, heat 2 inches oil over medium heat until temperature reaches 370°F on a deep-fat thermometer.

2. Pour milk into large bowl. In ziptight plastic bag, mix flour and salt. Dip one-fourth of onion rings in milk. With tongs, transfer to flour mixture; shake to coat.

3. Carefully drop coated onion rings into hot oil; fry until golden brown, 5 to 7 minutes. With slotted spoon, transfer to paper towels to drain. Repeat dipping, coating, and frying with remaining onion rings. Serve hot.

EACH SERVING: About 487 calories, 4g protein, 26g carbohydrate, 42g total fat (5g saturated), 1mg cholesterol, 298mg sodium.

# Home Fries

By the 1930s, mobile lunch wagons across America had turned into stationary eateries, which were originally called "dining cars," then later on "diners." Home fries, also known as "house fries" or "cottage fries" were then—and still are—a popular menu item. They begin with boiled potatoes that are chopped or sliced, often with onion, then fried in butter on the back of the grill. If you don't have a grill, a skillet works just fine.

**PREP:** 30 minutes plus cooling ★ **COOK:** 20 minutes
**MAKES** 4 accompaniment servings

4 medium all-purpose potatoes
(6 ounces each), not peeled

4 tablespoons butter or margarine

1 small onion, chopped

¼ teaspoon salt

1. In 4-quart saucepan, combine potatoes and enough *water* to cover; heat to boiling over high heat. Reduce heat; cover and simmer until tender, 15 to 20 minutes. Drain well.

2. Leave potato skins on, if you like. When cool enough to handle, cut potatoes into ¼-inch-thick slices.

3. In 12-inch skillet, melt butter over medium heat. Add potatoes and onion; cook until underside is golden, about 5 minutes. With wide spatula, turn potato mixture. Cook over medium heat, turning several times, until evenly browned. Sprinkle with the salt.

**EACH SERVING:** About 291 calories, 4g protein, 44g carbohydrate, 12g total fat (7g saturated), 31mg cholesterol, 269mg sodium.

# Chicago Mash with Onion and Bacon

In Chicago, down-home diners are a way of life. Chicagoans like their mashed potatoes with plenty of browned onion bits and bacon stirred in. Our recipe calls for making the potatoes with warm milk instead of cold. This keeps the potatoes hot and makes them fluffier because more air can be whipped into hot potatoes.

**PREP:** 15 minutes ★ **COOK:** 25 minutes
**MAKES** 8 accompaniment servings

4 slices bacon, chopped

1 large onion (12 ounces), chopped

3 pounds all-purpose potatoes (about 9 medium), peeled and cut into 1-inch pieces

1 bay leaf

1 teaspoon salt

¼ teaspoon coarsely ground black pepper

1 cup milk, warmed

1. In 10-inch skillet, cook bacon over medium heat until browned. With slotted spoon, transfer bacon to paper towels to drain; crumble.

2. To drippings in skillet, add onion; cook, stirring occasionally, over medium heat until onion is tender, about 15 minutes.

3. Meanwhile, in 3-quart saucepan, combine potatoes, bay leaf, and enough *water* to cover; heat to boiling over high heat. Reduce heat to low; cover and simmer until potatoes are tender, about 15 minutes. Drain.

4. Return potatoes to saucepan. Discard bay leaf. Mash potatoes with salt and pepper. Gradually add milk; mash until smooth and well blended. Stir in onion and bacon.

**EACH SERVING:** About 200 calories, 5g protein, 28g carbohydrate, 8g total fat (3g saturated), 12mg cholesterol, 370mg sodium.

# Potato Boats

Early American cookbooks often featured potatoes "baked in the half-shell." Today they're called by various names: twice-baked potatoes, stuffed baked potatoes, potato boats, and even 'tater boats.

**PREP:** 15 minutes  ★  **BAKE:** 1 hour 15 minutes
**MAKES** 4 accompaniment servings

**4 medium baking potatoes (8 ounces each), scrubbed**

**3 tablespoons butter or margarine**

**2 large green onions (12 ounces each), thinly sliced**

**½ cup sour cream**

**¼ teaspoon salt**

**¼ teaspoon ground black pepper**

**4 ounces sharp Cheddar cheese, shredded (1 cup)**

**¼ teaspoon paprika**

1. Preheat oven to 450°F. Prick potatoes with fork. Bake until tender, about 1 hour.

2. Meanwhile, in medium skillet, melt butter over medium heat. Add green onions and cook, stirring, until wilted, about 2 minutes. Set aside.

3. While potatoes are hot, using a pot holder, cut a thin lengthwise slice, about ½ inch thick, from each potato. With spoon, scoop out flesh into skillet; reserve shells. Scoop out flesh from tops into skillet. Mash potatoes, sour cream, salt, and pepper until smooth and well blended. Stir in ½ cup Cheddar. Spoon mixture into reserved shells, mounding slightly. Place on cookie sheet; sprinkle with remaining ½ cup Cheddar and paprika.

4. Bake potatoes until hot and cheese has melted, about 15 minutes.

**EACH SERVING:** About 459 calories, 14g protein, 49g carbohydrate, 24g total fat (15g saturated), 66mg cholesterol, 440mg sodium.

# Steak Fries

Steak fries became popular in the mid-twentieth century in diners and roadside cafés. The potatoes were thick cut with their skins left on. Their name derives from the fact that they are usually piled high next to one's steak as the ideal accompaniment.

**PREP:** 15 minutes plus chilling
**COOK:** 6 minutes per batch
**MAKES** 4 accompaniment servings

**2 pounds russet or baking potatoes (4 medium), scrubbed**

**3 cups peanut or vegetable oil**

**1 teaspoon kosher salt**

1. Cut each potato lengthwise into quarters, then cut each quarter into 4 long wedges. In large bowl, combine potatoes with enough *cold water* to cover. Refrigerate potatoes at least 2 hours or up to 8 hours.

2. Drain potatoes; transfer to paper towel–lined jelly-roll pan. Pat dry with paper towels.

3. In 5-quart Dutch oven or deep fryer, heat oil over medium heat until temperature reaches 325°F on deep-fat thermometer. Place one-fourth of potatoes in frying basket or fine-mesh sieve. Cook, turning occasionally, until potatoes are tender and edges are slightly crisp and pale golden, about 4 minutes. Transfer to paper towels to drain. Fry remaining potatoes.

4. Preheat oven to 300°F. Heat oil over medium heat until temperature reaches 375°F. Refry one-fourth of potatoes until crisp and golden, 1½ to 2 minutes. Transfer steak fries to paper towel–lined cookie sheet. Keep warm in oven while refrying remaining potatoes. Sprinkle with salt. Serve hot.

**EACH SERVING:** About 284 calories, 5g protein, 41g carbohydrate, 12g total fat (2g saturated), 0mg cholesterol, 500mg sodium.

# Scalloped Potatoes

At the turn of the twentieth century, scalloped potatoes began appearing at church suppers and holiday gatherings throughout America. Traditionally, scalloped potatoes were prepared with thinly sliced potatoes that were covered with white sauce and baked until the potatoes were meltingly tender and the top richly browned, as in our recipe. Early cookbooks often suggested lightly sprinkling bread crumbs on top of the dish to give it a nice crisp top.

**PREP:** 30 minutes ★ **BAKE:** 1 hour 30 minutes
**MAKES** 6 accompaniment servings

3 tablespoons butter or margarine

1 small onion, chopped

3 tablespoons all-purpose flour

1 teaspoon salt

$\frac{1}{8}$ teaspoon ground black pepper

1 $\frac{1}{2}$ cups milk, warmed

2 pounds all-purpose potatoes (6 medium),
    peeled and thinly sliced

**1.** Preheat oven to 375°F. Grease 9-inch square baking dish or shallow 2-quart casserole.

**2.** In heavy 2-quart saucepan, melt butter over low heat. Add onion and cook until tender, about 5 minutes. Add flour and cook, stirring, 1 minute. With wire whisk, gradually whisk in milk. Cook over medium heat, stirring constantly, until mixture has thickened and boils. Reduce heat; simmer, stirring frequently, 1 minute. Stir in salt and pepper; remove from heat.

**3.** Arrange half of potatoes in single layer in prepared dish; pour half of sauce on top. Repeat layers. Cover and bake 1 hour. Remove cover; bake until potatoes are tender and top is golden, about 30 minutes longer.

**EACH SERVING:** About 199 calories, 5g protein, 28g carbohydrate, 8g total fat (5g saturated), 24mg cholesterol, 484mg sodium.

## Southern Sweet Potatoes

*Boil six medium-sized sweet potatoes until nearly done. Peel and slice the long way into pieces about half an inch thick. Fill a baking dish with layers of the slices thickly covered with dark brown sugar and bits of butter. Pour over a half cup of boiling water. Cook in a hot oven for twenty or thirty minutes. This will fill a quart and a half baking dish.*

—**Good Housekeeping Everyday Cook Book**, 1903

# Bubbe's Potato Latkes

The tradition of serving potato pancakes at Chanukah began with the Ashkenazi Jews of Northern and Eastern European communities. The pancakes commemorate the Maccabees' defeat of the Syrian army and the reclaiming of the Temple of Jerusalem in 165 BC. The Maccabees found only enough oil in the temple to light their menorah for one night, but miraculously it burned for eight. The oil used to fry these traditional pancakes symbolizes this miracle.

**PREP:** 45 minutes ★ **COOK:** 45 minutes
**MAKES** about 20 latkes or 10 accompaniment servings

Homemade Applesauce (opposite)

4 large baking potatoes (about 2½ pounds), peeled

1 medium onion

1 large egg

2 tablespoons all-purpose flour or matzoh meal

1 tablespoon minced fresh parsley or dill

1 tablespoon fresh lemon juice

½ teaspoon baking powder

½ teaspoon salt

¼ teaspoon coarsely ground black pepper

¾ cup vegetable oil

**1.** Prepare Homemade Applesauce; cover and refrigerate until serving time.

**2.** Finely shred potatoes and onion into colander. With hands, squeeze to remove as much liquid as possible. Place potato mixture in medium bowl; stir in egg, flour, parsley, lemon juice, baking powder, salt, and pepper until well mixed.

**3.** Preheat oven to 250°F. In 12-inch skillet, heat 3 tablespoons vegetable oil over medium heat until hot but not smoking. Drop potato mixture by scant ¼ cups into hot oil to make 5 latkes.

With back of large spoon, flatten each latke into 3-inch round. Cook until underside is golden, 4 to 5 minutes. With slotted spatula, turn latkes and cook until second side is golden brown and crisp, 4 to 5 minutes longer. With spatula, transfer latkes to paper towel–lined cookie sheet to drain; keep warm in oven.

**4.** Repeat with remaining potato mixture, stirring potato mixture before frying each batch and using 3 tablespoons more oil for each new batch. Serve hot with Homemade Applesauce.

**EACH SERVING WITHOUT APPLESAUCE:** About 250 calories, 6g protein, 38g carbohydrate, 9g total fat (1g saturated), 43mg cholesterol, 270mg sodium.

## Homemade Applesauce

Peel and core *4 large Golden Delicious apples (2 pounds)*; cut each into eighths. In 3-quart saucepan, combine apples, *½ cup apple cider or juice*, *¼ cup sugar*, and *1 teaspoon fresh lemon juice*. Heat to boiling over high heat. Reduce heat to low; cover and simmer until apples are very tender, 20 to 25 minutes. Remove from heat; with potato masher, coarsely mash apples. Makes 3 cups.

**EACH SERVING:** About 69 calories, 0g protein, 18g carbohydrate, 0g total fat (0g saturated), 0mg cholesterol, 0mg sodium.

# Dixie Squash Pudding

The tender, sweet yellow squash of summer was one of the new vegetables the colonists learned how to cook in America. The squash was picked fresh and thinly sliced. It was then either boiled and mashed with cream and butter, dipped in batter and fried, or mashed and turned into fritters. In the South, squash pudding is a favorite dish that has changed over time. The squash can be thinly sliced, diced, or completely mashed. In some recipes, the pudding is seasoned with salt and pepper and topped with buttered cracker crumbs, while other recipes contain sautéed onion, crisp bacon, jalapeños, cream cheese, Cheddar, or Monterey Jack.

**PREP:** 25 minutes ★ **BAKE:** 20 minutes
**MAKES** 8 accompaniment servings

2 tablespoons butter or margarine

1 small onion, finely chopped

2 pounds yellow squash, cut into
    ½-inch-thick slices

½ teaspoon salt

1 package (3 ounces) cream cheese,
    cut into ½-inch pieces

¼ cup milk

4 ounces jalapeño Monterey Jack cheese,
    shredded (1 cup)

½ cup crushed round buttery crackers
    (about 12 crackers)

1. Preheat oven to 350°F. Lightly grease a shallow 2-quart baking dish.

2. In 12-inch nonstick skillet, melt butter over medium heat. Add onion and cook until translucent, about 2 minutes. Add squash and salt; cook, stirring, until tender, about 10 minutes. Remove from heat.

3. Stir cream cheese into squash mixture until melted. Stir in milk, ½ cup Monterey Jack cheese, and ¼ cup crushed crackers. Turn into prepared baking dish. Combine remaining cheese and crushed crackers; sprinkle over top. Bake until hot and top is golden brown, about 20 minutes. Let stand 5 minutes for easier serving.

**EACH SERVING:** About 192 calories, 7g protein, 10g carbohydrate, 14g total fat (8g saturated), 39mg cholesterol, 371mg sodium.

# Baked Acorn Squash

Native Americans introduced the colonists to *askutasquash* (squash). Translated literally it means "eaten raw," and that's how it was likely eaten at first. The colonists were pleased to find that the squashes in America were superior to those back home. Acorn squash is still a favorite, especially baked and glazed with brown sugar and butter.

**PREP:** 10 minutes ★ **BAKE:** 35 minutes
**MAKES** 4 accompaniment servings

2 small acorn squash (1 pound each), each cut
    lengthwise in half and seeded

2 tablespoons butter or margarine, cut
    into pieces

¼ cup packed brown sugar

1. Preheat the oven to 350°F. Grease a 13" by 9" baking dish.

2. Place squash, cut side down, in baking dish; bake 30 minutes. Turn cut side up. Place one-fourth of butter and brown sugar in each cavity. Bake until squash is tender and butter and brown sugar have melted, about 5 minutes longer.

**EACH SERVING:** About 181 calories, 1g protein, 31g carbohydrate, 7g total fat (4g saturated), 16mg cholesterol, 69mg sodium.

# Roasted Winter Vegetables

Settlers would bring in the fall harvest and store many of the vegetables in root cellars in anticipation of the long winter ahead. Most nineteenth-century cookbooks feature recipes for winter squash and other autumn vegetables. They are often boiled in salted water, then served hot with melted butter poured over. Today winter vegetables are often roasted in the oven with a little oil and seasoning until richly caramelized and flavorful.

**PREP:** 30 minutes ★ **ROAST:** about 45 minutes
**MAKES** 24 accompaniment servings

- **3 large red onions, each cut into 12 wedges**
- **2 pounds carrots, peeled and cut into 2" by 1" pieces**
- **2 pounds parsnips, peeled and cut into 2" by 1" pieces**
- **2 red or yellow peppers, cut into 1½-inch pieces**
- **1 whole head garlic, separated into cloves and peeled**
- **3 tablespoons olive oil**
- **2 teaspoons salt**
- **¼ teaspoon ground black pepper**

**1.** Preheat oven to 475°F. In large bowl, combine onions, carrots, parsnips, red peppers, and garlic cloves. Add oil, salt, and pepper; toss until evenly coated.

**2.** Divide vegetable mixture between two jelly-roll pans or large shallow roasting pans. Place pans on two oven racks; roast until vegetable are tender and golden, about 45 minutes, rotating pans between upper and lower racks halfway through cooking time and tossing once.

**EACH SERVING:** About 65 calories, 1g protein, 12g carbohydrate, 2g total fat (0g saturated), 0mg cholesterol, 210mg sodium.

# Vegetable Stir-Fry

In the mid-nineteenth century, many Chinese immigrants prepared meals and performed household chores for well-to-do families. Although they were not allowed to cook their native dishes, they did apply their Asian cooking techniques to many foods. Stir-frying vegetables in a wok allows them to keep their color, texture, and flavor and is a popular technique today.

**PREP:** 20 minutes ★ **COOK:** 18 minutes
**MAKES** 4 accompaniment servings

- **1 tablespoon vegetable oil**
- **2 garlic cloves, thinly sliced**
- **1 teaspoon minced, peeled fresh ginger**
- **1 small bunch broccoli (12 ounces), cut into flowerets (about 3 cups)**
- **1 cup water**
- **1 cup peeled and thinly sliced carrots**
- **1 yellow pepper, cut into ½-inch pieces**
- **6 mushrooms, trimmed and thinly sliced**
- **3 green onions, cut on diagonal into 1-inch pieces**
- **2 tablespoons hoisin sauce**
- **¼ teaspoon salt**

In nonstick 12-inch skillet, heat oil over medium-high heat until hot. Add garlic and ginger; cook, stirring frequently (stir-frying), 1 minute. Add broccoli; stir-fry 1 minute. Increase heat to high; add water and cook 3 minutes. Add carrots and yellow pepper; stir-fry until liquid has evaporated, about 6 minutes. Add mushrooms, green onions, hoisin sauce, and salt; stir-fry until vegetables are tender and almost all liquid has evaporated, about 5 minutes longer.

**EACH SERVING:** About 109 calories, 4g protein, 15g carbohydrate, 4g total fat (1g saturated), 0mg cholesterol, 355mg sodium.

# The Shaker Larder

In the nineteenth century, Shaker communities represented simple, unpretentious farm living at its best. The Shakers were a celibate sect who lived in isolated communities in New England and the Midwest. They worked hard and ate well, although they never prepared food on Sunday, as that was their day to rest. Their cooking was simple but very tasty.

Unlike other farming families, the Shakers enjoyed a wide variety of foods, many exported from faraway places and brought home by their trustees, who traveled widely. The Shakers loved growing, cooking, and preserving foods and were very fond of herbs. Excellent cooks and bakers, they took advantage of their resources to give everyday dishes an epicurean touch, such as apple pie with rosewater and spinach flavored with rosemary. Shaker larders were known to be superior to others of their day. The women canned their own fruits and vegetables and made jams, jellies, relishes, and preserves, always managing to capture a freshness and high quality second to none.

The noonday meal was always a wholesome feast: meat that was often fried and smothered with gravy, vegetables fresh from the garden or home canned, homemade pies (apple was a favorite), brown bread, spoon cakes, and cream cheese.

# Eggplant Parmigiana

Thomas Jefferson often gets the credit for introducing America to the eggplant. It took a while for folks to become familiar with how to peel it, slice it, fry it, scallop it, stuff it, and bake it. Although Fannie Farmer's 1923 cookbook offers seven recipes for eggplant, eggplant Parmesan is not one of them. Our authentic version undoubtedly gained its fame in the restaurants and groceries in Italian communities known as Little Italies that popped up in cities following World War II.

**PREP:** 1 hour 30 minutes ★ **BAKE:** 25 minutes
**MAKES** 6 main-dish servings

4 tablespoons olive oil

1 large onion, chopped

1 garlic clove, minced

2 cans (14 to 16 ounces each) tomatoes

2 teaspoons sugar

1/2 teaspoon dried oregano

1/2 teaspoon dried basil

1/2 teaspoon salt

1 cup plain dried bread crumbs

2 large eggs

2 tablespoons water

1 large eggplant (2 1/2 pounds), cut lengthwise into 1/2-inch-thick slices

1/2 cup freshly grated Parmesan cheese

1 package (8 ounces) mozzarella cheese, cut into 1/4-inch-thick slices

1. In 10-inch skillet, heat 2 tablespoons oil over medium heat until hot. Add onion and garlic; cook until tender, about 5 minutes. Add tomatoes, sugar, oregano, basil, and salt. Reduce heat; cover and simmer 30 minutes.

2. Place bread crumbs on waxed paper. In small bowl, with fork, beat eggs and water. Dip eggplant slices, one at a time, in egg mixture, then in bread crumbs; repeat to coat each slice twice.

3. Preheat the oven to 350°F. Grease a 13" by 9" baking dish.

4. In 12-inch skillet, heat remaining 2 tablespoons oil over medium heat. Add eggplant, a few slices at a time, and cook until golden brown, about 5 minutes per side, using slotted spatula to transfer slices to platter as they are browned, adding more oil if necessary.

5. Layer half of eggplant slices in prepared baking dish and cover with half of tomato mixture. Sprinkle with half of Parmesan and top with half of mozzarella. Repeat layers. Cover baking dish with foil; bake 15 minutes. Remove foil; bake until bubbling, about 10 minutes.

**EACH SERVING:** About 426 calories, 19g protein, 38g carbohydrate, 24g total fat (9g saturated), 107mg cholesterol, 917mg sodium.

# Fried Green Tomatoes

New Englanders liked their green tomatoes baked into a pie with a little sprinkling of sugar and spice and a splash of vinegar. Down South, green tomatoes were usually fried up with a crunchy cornmeal coating. Often served at bountiful plantation breakfasts, fried green tomatoes became a tradition that continues today.

**PREP:** 20 minutes ★ **COOK:** 3 minutes per batch
**MAKES** 6 accompaniment servings

**6 slices bacon**

**1 large egg white**

**¼ teaspoon salt**

**½ cup cornmeal**

**¼ teaspoon coarsely ground black pepper**

**3 medium green tomatoes (1 pound),
    cut into scant ½-inch-thick slices**

1. In 12-inch skillet, cook bacon over medium heat until browned. With slotted spoon, transfer bacon to paper towels to drain; crumble. Set aside skillet with drippings.

2. In pie plate, beat egg white and salt. On waxed paper, combine cornmeal and pepper. Dip tomatoes in egg mixture to coat both sides, then dip into cornmeal mixture, pressing so mixture adheres. Place on waxed paper.

3. Heat bacon drippings in skillet over medium-high heat. Cook tomatoes, in batches, until golden brown, about 1½ minutes per side, transferring them to paper towels to drain.

4. Transfer tomatoes to platter; top with bacon.

**EACH SERVING:** About 189 calories, 4g protein, 13g carbohydrate, 13g total fat (5g saturated), 15mg cholesterol, 270mg sodium.

# Chapter 5

# Breads

Corn always grew in America, and as might be expected, it was used for bread making, first by the Native Americans and then by the colonists. The natives baked bread (similar to tortillas) and corn pone (known as Indian bread). By 1750, the colonists had created their own corn bread.

Sometime later, yeast, which had been brought back from Europe enabled the colonists to create rye 'n' Injun bread.

Some innovations and inventions also encouraged bread baking. In the 1790s, it was discovered that when pearl ash, a refined form of potash, was added to quick-bread batter, the bread rose up light and high, something never before thought possible. By the 1850s, a leavening called baking powder made bread making almost foolproof and less labor intensive. And a new product called self-rising flour convinced homemakers that they could whip up delicious griddlecakes, cream biscuits, rolls, and all types of tea cakes with ease. Around this same time, Gold Rushers became acquainted with a San Francisco "wonder" bread called sourdough, and word of its goodness quickly spread. By 1886, Sarah T. Rorer declared in her *Philadelphia*

*Cook Book*: "Bread heads the list of foods for man." Another popular yeast bread was Sally Lunn. Butter and eggs made it rich, and a Turk's head mold made it decorative.

By 1868, yeast was commercially produced, and by the twentieth century, flour had become more refined. The coarser whole-wheat breads were enjoyed by the middle class, while the whiter breads were reserved for society's upper class. To ensure that all bread was nutritious, by the 1940s federal regulations required manufacturers to enrich their breads with the vitamins and minerals lost in the refining process.

Other products were also heading to market, including Wonder Bread sandwich loaf, heat-and-serve rolls, and refrigerated doughs. With time, bakeries began turning out coarser, more nutritious, artisanal breads that were often like those our forefathers had first baked.

# White Bread (Daily Loaf)

In the 1848 edition of *Directions for Cookery in Its Various Branches,* Eliza Leslie advised her readers to bake several loaves of bread at a time, as it was not worthwhile to heat a brick oven for just a loaf or two: "Take one peck or two gallons of fine wheat flour, and sift it into a kneading trough, or into a small clean tub, or a large broad earthen pan..." She suggested wrapping each baked loaf in a clean, coarse towel, then standing the breads on their ends to cool. She also advised sprinkling the towels with water to make the crust less dry and hard. Our recipe only makes two loaves, but you can double it, if you wish.

PREP: 25 minutes plus rising ★ BAKE: 30 minutes
MAKES 2 loaves, 12 slices each

½ cup warm water (105° to 115°F)

2 packages active dry yeast

1 teaspoon plus ¼ cup sugar

2¼ cups milk, heated to warm (105° to 115°F)

4 tablespoons butter or margarine, softened

1 tablespoon salt

about 7½ cups all-purpose or bread flour

1. In large bowl, combine warm water, yeast, and 1 teaspoon sugar; stir well to dissolve. Let stand until foamy, about 5 minutes. Add milk, butter, remaining ¼ cup sugar, salt, and 4 cups flour. Beat well with wooden spoon. Gradually stir in 3 cups flour to make soft dough.

2. Turn dough onto floured surface. Knead until smooth and elastic, about 8 minutes, working in enough of remaining ½ cup flour just to keep dough from sticking.

3. Shape dough into ball; place in greased large bowl, turning dough to grease top. Cover bowl with plastic wrap and let rise in warm place (80° to 85°F) until doubled in volume, about 1 hour.

4. Grease two 9" by 5" metal loaf pans. Punch down dough. Turn dough onto lightly floured surface and cut in half. Shape each half into rectangle about 12" by 7." Roll each up from a short side. Pinch seam and ends to seal. Place dough, seam side down, in prepared pans. Cover pans loosely with greased plastic wrap; let dough rise in warm place until almost doubled, about 1 hour.

5. Meanwhile, preheat oven to 400°F. Bake until browned and loaves sound hollow when lightly tapped on bottom, 30 to 35 minutes. Remove loaves from pans and cool on wire racks.

EACH SLICE: About 187 calories, 5g protein, 34g carbohydrate, 3g total fat (2g saturated), 8mg cholesterol, 323mg sodium.

## Cinnamon-Raisin Bread

Prepare as directed but stir *2 cups dark seedless raisins* into yeast mixture with milk. Spread each rectangle with *2 tablespoons butter or margarine,* softened, leaving ½-inch border. In small cup, combine *⅓ cup packed brown sugar* and *1 tablespoon ground cinnamon*; sprinkle over butter. Roll up each loaf from a short side. Pinch seam and ends to seal. Makes 2 loaves, 12 slices each.

EACH SLICE: About 244 calories, 5g protein, 47g carbohydrate, 4g total fat (2g saturated), 11mg cholesterol, 335mg sodium.

# Mashed-Potato Loaf

Early American cookbooks often gave instructions for making Irish potato yeast from a boiled potato and yeast, which included a recommendation to let the starter work for half a day before using it to make a loaf of bread for the next day's breakfast. Recipes suggested using some of the potato water for the bread's liquid. Cookbook author Annabella P. Hill gives a recipe in her 1872 book *Southern Practical Cookery and Receipt Book* that includes six Irish potatoes that have been pushed through a sieve. She advises: "This bread keeps well." We agree. Potato breads store well and are nice and moist.

---

**PREP:** 1 hour 30 minutes plus rising
**BAKE:** 25 minutes
**MAKES** 2 loaves, 12 slices each

---

**3 medium all-purpose potatoes (about 1 pound), peeled and cut into 1-inch pieces**

**1 cup warm water (105° to 115°F)**

**2 packages active dry yeast**

**2 tablespoons sugar**

**4¼ teaspoons salt**

**4 tablespoons butter or margarine, softened**

**about 9¾ cups all-purpose flour or 8¾ cups bread flour**

**2 large eggs**

1. In 2-quart saucepan, combine potatoes and *4 cups water;* heat to boiling over high heat. Reduce heat; cover and simmer until potatoes are tender, about 15 minutes. Drain, reserving 1 cup potato water. Return potatoes to saucepan; mash until smooth.

2. In large bowl of electric mixer, combine warm water, yeast, and 1 tablespoon sugar; stir to dissolve. Let stand until foamy, about 5 minutes. Stir in 4 teaspoons salt, remaining 1 tablespoon sugar, butter, reserved potato water, and 3 cups flour.

3. With mixer at low speed, beat just until blended. Increase speed to medium; beat 2 minutes, occasionally scraping bowl with rubber spatula. Separate 1 egg. Cover egg white and reserve in refrigerator. Beat in remaining egg, egg yolk, and 1 cup flour to make thick batter; continue beating 2 minutes, frequently scraping bowl. With wooden spoon, stir in mashed potatoes, then 5 cups all-purpose flour or 4 cups bread flour, 1 cup at a time, to make soft dough. (You may want to transfer mixture to larger bowl for easier mixing.)

4. Turn dough onto well-floured surface. Knead until smooth and elastic, about 10 minutes, working in enough of remaining ¾ cup flour just to keep dough from sticking.

5. Shape dough into ball; place in greased large bowl, turning dough to grease top. Cover bowl with plastic wrap and let rise in warm place (80° to 85°F) until doubled in volume, about 1 hour.

6. Grease two 9" by 5" metal loaf pans. Punch down dough. Turn dough onto lightly floured surface and cut in half. Shape each dough half into rectangle about 12" by 7." Roll up from a short side. Pinch seam and ends to seal. Place dough, seam side down, in prepared pans. Cover pans with greased plastic wrap and let dough rise in warm place until doubled, about 40 minutes, or refrigerate up to overnight.

7. Meanwhile, preheat oven to 400°F. (If dough has been refrigerated, remove plastic wrap and let stand about 10 minutes before baking.) Beat reserved egg white with remaining ¼ teaspoon salt; brush over loaves. Bake until golden and loaves sound hollow when lightly tapped on bottom, 25 to 30 minutes. Remove loaves from pans; cool on wire racks.

---

**EACH SLICE:** About 231 calories, 6g protein, 43g carbohydrate, 3g total fat (1g saturated), 23mg cholesterol, 439mg sodium.

# The Baker's First Ovens

The first baker's oven was a sheet of tin attached to the hearth that reflected the fire's heat onto the bread to brown the top crust, while the heat from the hearthstone browned the bottom. Next came the Dutch oven: a portable metal box that was set on the hearth with one open side facing the fire. Usually the box was fitted with shelves, so several breads, cakes, or pies could be baked at the same time. Last came the reflecting oven: about a foot square box made of tin, with a shining rear wall that reflected the heat from the fire back into the oven. It could be heated to a higher temperature than previous ovens, as its curved canopy radiated even more heat back into the oven. This oven was also frequently used for roasting.

In the seventeenth century, fixed brick ovens began appearing—a brick compartment built into the wall of the fireplace. A fire was lit inside the oven and allowed to burn until the oven was the right temperature for baking. The ashes were then scraped out and the food put in. The food that needed the longest baking time was slid to the back, while cakes, pies, and cookies were placed in the front. A tight-fitting wooden shield closed off the oven's open side, and the food was then baked by the heat from the hearth. As homes became larger, separate bake ovens were often built. The height of luxury was a bake oven with a hinged iron door and a damper that could be opened and closed to regulate the flow of air, the intensity of the fire, and the temperature inside the oven.

## Sourdough Starter

**PREP:** 10 minutes plus 3 days
**MAKES** about 2 ⅔ cups starter

2 cups warm water (105° to 115°F)

1 package active dry yeast

1 tablespoon honey

2 cups unbleached all-purpose flour or
   bread flour

**1.** In large glass or ceramic bowl, combine warm water, yeast, and honey; stir to dissolve. Let stand until foamy, about 5 minutes. Gradually stir in flour. Cover bowl with clean kitchen towel and let stand in warm place (80° to 85°F) until starter stops bubbling and has a pleasant yeasty, sour aroma, 3 to 4 days. A clear amber liquid will separate from mixture; stir back into starter once a day. Pour starter into clean jar with lid. Place lid loosely on jar and refrigerate until ready to use.

**2.** To maintain starter, "feed" it once every 2 weeks: Remove jar from refrigerator and pour starter into large glass or ceramic bowl. Whisk in liquid that has separated. Measure out amount of starter needed for recipe. Replace amount used with equal amounts of flour and water. (For example, if recipe uses 1 cup starter, stir in 1 cup unbleached flour and 1 cup water.) Let starter stand at room temperature to become active again, 8 to 12 hours. Use immediately or refrigerate to use within 2 weeks before feeding again.

**3.** If not baking with starter every 2 weeks, discard or give away 1 cup before feeding. If at any point starter seems sluggish and breads are not rising well, stir 1 teaspoon active dry yeast dissolved in ¼ cup warm water (105° to 115°F) into starter and let stand at room temperature overnight.

# San Francisco Sourdough

This special bread became popular thanks to prospectors who carried sourdough starter in their packs so they could bake a batch of bread where and whenever they wanted.

**PREP:** 30 minutes plus 8 hours for starter plus rising
**BAKE:** 25 minutes per loaf
**MAKES** 2 loaves, 8 slices each

1 cup Sourdough Starter (opposite)

1¾ cups warm water (105° to 115°F)

about 6 cups unbleached all-purpose flour or bread flour

1 teaspoon active dry yeast

1 tablespoon sugar

1 tablespoon plus ¼ teaspoon salt

cornmeal for sprinkling

1 large egg white

1. Prepare Sourdough Starter. Place 1 cup of starter in large glass or ceramic bowl. Add 1½ cups warm water and 3 cups flour; stir vigorously with wooden spoon. Cover bowl with plastic wrap; let stand in draft-free place 8 to 24 hours. (The longer the starter sits, the tangier the bread.)

2. In small bowl, combine remaining ¼ cup warm water, yeast, and sugar; stir to dissolve. Let stand until foamy, about 5 minutes. Stir 2 cups flour, yeast mixture, and 1 tablespoon salt into starter to make soft dough. Turn dough onto floured surface. Knead until smooth and elastic, for about 8 minutes, working in enough of remaining 1 cup flour to make firm dough. Shape dough into ball; place in greased large bowl, turning dough to grease top of dough. Cover bowl with plastic wrap and let rise in warm place (80° to 85°F) until doubled in volume, about 2 hours.

3. Grease 2 large cookie sheets and sprinkle with cornmeal. Punch down dough. Turn dough onto lightly floured surface and cut in half. Shape each half into smooth round ball. Place 1 ball on each prepared cookie sheet. Cover loosely with greased plastic wrap and let dough rise until doubled, about 1 hour 30 minutes.

4. Meanwhile, preheat oven to 425°F. In small bowl, beat egg white with remaining ¼ teaspoon salt; brush over 1 loaf. With serrated knife or single-edge razor blade, cut six ¼-inch-deep slashes in top of 1 loaf to make crisscross pattern. Place 12 ice cubes in 13" by 9" baking pan. Place pan in bottom of oven. Bake slashed loaf until well browned and loaf sounds hollow when lightly tapped on bottom, 25 to 30 minutes. Transfer loaf to wire rack to cool completely. Repeat with remaining loaf.

**EACH SLICE:** About 205 calories, 6g protein, 41g carbohydrate, 1g total fat (0g saturated), 0mg cholesterol, 475mg sodium.

## Sourdough Rolls

Prepare dough as directed through Step 2, but after first rising, cut dough into 24 equal pieces. Shape each piece into smooth round ball and place, 2 inches apart, on greased cookie sheets. Cover loosely with greased plastic wrap and let dough rise until doubled, about 1 hour. Brush with egg-white glaze. Bake until well browned, 20 to 25 minutes. Cool on wire rack. Makes 24 rolls.

**EACH ROLL:** About 135 calories, 4g protein, 28g carbohydrate, 1g total fat (0g saturated), 0mg cholesterol, 320mg sodium.

# Cloverleaf Rolls

*(pictured on page 96)*

Although these rolls are not mentioned in the first edition of *The Boston Cooking-School Cook Book,* later editions did include clover leaves [*sic*] in the list of possible shapes for dinner rolls. Muffin-pan cups help the rolls to hold their shape and enable them to puff up high.

**PREP:** 30 minutes plus rising ★ **BAKE:** 10 minutes
**MAKES** 24 rolls

½ cup warm water (105° to 115°F)

2 packages active dry yeast

1 teaspoon plus ⅓ cup sugar

¾ cup milk, heated to warm (105° to 115°F)

4 tablespoons butter or margarine, softened

about 3¾ cups all-purpose flour

1½ teaspoons salt

2 large eggs

1 egg yolk mixed with 1 tablespoon water

1. In large bowl, combine warm water, yeast, and 1 teaspoon sugar; stir to dissolve. Let stand until foamy, about 5 minutes.

2. With wooden spoon or mixer at low speed, beat in warm milk, butter, ½ cup flour, remaining ⅓ cup sugar, salt, and eggs to make thick batter; continue beating 2 minutes, frequently scraping bowl with rubber spatula. Gradually stir in 3 cups flour to make soft dough.

3. Turn dough onto lightly floured surface. Knead until smooth and elastic, about 10 minutes, working in enough of remaining ¼ cup flour just to keep dough from sticking.

4. Shape dough into ball; place in greased large bowl, turning dough to grease top. Cover bowl with plastic wrap and let dough rise in warm place (80° to 85°F) until doubled in volume, about 1 hour.

5. Punch down dough; turn onto lightly floured surface; cover and let rest 15 minutes.

6. Grease twenty-four 2½-inch muffin-pan cups. Divide dough in half. Cut 1 dough half into 36 equal pieces; shape each piece into ball. Place 3 balls in each prepared muffin-pan cup. Repeat with remaining dough. Cover and let rise in warm place until doubled, about 30 minutes.

7. Meanwhile, preheat oven to 400°F. Brush rolls with egg-yolk mixture. Bake until golden and rolls sounds hollow when lightly tapped on bottom, 10 to 20 minutes, rotating sheets between upper and lower racks halfway through baking. Serve warm, or cool on wire racks to serve later.

**EACH ROLL:** About 130 calories, 3g protein, 19g carbohydrate, 4g total fat (2g saturated), 33mg cholesterol, 175mg sodium.

# Parker House Rolls

The story is that a German baker in the newly opened Parker House Hotel in Boston in 1855 grew annoyed when a guest became unpleasant. He threw his unfinished rolls into the oven, where they puffed up into light, delicious buns that went on to make his employer, Harvey Parker, famous. Fannie Farmer offers this tip: "Parker House Rolls may be shaped by cutting or tearing off small pieces of dough, and shaping round like a biscuit…let rise fifteen minutes. With handle of large wooden spoon, or toy rolling-pin, roll through centre of each biscuit, brush edge of lower halves with melted butter, fold, press lightly, place in buttered pan one inch apart, cover, let rise, and bake." The rolls resemble little pocketbooks, which is another name for these delectable morsels. Our recipe features an ever-popular refrigerator dough, which can be chilled overnight or baked up right away,

**PREP:** 35 minutes plus rising ★ **BAKE:** 18 minutes
**MAKES** 40 rolls

**1½ cups warm water (105° to 115°F)**

**2 packages active dry yeast**

**1 teaspoon plus ½ cup sugar**

**1 cup butter or margarine (2 sticks), softened**

**2 teaspoons salt**

**about 6 cups all-purpose flour**

**1 large egg**

**vegetable oil for brushing**

**1.** In large bowl, combine ½ cup warm water, yeast, and 1 teaspoon sugar; stir to dissolve. Let stand until foamy, about 5 minutes. Stir in remaining 1 cup warm water, ½ cup butter, remaining ½ cup sugar, salt, and 2¼ cups flour. With wooden spoon or mixer at low speed, beat in egg and ¾ cup flour; continue beating 2 minutes, frequently scraping bowl with rubber spatula. Stir in 2½ cups flour to make soft dough.

**2.** Turn dough onto lightly floured surface. Knead until smooth and elastic, about 10 minutes, working in enough of remaining ½ cup flour just to keep dough from sticking.

**3.** Shape dough into ball; place in greased large bowl, turning dough to grease top. Cover bowl with plastic wrap and let rise in warm place (80° to 85°F) until doubled in volume, about 1½ hours.

**4.** Punch down dough and turn over; brush with oil. Cover bowl tightly with greased plastic wrap and refrigerate overnight or up to 24 hours. (Or, if you like, after punching down dough, shape into rolls as in Step 5. Cover and let rise until doubled, about 45 minutes, and bake as in Step 6.)

**5.** About 2½ hours before serving, melt remaining ½ cup butter in large deep roasting pan (17" by 11½"). On lightly floured surface, with floured rolling pin, roll out dough ½ inch thick. With floured 2¾-inch round biscuit cutter, cut out as many rounds as possible. Knead trimmings together; reroll and cut out more rounds. Dip both sides of each dough round into melted butter; fold rounds in half and arrange in rows in prepared pan, letting rolls touch each other. Cover and let rise in warm place until doubled, about 1½ hours.

**6.** Meanwhile, preheat oven to 400°F. Bake until golden and rolls sound hollow when lightly tapped on bottom, 18 to 20 minutes. Serve warm, or cool on wire racks to serve later.

---

**EACH ROLL:** About 125 calories, 2g protein, 17g carbohydrate, 5g total fat (3g saturated), 18mg cholesterol, 165mg sodium.

# Finger Rolls

*Mix one cup of scalded milk with one tablespoon of butter. When cool, add one teaspoon of sugar, one-half teaspoon of salt, four tablespoons of liquid yeast (one-fourth cup), and flour enough to make a soft dough—about three cups. Mix well, knead for fifteen minutes and set in a warm place to rise for three or four hours. When light, knead again. Shape small pieces of dough into balls, then roll on the molding board into a small, long finger roll, pointing the ends. Place the rolls in a shallow pan, let them rise for one hour, or until double in size, brush them over with a little beaten egg to give a glaze, and bake in a hot oven for ten or fifteen minutes.*

**—Good Housekeeping Everyday Cook Book, 1903**

# Hot Cross Buns

Fannie Farmer's original recipe contains raisins and currants but no candied fruit. After the rolls are baked she decorates them with a simple ornamental-frosting cross. Americans have been baking these buns on Good Friday for generations.

**PREP:** 45 minutes plus rising ★ **BAKE:** 20 minutes
**MAKES** 25 buns

1 cup warm water (105° to 115°F)

2 packages active dry yeast

1 teaspoon plus ½ cup granulated sugar

1½ teaspoons ground cardamom

1½ plus ⅛ teaspoon salt

½ cup butter or margarine (1 stick), softened

about 4¾ cups all-purpose flour

2 large eggs

½ cup golden raisins

½ cup diced mixed candied fruit

1 cup confectioners' sugar

4 teaspoons water

1. In large bowl, combine warm water, yeast, and 1 teaspoon granulated sugar; stir to dissolve. Let stand until foamy, about 5 minutes. Stir in cardamom, 1½ teaspoons salt, butter, remaining ½ cup granulated sugar, and 1½ cups flour until mixed well. With mixer at low speed, beat just until blended.

2. Separate 1 egg. Cover egg white and reserve in refrigerator. Beat remaining egg, egg yolk, and ½ cup flour into flour mixture. With wooden spoon, stir in 2¼ cups flour to make soft dough.

3. Turn dough onto lightly floured surface. Knead until smooth and elastic, about 10 minutes, working in enough of remaining ½ cup flour just to keep dough from sticking.

4. Shape dough into a ball; place in greased large bowl, turning dough to grease top. Cover bowl with plastic wrap and let rise in warm place (80° to 85°F) until doubled in volume, about 1 hour.

5. Punch down dough. Knead in raisins and candied fruit. Cut dough into 25 equal pieces; cover loosely and let rest 15 minutes.

6. Grease large cookie sheet. Shape dough into balls. Arrange balls, ½ inch apart to allow for rising, in square shape, on prepared cookie sheet. Cover loosely and let rise in warm place until doubled, about 40 minutes.

7. Meanwhile, preheat oven to 375°F. In cup, with fork, beat reserved egg white with remaining ⅛ teaspoon salt; brush over buns. Bake until golden and buns sound hollow when lightly tapped on bottom, about 20 minutes. Transfer to wire racks to cool.

8. When buns are cool, prepare icing: In small bowl, mix confectioners' sugar and water until smooth. Spoon icing into small ziptight plastic bag; snip off one corner (or use a pastry bag fitted with a very small tip) and pipe cross on each bun. Let icing set before serving.

**EACH BUN:** About 190 calories, 3g protein, 34g carbohydrate, 5g total fat (3g saturated), 27mg cholesterol, 210mg sodium.

## Festive Christmas Tree Buns

Prepare dough as directed through Step 5 and shape into balls. To make Christmas tree: Place 1 dough ball at top of lightly greased large cookie sheet. Make second row by centering 2 dough balls directly under first ball, placing them about ¼ inch apart to allow space for rising. Continue making rows, increasing each row by one ball and centering balls directly under previous row, until there are 6 rows in all. Leave space for rising. Use last 4 balls to make trunk of tree. Center 2 rows of 2 balls each under last row. Cover loosely and let rise in warm place until doubled, about 40 minutes. Brush with egg-white mixture and bake as directed. When buns are cool, prepare icing and pipe in zigzag pattern over tree.

**EACH BUN:** About 190 calories, 3g protein, 34g carbohydrate, 5g total fat ( 3g saturated), 27mg cholesterol, 210mg sodium.

# Southern Sally Lunn

A recipe for this popular bread was often included in early cookbooks. Several stories exist regarding its origin. One of the more intriguing stories tells of an English girl who sold bread on the streets of Bath by crying *"Sol et Lune! Soleilune."* Another tale suggests that the name comes from *soleil et lune,* French for "sun and moon," referring to the golden top and the whitish bottom of the buns. By the time the tales and bread showed up in America in the nineteenth century, it was called Sally Lunn. Traditionally it is baked in a kugelhopf pan, which is a turban-shaped tube mold with swirled sides.

**PREP:** 20 minutes plus rising ★ **BAKE:** 40 minutes
**MAKES** I loaf, 16 slices

¹⁄₃ **cup warm water (105° to 115°F)**

**I package active dry yeast**

**I teaspoon plus ¹⁄₃ cup sugar**

¹⁄₂ **cup milk, heated to warm (105° to 115°F)**

¹⁄₂ **cup butter or margarine (1 stick), softened**

I¹⁄₄ **teaspoons salt**

3¹⁄₄ **cups all-purpose flour**

**3 large eggs**

**I.** In large bowl, combine warm water, yeast, and 1 teaspoon sugar; stir to dissolve. Let stand until foamy, about 5 minutes.

**2.** With mixer at low speed or with wooden spoon, beat warm milk, butter, salt, remaining ¹⁄₃ cup sugar, and 1¹⁄₄ cups flour into yeast mixture. Increase mixer speed to medium; beat 2 minutes, occasionally scraping bowl with rubber spatula. Beat in eggs, one at a time, and 1 cup flour; continue beating 2 minutes, occasionally scraping bowl. With spoon, stir in remaining 1 cup flour. Cover bowl with slightly damp clean kitchen towel; let dough rise in warm place (80° to 85°F) until doubled in volume, about 1 hour.

**3.** Grease and flour 9- to 10-inch tube pan or kugelhopf mold. With spoon, stir down dough; spoon into prepared pan. With well-greased hands, pat dough evenly into pan. Cover pan with slightly damp towel; let rise in warm place until doubled, about 45 minutes.

**4.** Meanwhile, preheat oven to 350°F. Bake bread until golden and loaf sounds hollow when lightly tapped on bottom, 40 to 45 minutes. With narrow metal spatula, loosen bread from side of pan; remove from pan to cool on wire rack.

**EACH SLICE:** About 190 calories, 4g protein, 25g carbohydrate, 8g total fat (4g saturated), 56mg cholesterol, 255mg sodium.

# Monkey Bread

Recipes for Monkey Bread (also known as bubble loaf) began appearing in women's magazines in the mid-1950s. Before long, it was served at brunches and lunches across America. It's made from balls (bubbles) of dough that are dipped in butter, coated with cinnamon-sugar, and layered in a tube pan. There are several tales regarding the origin of the name Monkey Bread. One connects this popular bread with the monkey-puzzle tree (*Araucaria araucana*) which has prickly branches that are not easy to climb. Another legend links it to the fruit of the baobab tree (*Adansonia digitata*) of Africa, which is called monkey bread, while another connects the name to the fact that the bread resembles a pack of monkeys jumbled together. During the Reagan years, the First Lady made it a tradition to serve Monkey Bread at White House Christmas celebrations. She believed that the name of the bread reflected the fact that as you make it you have to monkey around with the dough.

PREP: 40 minutes plus rising  ★  BAKE: 45 minutes
MAKES 16 servings

¾ cup warm water (105° to 115°F)

2 packages active dry yeast

1 teaspoon plus ¾ cup granulated sugar

¾ cup butter or margarine (1½ sticks), softened

1 teaspoon salt

about 5½ cups all-purpose flour

3 large eggs

½ cup packed brown sugar

1 teaspoon ground cinnamon

1. In large bowl, combine ½ cup warm water, yeast, and 1 teaspoon granulated sugar; stir to dissolve. Let stand until foamy, about 5 minutes. Add remaining ¼ cup warm water and ½ cup butter; mix well. With wooden spoon, stir in remaining ¾ cup granulated sugar, salt, and 2 cups flour just until blended. Gradually beat in eggs and 1 cup flour. Stir in 2¼ cups flour.

2. Turn dough onto lightly floured surface. Knead until smooth and elastic, 8 to 10 minutes, working in enough of remaining ¼ cup flour just to keep dough from sticking. Cut dough in half and cut each half into 16 equal pieces. Cover dough and let rest 15 minutes.

3. Meanwhile, in small bowl, combine brown sugar and cinnamon. Melt remaining ¼ cup butter; set aside. Grease 9- to 10-inch tube pan.

4. Shape each piece of dough into tight ball. Place half of balls in prepared pan; brush with half of melted butter and sprinkle with half of sugar mixture. Repeat with remaining dough, melted butter, and sugar mixture. Cover pan with plastic wrap and let dough rise in warm place (80° to 85°F) until doubled in volume, about 1 hour.

5. Meanwhile, preheat oven to 350°F. Bake until browned and bread sounds hollow when lightly tapped, about 45 minutes. If top browns too quickly, cover with foil during last 15 minutes of baking. Cool in pan on wire rack 10 minutes; remove from pan. Serve warm, or cool on wire rack to serve later. Reheat if desired.

EACH SERVING: About 319 calories, 6g protein, 50g carbohydrate, 11g total fat (6g saturated), 63mg cholesterol, 249mg sodium.

# Pennsylvania-Dutch Sticky Buns

The Pennsylvania Dutch became famous for their food specialties, especially these sticky buns made with a rich yeast dough rolled up with currant filling, sliced, and then baked on top of a brown sugar–pecan mixture. Some believe that the first sticky buns appeared at about the same time that light corn syrup was introduced in 1912.

**PREP:** 1 hour plus rising and overnight to chill
**BAKE:** 30 minutes  ★  **MAKES** 20 buns

## DOUGH

¼ cup warm water (105° to 115°F)
1 package active dry yeast
1 teaspoon plus ¼ cup granulated sugar
¾ cup milk
4 tablespoons butter or margarine, softened
1 teaspoon salt
3 large egg yolks
about 4 cups all-purpose flour

## FILLING

½ cup packed dark brown sugar
¼ cup dried currants
1 tablespoon ground cinnamon
4 tablespoons butter or margarine, melted

## TOPPING

⅔ cup packed dark brown sugar
3 tablespoons butter or margarine
2 tablespoons light corn syrup
2 tablespoons honey
1¼ cups pecans (5 ounces), coarsely chopped

**1.** Prepare dough: In cup, combine warm water, yeast, and 1 teaspoon granulated sugar; stir to dissolve. Let stand until foamy, about 5 minutes.

**2.** In large bowl, with mixer at low speed, blend yeast mixture with milk, butter, remaining ¼ cup granulated sugar, salt, egg yolks, and 3 cups flour until blended. With wooden spoon, stir in ¾ cup flour.

**3.** Turn dough onto lightly floured surface and knead until smooth and elastic, about 5 minutes, working in enough of remaining ¼ cup flour just to keep dough from sticking.

**4.** Shape dough into ball; place in greased large bowl, turning dough to grease top. Cover bowl with plastic wrap and let dough rise in warm place (80° to 85°F) until doubled in volume, about 1 hour.

**5.** Meanwhile, prepare filling: In bowl, combine brown sugar, currants, and cinnamon. Reserve melted butter.

**6.** Prepare topping: In 1-quart saucepan, combine brown sugar, butter, corn syrup, and honey. Heat over low heat, stirring, until brown sugar and butter have melted. Grease 13" by 9" baking pan; pour brown-sugar mixture into pan and sprinkle evenly with pecans; set aside.

**7.** Punch down dough. Turn dough onto lightly floured surface; cover and let rest 15 minutes. Roll dough into 18" by 12" rectangle. Brush with reserved melted butter and sprinkle with currant mixture. Starting at a long side, roll up jelly-roll fashion; place, seam side down, on surface. Cut dough crosswise into 20 equal slices.

**8.** Place slices, cut side down, on brown-sugar mixture in prepared baking pan, making four rows of five slices each. Cover pan and refrigerate at least 12 hours or up to 15 hours.

**9.** Preheat oven to 375°F. Bake buns until golden, about 30 minutes. Immediately place serving tray or jelly-roll pan over top of baking pan and invert; remove pan. Let buns cool slightly to serve warm, or cool on wire rack to serve later.

**EACH BUN:** About 290 calories, 4g protein, 42g carbohydrate, 12g total fat (5g saturated), 50mg cholesterol, 195mg sodium.

## Cinnamon Buns

Prepare and shape dough as directed, omitting topping; bake as directed. Invert baked buns onto cookie sheet; remove baking pan and invert buns onto wire rack. In small bowl, mix *1 cup confectioners' sugar* and *5 teaspoons water* until smooth; drizzle over hot buns.

**EACH BUN:** About 215 calories, 4g protein, 36g carbohydrate, 6g total fat (3g saturated), 46mg cholesterol, 170mg sodium.

# Soft Pretzels

These knot-shaped salted treats can be traced back to Roman times and have long been traditional in Germany and Alsace. The word *pretzel* is German, which some link to the Latin word *pretium,* meaning "reward" or "little gift." Legend has it that a monk from Alsace or northern Italy first twisted the pretzel into its unusual shape so it resembled the folded arms of a person at prayer. The Dutch are usually credited with bringing pretzels to America. The word *pretzel* first appeared here in print around 1824. The first pretzel bakery was founded in Lititz, Pennsylvania, in 1861. And since 1933, most pretzels have been twisted by machine.

**PREP:** 30 minutes plus rising ★ **BAKE** 16 minutes
**MAKES** 12 pretzels

2 cups warm water (105° to 115°F)

1 package active dry yeast

1 teaspoon sugar

about 4 cups all-purpose flour

1 teaspoon table salt

2 tablespoons baking soda

1 tablespoon kosher or coarse sea salt

**1.** In large bowl, combine 1½ cups warm water, yeast, and sugar; stir to dissolve. Let stand until foamy, about 5 minutes. Add 2 cups flour and table salt; beat well with wooden spoon. Gradually stir in 1½ cups flour to make soft dough.

**2.** Turn dough onto floured surface. Knead until smooth and elastic, about 6 minutes, working in enough of remaining ½ cup flour just to keep dough from sticking.

**3.** Shape dough into ball; place in greased large bowl, turning dough to grease top. Cover bowl with plastic wrap and let rise in warm place (80° to 85°) until doubled in volume, about 30 minutes.

**4.** Meanwhile, preheat oven to 400°F. Grease two large cookie sheets. Punch down dough and cut into 12 equal pieces. Roll each piece into 24-inch-long rope. Shape ropes into loop-shaped pretzels.

**5.** In small bowl, whisk remaining ½ cup warm water and baking soda until soda has dissolved.

**6.** Dip pretzels in baking soda mixture and place, 1½ inches apart, on prepared cookie sheets; sprinkle lightly with kosher salt. Bake until browned, 16 to 18 minutes, rotating sheets between upper and lower racks halfway through baking. Serve pretzels warm, or cool on wire racks to serve later.

**EACH PRETZEL:** About 165 calories, 5g protein, 33g carbohydrate, 1g total fat (0g saturated), 0mg cholesterol, 1190mg sodium.

## Soft Pretzel Sticks

Prepare dough as directed, but roll each piece into 8-inch-long rope. Dip ropes in baking-soda mixture and place, 2 inches apart, on prepared cookie sheets. Sprinkle with kosher salt. Bake as directed.

# Bee-Sting Cake

As the tale goes, a German baker made this cake glazed with honey, butter, and cream. The sweet glaze attracted a bee, which then stung the baker.

**PREP:** 40 minutes plus rising and cooling
**BAKE:** 20 minutes ★ **MAKES** 16 servings

## CAKE

¼ **cup warm water (105° to 115°F)**

1 **package active dry yeast**

1 **teaspoon plus** ⅓ **cup sugar**

6 **tablespoons butter or margarine, softened**

1 **large egg**

1 **large egg yolk**

⅓ **cup milk**

1 **teaspoon vanilla extract**

¼ **teaspoon salt**

**about 3 cups all-purpose flour**

## GLAZE

½ **cup sugar**

6 **tablespoons butter or margarine**

⅓ **cup honey**

3 **tablespoons heavy or whipping cream**

1½ **teaspoons fresh lemon juice**

1⅓ **cups sliced natural almonds**

1. Prepare cake: In cup, combine yeast, warm water, and 1 teaspoon sugar; stir to dissolve. Let mixture stand until foamy, about 5 minutes.

2. Meanwhile, in large bowl, with mixer at medium speed, beat butter and remaining ⅓ cup sugar until blended, frequently scraping bowl with rubber spatula. Beat until creamy, about 1 minute. Reduce speed to low; beat in egg and egg yolk (mixture may look curdled). Beat in yeast mixture, milk, vanilla, salt, and 2½ cups flour until blended.

3. Turn dough onto floured surface and knead until smooth and elastic, about 5 minutes, working in enough of remaining ½ cup flour to make slightly sticky dough.

4. Shape dough into ball; place in greased large bowl, turning dough to grease top. Cover bowl with plastic wrap and let rise in warm place (80° to 85°F) until doubled in volume, about 1 hour.

5. Punch down dough; cover and let rest 15 minutes. Meanwhile, grease 13" by 9" baking pan. Line bottom and sides with foil; grease foil.

6. Turn dough into prepared pan. With hands, press dough evenly into pan, making sure to press dough into corners. Cover pan with plastic wrap; let dough rise in warm place until doubled; 1 hour.

7. Meanwhile, preheat oven to 375°F. Prepare glaze: In 2-quart saucepan, combine sugar, butter, honey, and cream; heat to boiling over medium heat, stirring frequently. When butter has melted, remove from heat; stir in lemon juice. Set aside to cool slightly, about 5 minutes.

8. Evenly pour all but 3 tablespoons glaze over dough; scatter almonds over top. Drizzle remaining glaze over almonds. Place two sheets of foil underneath pan; crimp foil edges to form a rim to catch any overflow during baking. Bake cake until top is brown, 20 to 25 minutes. Cool in pan on wire rack 15 minutes. Run small knife between foil and edges of pan to loosen, then invert cake onto large cookie sheet. Gently peel off foil and discard. Immediately invert cake, almond side up, onto wire rack to cool completely.

**EACH SERVING:** About 297 calories, 5g protein, 36g carbohydrate, 15g total fat (7g saturated), 54mg cholesterol, 133mg sodium.

# Coffee Cake Wreath

**D**uring the 1950s, national cooking contests encouraged home cooks to develop their own recipes and to enter them into competitions for blue ribbons, prizes, and trips to bake-offs. Women's magazines and food corporations often inspired readers with elaborate creations. This recipe, which is reminiscent of that era, turns a rich yeast coffee cake dough into a Christmas wreath that can be filled with either a sweet almond or cinnamon-sugar filling—perfect for Christmas morning. It's typical of the spectacular food presentations of the '50s that turned ordinary cooks into "stars" in their communities and sometimes beyond.

**PREP:** 40 minutes plus rising ★ **BAKE:** 30 minutes
**MAKES** 1 coffee cake, about 16 slices

## CAKE
½ cup warm water (105° to 115°F)

2 packages active dry yeast

1 teaspoon plus ½ cup sugar

½ cup butter or margarine (1 stick), softened

1 large egg

½ teaspoon salt

about 3¼ cups all-purpose flour

choice of filling (opposite)

## ICING (OPTIONAL)
1 cup confectioners' sugar

2 tablespoons milk

**1.** In cup, combine warm water, yeast, and 1 teaspoon sugar; stir to dissolve. Let stand until mixture is foamy, about 5 minutes.

**2.** Meanwhile, in large bowl, with mixer at low speed, beat butter and remaining ½ cup sugar until blended. Increase speed to high; beat until light and fluffy, about 2 minutes, scraping bowl with rubber spatula. Reduce speed to low; beat in egg until blended. Beat in yeast mixture, salt, and ½ cup flour just until blended (batter will look curdled). With wooden spoon, stir in 2½ cups flour until blended.

**3.** Turn dough onto lightly floured surface. Knead until smooth and elastic, about 8 minutes, working in enough of remaining ¼ cup flour just to keep dough from sticking.

**4.** Shape dough into ball; place in greased large bowl, turning dough to grease top. Cover bowl with plastic wrap and let dough rise in warm place (80° to 85°F) until doubled in volume, about 1 hour.

**5.** Meanwhile, prepare filling of choice; cover and refrigerate until ready to use.

**6.** Punch down dough. Turn dough onto lightly floured surface; cover and let rest 15 minutes. Meanwhile, grease large cookie sheet.

**7.** With floured rolling pin, roll dough into 18" by 12" rectangle. Spread filling of choice over dough to within ½ inch of edges.

**8.** Starting at a long side, roll up dough jelly-roll fashion. Carefully lift roll and place, seam side down, on prepared cookie sheet. Shape roll into ring; press ends together to seal. With knife or kitchen shears, cut ring at 1½-inch intervals, up to but not completely through inside dough edge. Gently pull and twist each cut piece to show filling. Dough will be soft; use small metal spatula to help lift pieces. Cover and let dough rise in warm place until risen slightly, about 1 hour.

**9.** Meanwhile, preheat oven to 350°F. Bake wreath until golden, 30 to 35 minutes. Transfer to wire rack to cool.

**10.** Prepare icing, if using: In small bowl, mix confectioners' sugar with milk until smooth. When wreath is cool, drizzle with icing.

---

**EACH SLICE WITHOUT FILLING AND ICING:** About 176 calories, 3g protein, 26g carbohydrate, 6g total fat (4g saturated), 29mg cholesterol, 136mg sodium.

# Sweet Almond Filling

In food processor with knife blade attached, process *½ cup whole blanched almonds* and *¼ cup packed brown sugar* until almonds are finely ground. Add *4 ounces almond paste*, broken into chunks, and *2 large egg whites*; process until mixture is smooth. Makes about 1 cup.

---

**EACH TABLESPOON:** About 71 calories, 2g protein, 7g carbohydrate, 4g total fat (0g saturated), 0mg cholesterol, 9mg sodium.

# Cinnamon-Sugar Filling

In small bowl, combine *½ cup packed brown sugar, ½ cup whole blanched almonds*, toasted and chopped, and *½ teaspoon ground cinnamon*. After rolling out dough, brush with *2 tablespoons butter or margarine*, melted, and sprinkle with sugar mixture. Makes about 1 cup.

---

**EACH TABLESPOON:** About 65 calories, 1g protein, 8g carbohydrate, 4g total fat (1g saturated), 4mg cholesterol, 18mg sodium.

# Cheese Pizza

Raffaele Esposito supposedly created the first pizza made with pizza dough, tomato, basil, and mozzarella in Naples, Italy, in 1889. Neapolitan immigrants who settled in New York City in the early twentieth century made oversized pizzas—eighteen inches or more in diameter—and sold them by the slice, which made pizza perfect for a quick lunch or snack. Back in Italy, pizzas were nine to ten inches in diameter, served on dinner plates, and eaten with a knife and fork. Brick-oven pizzerias appeared as early as 1905 in Little Italy communities (Lombardi's was the first one in Manhattan). If you have a pizza stone, use it, as it helps to create a crispier crust.

**PREP:** 50 minutes plus dough rising and resting
**BAKE:** 15 minutes
**MAKES** 2 pizzas, 8 main-dish servings

## PIZZA DOUGH

1¼ cups warm water (105° to 115°F)

1 package active dry yeast

1 teaspoon sugar

2 tablespoons olive oil

2 teaspoons salt

about 4 cups all-purpose flour or
 3½ cups bread flour

## PIZZA SAUCE

1 tablespoon olive oil

1 large garlic clove, finely chopped

1 can (28 ounces) tomatoes in
 thick puree, chopped

¼ teaspoon salt


cornmeal for sprinkling

¼ cup freshly grated Parmesan cheese

8 ounces mozzarella cheese, shredded (2 cups)

**1.** Prepare pizza dough: In large bowl, combine ¼ cup warm water, yeast, and sugar; stir to dissolve. Let stand until foamy, about 5 minutes. With wooden spoon, stir in remaining 1 cup warm water, oil, salt, and 1½ cups flour until smooth. Gradually add 2 cups all-purpose flour or 1½ cups bread flour, stirring until dough comes away from side of bowl.

**2.** Turn dough onto lightly floured surface. Knead until smooth and elastic, about 10 minutes, working in enough of remaining ½ cup flour just to keep dough from sticking. Shape dough into ball; place in greased large bowl, turning dough to grease top. Cover bowl with plastic wrap and let rise in warm place (80° to 85°F) until doubled in volume, about 1 hour.

**3.** Meanwhile, prepare pizza sauce: In 2-quart saucepan, heat oil over medium-high heat. Add garlic and cook, stirring often, until golden, about 30 seconds. Add tomatoes with puree and salt; heat to boiling over high heat. Reduce heat and simmer, uncovered, 10 minutes. Makes about 3 cups.

**4.** Punch down dough. Turn onto lightly floured surface and cut in half. Cover and let rest 15 minutes. Or, if not using right away, place dough in large greased bowl, cover loosely with greased plastic wrap, and refrigerate up to 24 hours.

**5.** Meanwhile, preheat oven to 450°F. Sprinkle two large cookie sheets with cornmeal. Shape each dough half into ball. On one prepared cookie sheet, with floured rolling pin, roll 1 ball of dough into 14" by 10" rectangle. Fold edges in to make 1-inch rim. Repeat with remaining dough ball.

**6.** Sprinkle dough with Parmesan. Spread pizza sauce over Parmesan and top with mozzarella. Let pizzas rest 20 minutes. Bake pizzas until crust is golden, 15 to 20 minutes, rotating cookie sheets between upper and lower oven racks halfway through baking.

**EACH SERVING:** About 400 calories, 15g protein, 56g carbohydrate, 13g total fat (5g saturated), 25mg cholesterol, 976mg sodium.

# Hush Puppies

Several legends explain how these fried balls of corn bread became known as hush puppies. One tale dates back to the Civil War. Confederate soldiers frequently cooked dinner over an open fire. Whenever Yankee soldiers were nearby, the Southerners would fry up bits of corn bread and throw them to the dogs, giving the command "Hush, puppies!" in order to keep them quiet. Another legend cites the hounds that often went along on hunting and fishing expeditions in the South. Whenever the hounds smelled fish frying, they would loudly yelp. To quiet them, the hunters fried bits of cornmeal batter alongside the fish, then tossed the corn-bread balls to the dogs, while saying "Hush, puppies!" Hush puppies flavored with onion remain a tradition in the South and are often served on the same platter with fried fish or wrapped inside a paper napkin carried in a wicker breadbasket.

**PREP:** 15 minutes plus standing
**COOK:** 3 minutes per batch
**MAKES** about 36 hush puppies, 9 servings

vegetable oil for frying

1¾ cups cornmeal, preferably stone ground

¼ cup all-purpose flour

2 teaspoons sugar

1½ teaspoons baking powder

¾ teaspoon salt

½ teaspoon baking soda

¼ teaspoon ground black pepper

pinch ground red pepper (cayenne)

1 cup buttermilk

1 medium onion, grated (½ cup)

2 large eggs

1. In 5- to 6-quart Dutch oven, heat 2 inches oil over medium heat until temperature reaches 350°F on deep- fat thermometer.

2. Meanwhile, in large bowl, combine cornmeal, flour, sugar, baking powder, salt, baking soda, black pepper, and ground red pepper. Whisk until blended.

3. In medium bowl, with wire whisk, whisk buttermilk, onion, and eggs until blended. Add buttermilk mixture to cornmeal mixture; stir until blended. Let batter stand 5 minutes.

4. Meanwhile, preheat oven to 200°F. Line cookie sheet with paper towels. In batches, drop batter by rounded teaspoons into hot oil, using another teaspoon to push batter from spoon. Cook, turning once, until browned and cooked through, 2 to 3 minutes. With slotted spoon, transfer to paper towel–lined cookie sheet; keep warm in oven. Repeat with remaining batter. Serve immediately.

**EACH SERVING:** About 253 calories, 5g protein, 27g carbohydrate, 14g total fat (2g saturated), 48mg cholesterol, 388mg sodium.

## Boston Brown Bread

*One cup of sour milk, one-half cup of New Orleans molasses, one egg, butter size of walnut, one teaspoon of soda in the milk, and enough graham flour to thicken like cake. Steam three hours; start over cold water.*

—Good Housekeeping
Everyday Cook Book, 1903

# Spoonbread

This popular southern specialty is more like a tender, custardy soufflé than a bread. Some historians believe that its name comes from the Native American word *suppawn,* meaning "porridge." Others think its name is derived from the fact that it's eaten with a spoon. Curiously, this recipe did not appear in cookbooks until the twentieth century.

PREP: 15 minutes plus standing ★ BAKE: 40 minutes
MAKES 8 accompaniment servings

3 cups milk

$^1/_2$ teaspoon salt

$^1/_4$ teaspoon ground black pepper

I cup cornmeal

4 tablespoons butter or margarine,
    cut into pieces

3 large eggs, separated

1. Preheat oven to 400°F. Generously grease shallow $1^1/_2$-quart baking dish.

2. In 4-quart saucepan, combine milk, salt, and pepper; heat to boiling over medium-high heat. Remove from heat; with wire whisk, whisk in cornmeal. Add butter, stirring until melted. Let stand 5 minutes.

3. Whisk egg yolks, one at a time, into cornmeal mixture, until blended. In small bowl, with mixer at high speed, beat egg whites just until soft peaks form when beaters are lifted. Gently fold egg whites, one-half at a time, into cornmeal mixture. Pour into prepared baking dish; spread evenly. Bake until spoonbread is set, about 40 minutes. Serve immediately.

EACH SERVING: About 203 calories, 7g protein, 18g carbohydrate, 11g total fat (6g saturated), 108mg cholesterol, 272mg sodium.

# Golden Corn Bread

The colonists often used corn for bread instead of the more scarce whole-wheat flour. Corn pone, made from cornmeal, water, and salt, was baked directly over hot coals in a spider: a cast-iron skillet with three short legs. In the South, corn bread is still baked in a cast-iron skillet, which is coated with a little shortening or bacon fat and heated up until sizzling hot. When the cold batter is poured in, it starts cooking immediately and a tempting golden crust forms. Even today, the best recipes instruct cooks to preheat the pan before adding the batter.

PREP: 10 minutes ★ BAKE: 25 minutes
MAKES 8 servings

4 tablespoons butter or margarine

$1^1/_2$ cups cornmeal

I cup all-purpose flour

2 teaspoons baking powder

I teaspoon salt

$^1/_4$ teaspoon baking soda

$1^3/_4$ cups buttermilk

2 large eggs

1. Preheat oven to 450°F. Place butter in 10-inch cast-iron skillet or 9-inch square baking pan; place in oven just until butter melts, 3 to 5 minutes. Tilt skillet to coat.

2. Meanwhile, in large bowl, combine cornmeal, flour, baking powder, salt, and baking soda. In bowl, with fork, beat buttermilk and eggs until blended. Add melted butter to buttermilk mixture, then add to flour mixture. Stir just until flour is moistened (batter will be lumpy).

3. Pour batter into prepared skillet. Bake until golden at edge and toothpick inserted in center comes out clean, about 25 minutes. Serve warm.

EACH SERVING: About 243 calories, 7g protein, 35g carbohydrate, 8g total fat (4g saturated), 71mg cholesterol, 584mg sodium.

# Buttermilk Biscuits

In the 1872 edition of Annabella P. Hill's *Southern Practical Cookery and Receipt Book,* she instructs bakers to sift together the flour and super-carb soda, then to "rub into the flour thoroughly a piece of butter the size of a hen's egg; salt to taste; wet the flour with sour milk until a soft dough is formed; make it into thin biscuit, and bake in a quick oven. Work it very little. Always reserve a little flour before putting in the soda to work into the dough, and flour the board." This good advice holds true even today.

**PREP:** 15 minutes ★ **BAKE:** 12 minutes
**MAKES** about 18 high biscuits or 36 thin biscuits

**2 cups all-purpose flour**

**2¹⁄₂ teaspoons baking powder**

**¹⁄₂ teaspoon baking soda**

**¹⁄₂ teaspoon salt**

**¹⁄₄ cup vegetable shortening**

**³⁄₄ cup buttermilk**

**1.** Preheat oven to 450°F. In large bowl, combine flour, baking powder, baking soda, and salt. With pastry blender or two knives used scissor-fashion, cut in shortening until mixture resembles coarse crumbs. Stir in buttermilk, stirring just until mixture forms soft dough that leaves side of bowl.

**2.** Turn dough onto lightly floured surface; knead 6 to 8 times, just until smooth. With floured rolling pin, roll dough ¹⁄₂ inch thick for high, fluffy biscuits or ¹⁄₄ inch thick for thin, crusty buttermilk biscuits.

**3.** With floured 2-inch biscuit cutter, cut out rounds, without twisting cutter. Arrange biscuits on ungreased cookie sheet, 1 inch apart for crusty biscuits or nearly touching for soft-sided biscuits.

**4.** Press trimmings together. Reroll; cut out additional biscuits. Bake biscuits until golden, 12 to 15 minutes. Serve biscuits warm.

**EACH HIGH BISCUIT:** About 83 calories, 2g protein, 12g carbohydrate, 3g total fat (1g saturated), 0mg cholesterol, 178mg sodium.

## Baking Powder Biscuits

Prepare as directed but substitute ³⁄₄ *cup milk* for buttermilk and use *1 tablespoon baking powder;* omit baking soda. Makes about 18 biscuits.

# Angel Biscuits

As the name suggests, these can best be described in one word: heavenly! Our never-fail recipe recommends patting out the dough to three-quarter-inch thickness, in contrast to regular biscuits that are patted out one-quarter to one-half inch thick.

**PREP:** 15 minutes plus rising ★ **BAKE:** 17 minutes
**MAKES** 2 dozen biscuits

**¹⁄₄ cup warm water (105° to 115°F)**

**1 package active dry yeast**

**1 teaspoon sugar**

**3 cups all-purpose flour**

**1¹⁄₂ teaspoons baking powder**

**¹⁄₂ teaspoon baking soda**

**¹⁄₄ teaspoon salt**

**4 tablespoons cold butter or margarine, cut into pieces**

**2 tablespoons vegetable shortening**

**1 cup plus 2 tablespoons buttermilk**

**1.** In small bowl, combine warm water, yeast, and sugar; stir to dissolve. Let stand until foamy, about 5 minutes.

**2.** In large bowl, combine flour, baking powder, baking soda, and salt. Stir until well combined.

With pastry blender or two knives used scissor-fashion, cut in butter and shortening until mixture resembles coarse crumbs. Make well in center of mixture; pour in buttermilk and yeast mixture. Stir until well combined.

**3.** Turn dough onto lightly floured surface; knead several times, just until dough holds together and is smooth and elastic. Place in greased bowl, turning dough to grease top. Cover bowl with plastic wrap and let stand in warm place (80° to 85°F) until doubled in volume, about 1 hour.

**4.** Punch down dough. Cover and let stand 10 minutes.

**5.** On lightly floured surface, with floured hands, pat dough out until ¾ inch thick. With 2-inch round biscuit cutter, cut out rounds without twisting cutter. Place the biscuits, 2 inches apart, on 2 ungreased large cookie sheets. Reserve trimmings for rerolling. Cover biscuits and let rise until almost doubled, about 30 minutes.

**6.** Meanwhile, preheat oven to 400°F. Bake biscuits until tops are pale golden, 17 to 20 minutes, rotating sheets between upper and lower racks halfway through baking. Serve warm.

**EACH BISCUIT:** About 95 calories, 2g protein, 14g carbohydrate, 3g total fat (2g saturated), 6mg cholesterol, 110mg sodium.

# Tex-Mex Cheese Biscuits

Annabella P. Hill suggested making cheese biscuits from "One pound of flour, half a pound of butter, half a pound of grated cheese; make up quick, and with very little handling, as puff paste. Roll thin; cut and bake in a quick oven. Salt to taste." The problem with adding cheese to biscuit dough was that the rich cheese tended to prevent biscuits from becoming light and flaky. It's no wonder then that cheese biscuits were slow to catch on. But when Tex-Mex food achieved its rightful status as a unique cuisine it is not surprising that cheesy biscuits were teamed up with chile peppers in true Tex-Mex style.

**PREP:** 15 minutes ★ **BAKE:** 13 minutes
**MAKES** 20 biscuits

**2 cups all-purpose flour**

**1 tablespoon baking powder**

**½ teaspoon paprika**

**½ teaspoon salt**

**3 tablespoons cold butter or margarine, cut into pieces**

**2 tablespoons vegetable shortening**

**4 ounces shredded sharp or extrasharp Cheddar cheese (1 cup)**

**3 tablespoons drained and chopped pickled jalapeño chiles**

**¾ cup milk**

**1.** Preheat oven to 450°F. In large bowl, combine flour, baking powder, paprika, and salt. With pastry blender or two knives used scissor-fashion, cut in butter and shortening until mixture resembles coarse crumbs. Stir cheese, chiles, and milk into flour mixture just until ingredients are blended and mixture forms a soft dough that leaves side of the bowl.

**2.** Turn dough onto lightly floured surface. With lightly floured hands, pat dough into 10" by 4" rectangle. With floured knife, cut rectangle lengthwise in half, then cut each half crosswise to make five 2-inch squares. Cut each square diagonally in half to make 20 triangles in all. Place biscuits, 1 inch apart, on ungreased large cookie sheet.

**3.** Bake until golden, 13 to 15 minutes. Serve biscuits warm, or cool on wire rack to serve later.

**EACH BISCUIT:** About 104 calories, 3g protein, 11g carbohydrate, 5g total fat (3g saturated), 12mg cholesterol, 207mg sodium.

# Yankee Popovers

In Fannie Farmer's 1896 cookbook, she suggests using a Dover egg-beater for mixing the Popover [sic] batter. Her directions for baking popovers are clear: "...turn [batter] into hissing hot buttered iron gem pans, and bake thirty to thirty-five minutes in a hot oven. They may be baked in buttered earthen cups, when the bottom will have a glazed appearance. Small round iron gem pans are best for Pop-overs."

**PREP:** 10 minutes ★ **BAKE:** 1 hour
**MAKES** 8 medium or 12 small popovers

3 large eggs

1 cup milk

3 tablespoons butter or margarine, melted

1 cup all-purpose flour

½ teaspoon salt

1. Preheat oven to 375°F. Generously grease eight 6-ounce custard cups or twelve 2½" by 1¼" muffin-pan cups. Place custard cups in jelly-roll pan for easier handling.

2. In medium bowl, with mixer at low speed, beat eggs until frothy. Beat in milk and melted butter until blended. Gradually beat in flour and salt. (Or, in blender, combine eggs, milk, butter, flour, and salt. Blend until smooth.)

3. Pour about ⅓ cup batter into each prepared custard cup or fill muffin-pan cups half full. Bake 50 minutes, then with tip of knife, quickly cut small slit in top of each popover to release steam; bake 10 minutes longer. Immediately remove popovers from cups, loosening popovers with spatula if necessary. Serve hot.

**EACH MEDIUM POPOVER:** About 160 calories, 5g protein, 14g carbohydrate, 9g total fat (5g saturated), 101mg cholesterol, 250mg sodium.

**EACH SMALL POPOVER:** About 105 calories, 3g protein, 9g carbohydrate, 6g total fat (3g saturated), 67mg cholesterol, 165mg sodium.

## Herb Popovers

Prepare as directed, adding *2 tablespoons chopped chives or green onion* to batter in Step 2. Bake as directed.

# Blueberry Hill Scones

Originally a Scottish word, *scone* probably comes from the word *schoonbrot* or *sconbrot*, meaning "fine white bread." To the colonists, scones were small, fairly plain cakes that were leavened either with baking soda and an acid ingredient such as sour milk or with baking powder. They were meant to be eaten piping hot with butter, then later on were enjoyed with clotted cream and jam. Scones were always served at afternoon tea. Traditionally they were baked on a *girdle* (griddle), but today they're usually baked in the oven. Scones did not often appear in early-nineteenth-century American cookbooks, although recipes for biscuits were almost always present.

**PREP:** 15 minutes ★ **BAKE:** 22 minutes
**MAKES** 12 scones

2 cups all-purpose flour

¼ cup sugar

1 tablespoon baking powder

¼ teaspoon salt

4 tablespoons cold butter or margarine,
   cut into pieces

1 cup blueberries

⅔ cup heavy or whipping cream

1 large egg

½ teaspoon freshly grated lemon peel

1. Preheat oven to 375°F. In large bowl, with fork, mix flour, sugar, baking powder, and salt. With pastry blender or two knives used scissor-fashion, cut butter into dry ingredients until mixture resembles coarse crumbs. Add blueberries and toss to mix.

2. In small bowl, with fork, mix cream, egg, and lemon peel until blended. Slowly pour cream mixture into dry ingredients and stir with rubber spatula just until soft dough forms.

3. With lightly floured hand, knead dough 3 to 4 times in bowl, just until it comes together; do not overmix. Divide dough in half. On lightly floured surface, shape each half into 6-inch round. With floured knife, cut each round into 6 wedges. Place the wedges, 1 inch apart, on ungreased large cookie sheet.

4. Bake scones until golden brown, 22 to 25 minutes. Serve scones warm, or cool on wire rack to serve later.

**EACH SCONE:** About 190 calories, 3g protein, 23g carbohydrate, 9g total fat (6g saturated), 46mg cholesterol, 220mg sodium.

# Homemade Muffins

Early American cookbooks often provided two types of muffin recipes: one that used yeast and another that used baking soda, beaten egg yolks, and stiffly beaten egg whites, which made the muffins as light as yeast ones. Muffins were rather plain, varying only in the type of flour (or meal) used, usually corn, whole-wheat, or rye. In the nineteenth century, Gems became popular. These muffins were always made with graham or whole-wheat flour and resembled today's bran muffins. Occasionally fresh fruit was added to the batter, turning them into Fruit Gems. Gems were always baked in a Gem pan: a heavy cast-iron pan that contains shallow, rounded-bottom, oblong cups. Until the late twentieth century, the American muffin menu was limited to varieties such as oatmeal, date, apple, and corn. Then in the '70s and '80s, muffin mania set in. No longer were muffins simple. Before being baked, extra ingredients, such as shredded vegetables, fruit, jams or jellies, nuts, and even chocolate, were added to the batter. Sometimes the muffins were showered with chocolate chips or coconut, glazed or frosted, or covered with a rich cinnamon streusel. Muffins as we know them today had arrived.

**PREP:** 10 minutes ★ **BAKE:** 20 minutes
**MAKES** 12 muffins

2¹/₂ **cups all-purpose flour**

¹/₂ **cup sugar**

1 **tablespoon baking powder**

¹/₂ **teaspoon salt**

1 **cup milk**

¹/₂ **cup butter or margarine (1 stick), melted**

1 **large egg**

1 **teaspoon vanilla extract**

1. Preheat oven to 400°F. Grease twelve 2¹/₂" by 1¹/₄" muffin-pan cups. In large bowl, combine flour, sugar, baking powder, and salt. In medium bowl, with fork, beat milk, melted butter, egg, and vanilla until blended. Add to flour mixture, stirring just until flour is moistened (batter will be lumpy).

2. Spoon batter into prepared muffin-pan cups. Bake until toothpick inserted in center of muffin comes out clean, 20 to 25 minutes. Immediately remove muffins from pan. Serve muffins warm, or cool on wire rack to serve later.

**EACH MUFFIN:** About 225 calories, 4g protein, 30g carbohydrate, 10g total fat (6g saturated), 41mg cholesterol, 312mg sodium.

## Jam-Filled Muffins

Prepare as directed but fill muffin-pan cups one-third full with batter. Drop *1 rounded teaspoon strawberry or raspberry preserves* in center of each; top with remaining batter. Bake as directed.

## Blueberry or Raspberry Muffins

Prepare as directed; stir *1 cup blueberries or raspberries* into batter.

## Walnut or Pecan Muffins

Prepare as directed; stir *¹/₂ cup chopped toasted walnuts or pecans* into batter. Sprinkle with *2 tablespoons sugar* before baking.

# Cape Cod Cranberry-Nut Loaf

**D**uring that first winter in Plymouth, the Pilgrims found several foods growing wild, including cranberries, which grew along the sandy coastline. With the introduction of baking powder in 1856, breads known as lightnin' breads, aerated breads, or quick breads, became popular. Double-acting baking powder, which showed up on the market in 1889, produced a lighter, higher loaf because it made the batter rise once when the liquid and dry ingredients were combined and a second time in the oven, hence its name.

**PREP:** 20 minutes plus cooling ★ **BAKE:** 55 minutes
**MAKES** 1 loaf, 12 slices

1 large orange

2$\frac{1}{2}$ cups all-purpose flour

1 cup sugar

2 teaspoons baking powder

$\frac{1}{2}$ teaspoon baking soda

$\frac{1}{2}$ teaspoon salt

2 large eggs

4 tablespoons butter or margarine, melted

2 cups fresh or frozen cranberries, coarsely chopped

$\frac{3}{4}$ cup walnuts, chopped (optional)

**1.** Preheat oven to 375°F. Grease 9" by 5" metal loaf pan. From orange, grate peel and squeeze $\frac{1}{2}$ cup of juice.

**2.** In large bowl, combine flour, sugar, baking powder, baking soda, and salt. In small bowl, with wire whisk or fork, beat eggs, butter, and orange peel and juice. With wooden spoon, stir egg mixture into flour mixture just until blended (batter will be stiff). Fold in the cranberries and walnuts, if using.

**3.** Spoon batter into prepared pan. Bake until toothpick inserted in center comes out clean, 55 to 60 minutes. Cool bread in pan on wire rack 10 minutes; remove from pan and cool completely on wire rack.

**EACH SLICE WITHOUT WALNUTS:**
About 223 calories, 4g protein, 40g carbohydrate, 5g total fat (3g saturated), 46mg cholesterol, 281mg sodium.

# Banana Bread

**A**t the Philadelphia Centennial Exposition of 1876, the owners of the Boston Fruit Company introduced the banana, which was wrapped in foil and sold as an exotic fruit for a dime. The company imported large shipments of bananas from Jamaica and other places and wanted to increase the demand for the fruit—and it worked. By the turn of the century, bananas were being shipped nationwide.

**PREP:** 20 minutes ★ **BAKE:** 1 hour 10 minutes
**MAKES** 1 loaf, 12 slices

2¹⁄₂ cups all-purpose flour

2 teaspoons baking powder

³⁄₄ teaspoon salt

¹⁄₂ teaspoon baking soda

1¹⁄₂ cups mashed very ripe bananas (3 medium)

¹⁄₄ cup milk

2 teaspoons vanilla extract

¹⁄₂ cup butter or margarine (1 stick), softened

1 cup sugar

2 large eggs

1. Preheat oven to 350°F. Grease 9" by 5" metal loaf pan. In medium bowl, combine flour, baking powder, salt, and baking soda. In small bowl, combine bananas, milk, and vanilla.

2. In large bowl, with mixer at medium speed, beat butter and sugar until light and fluffy. Beat in eggs, one at a time. Reduce speed to low; alternately add flour mixture and banana mixture, beginning and ending with flour mixture, occasionally scraping bowl with rubber spatula. Beat just until blended.

3. Pour batter into prepared pan. Bake until toothpick inserted in center comes out clean, about 1 hour 10 minutes. Cool in pan on wire rack for 10 minutes; remove from pan and cool completely on wire rack.

**EACH SLICE:** About 274 calories, 4g protein, 44g carbohydrate, 9g total fat (5g saturated), 57mg cholesterol, 371mg sodium.

## Banana-Nut Bread

Prepare bread as directed but fold *1 cup walnuts or pecans (4 ounces)*, coarsely chopped, into batter before baking.

# Bishop's Bread

**D**uring the nineteenth century, clergymen frequently visited parishioners on horseback. As the story goes, early one Sunday morning, a circuit-riding bishop unexpectedly stopped by the home of a Kentucky parishioner just in time for breakfast. His hostess threw together this quick bread from foods she found in her cupboard. Reportedly her bread contained fruit and nuts. Our version also has chocolate bits.

**PREP:** 20 minutes ★ **BAKE:** 55 minutes
**MAKES** 1 loaf, 12 slices

1¹⁄₂ cups all-purpose flour

1 teaspoon baking powder

¹⁄₄ teaspoon salt

1 cup walnuts or pecans (4 ounces), chopped

¹⁄₂ cup red candied cherries, halved

¹⁄₂ cup pitted dates, finely chopped

¹⁄₂ cup semisweet chocolate chips

4 tablespoons butter or margarine, softened

1 cup sugar

3 large eggs

1. Preheat oven to 325°F. Grease and flour 9" by 5" metal loaf pan. In medium bowl, combine flour, baking powder, and salt. In small bowl, combine walnuts, cherries, dates, and chocolate chips.

2. In large bowl, with mixer at low speed, beat butter and sugar until well blended and texture of wet sand, about 2 minutes. Add eggs, one at a time, beating well after each addition. Add flour mixture and beat just until blended. Stir in fruit mixture.

3. Turn batter into prepared pan. Bake until toothpick inserted in center comes out clean, 55 to 60 minutes. Cool in pan on wire rack 10 minutes; remove from pan and cool completely on wire rack. Bread is best if wrapped and served the next day.

**EACH SLICE:** About 319 calories, 5g protein, 46g carbohydrate, 14g total fat (5g saturated), 63mg cholesterol, 146mg sodium.

# Lemon Tea Bread

The early settlers brought their memories of afternoon tea, plus recipes for tea sandwiches and sweet treats, to the New World. From 1860 to 1900, many well-to-do families entertained frequently, as they had servants. Since people often had to travel long distances to visit, dinner parties were replaced by afternoon tea parties for the ladies: low tea, which included a plate of thin sandwiches or cakes, and high tea, which featured more substantial foods, such as lobster in pastry. This lemon tea bread is typical of the kind of sweets that were often taken with a cup of tea. It is more like cake than bread, so it can be cut into small squares and set out alongside other pastries.

**PREP:** 25 minutes ★ **BAKE:** 1 hour 5 minutes
**MAKES** 1 loaf, 16 slices

2½ cups all-purpose flour
1½ teaspoons baking powder
½ teaspoon baking soda
½ teaspoon salt
½ cup butter or margarine (1 stick), softened
1¼ cups sugar
2 teaspoons freshly grated lemon peel
2 large eggs
1 container (8 ounces) sour cream
1 teaspoon vanilla extract

1. Preheat oven to 350°F. Grease 9" by 5" metal loaf pan; dust with flour.

2. In medium bowl, combine flour, baking powder, baking soda, and salt. In large bowl, with mixer at low speed, beat butter until creamy. Add sugar and lemon peel and beat until fluffy, about 2 minutes.

3. Reduce speed to low and add eggs, one at a time, beating well after each addition, occasionally scraping bowl with rubber spatula. Add flour mixture alternately with sour cream, beginning and ending with flour mixture. Add vanilla. Beat just until smooth, scraping bowl.

4. Spoon batter into prepared pan; spread evenly. Bake until toothpick inserted in center of loaf comes out clean, about 1 hour 5 minutes. Cool loaf in pan on wire rack 10 minutes. Remove from pan and cool completely on wire rack.

**EACH SLICE:** About 225 calories, 3g protein, 31g carbohydrate, 10g total fat (6g saturated), 48mg cholesterol, 230mg sodium.

# Sour Cream Coffee Cake

how-off cakes, such as this buttery sour-cream version with cinnamon-nut swirls, often appeared in women's magazines between 1945 and 1960. They had the wow factor to impress family and friends and a melt-in-your-mouth flavor. Home economists in magazine test kitchens tested recipes and wrote them out so precisely that even novice bakers (of which there were many) could become star hostesses.

**PREP:** 30 minutes ★ **BAKE:** I hour 20 minutes
**MAKES** 16 servings

⅔ **plus 1¾ cups sugar**

⅔ **cup walnuts, finely chopped**

**I teaspoon ground cinnamon**

**3¾ cups all-purpose flour**

**2 teaspoons baking powder**

**I teaspoon baking soda**

¾ **teaspoon salt**

½ **cup butter or margarine (I stick), softened**

**3 large eggs**

**2 teaspoons vanilla extract**

**I container (16 ounces) sour cream**

1. Preheat oven to 350°F. Grease and flour 9- to 10-inch tube pan with removable bottom. In small bowl, combine ⅔ cup sugar, walnuts, and cinnamon. In medium bowl, combine flour, baking powder, baking soda, and salt.

2. In large bowl, with mixer at low speed, beat butter and remaining 1¾ cups sugar until blended, frequently scraping bowl with rubber spatula. Increase speed to high; beat until light and fluffy, about 2 minutes, occasionally scraping bowl. Reduce speed to low; add eggs, one at a time, beating well after each addition. Beat in vanilla.

3. With mixer at low speed, alternately add flour mixture and sour cream, beginning and ending with flour mixture. Beat until smooth, occasionally scraping bowl.

4. Spoon one-third of batter into prepared pan. Sprinkle about ½ cup nut mixture evenly over batter, then top with half of remaining batter. Sprinkle evenly with ½ cup more nut mixture; top with remaining batter, then sprinkle with the remaining nut mixture.

5. Bake coffee cake until toothpick inserted in center comes out clean, about 1 hour 20 minutes. Cool in pan on wire rack 10 minutes. Run thin knife around cake to loosen from side and center tube of pan; lift tube to separate cake from pan side. Invert cake onto plate; slide knife under cake to separate from bottom of pan. Turn cake, nut-mixture side up, onto wire rack to cool completely.

**EACH SERVING:** About 388 calories, 6g protein, 55g carbohydrate, 17g total fat (8g saturated), 68mg cholesterol, 336mg sodium.

# Sour Cream-Pear Coffee Cake

Early cookbooks did not contain the kinds of coffee cakes we are familiar with today, but there were recipes for muffins, batter cakes, and Sally Lunn. By most accounts, coffee klatches and the cakes served at them were a twentieth-century phenomenon. After World War II, the boom years brought families to suburbia, where making friends with neighbors was a new adventure. On weekdays when husbands were at work, taking time to visit with the ladies over coffee was a frequent affair. Quick coffee cakes, such as this cinnamon-crumb classic, were often the featured specialty.

**PREP:** 25 minutes ★ **BAKE:** 40 minutes
**MAKES** 16 servings

## STREUSEL

⅔ **cup packed light brown sugar**

½ **cup all-purpose flour**

1 **teaspoon ground cinnamon**

4 **tablespoons butter or margarine, softened**

⅔ **cup walnuts, toasted and chopped**

## CAKE

2½ **cups all-purpose flour**

1½ **teaspoons baking powder**

½ **teaspoon baking soda**

½ **teaspoon salt**

6 **tablespoons butter or margarine, softened**

1¼ **cups granulated sugar**

2 **large eggs**

1½ **teaspoons vanilla extract**

1⅓ **cups sour cream**

3 **firm but ripe Bosc pears (about 1¼ pounds),** *
   **peeled, cored, and cut into 1-inch pieces**

1. Preheat oven to 350°F. Grease 13" by 9" baking pan; dust with flour.

2. Prepare streusel: In medium bowl, with fork, mix brown sugar, flour, and cinnamon until well blended. With fingertips, work in butter until evenly distributed. Add walnuts and toss to mix; set aside.

3. Prepare cake: In another medium bowl, combine flour, baking powder, baking soda, and salt. In large bowl, with mixer at low speed, beat butter with sugar until blended, frequently scraping bowl with rubber spatula. Increase speed to high; beat until fluffy, about 2 minutes, occasionally scraping bowl. Reduce speed to low; add eggs, one at a time, beating well after each addition. Beat in vanilla.

4. Reduce speed to low. Add flour mixture alternately with sour cream, beginning and ending with flour mixture. Beat until batter is smooth, occasionally scraping bowl. With rubber spatula, gently fold in pears.

5. Spoon batter into prepared pan; spread evenly. Evenly sprinkle with streusel mixture. Bake until toothpick inserted in center comes out clean, 40 to 45 minutes. Cool cake in pan on wire rack 1 hour to serve warm, or cool cake completely in pan to serve later.

* The pears can be replaced with an equal amount of apples, peaches, or plums, or with 2 cups of blueberries.

**EACH SERVING:** About 352 calories, 5g protein, 50g carbohydrate, 16g total fat (8g saturated), 54mg cholesterol, 253mg sodium.

# Cinnamon Doughnuts

**B**efore leaving for the New World, the Pilgrims and the early Dutch colonists spent several years in Holland, where many learned to make doughnuts. They were described in Washington Irving's 1809 *History of New York* as "balls of sweetened dough, fried in hog's fat, and called doughnuts or *oly koeks* [oil cakes]..." It is believed that doughnuts originated in Germany, home of the Pennsylvania-Dutch settlers. Doughnuts called *fossnocks* or *fasnachts* were served on Shrove Tuesday: they were the last sweet allowed before Lent. It is thought that the Pennsylvania Dutch were probably the first to make doughnuts with holes, perfect for dunking into a cup of steaming hot coffee.

**PREP:** 30 minutes plus chilling
**COOK:** 2 minutes per batch
**MAKES** 24 doughnuts

3 cups all-purpose flour

1 cup sugar

1/3 cup buttermilk

2 large eggs

2 tablespoons vegetable shortening

1 tablespoon baking powder

1 teaspoon baking soda

1 teaspoon salt

1/2 teaspoon ground nutmeg

vegetable oil for frying

1 cup sugar

1 teaspoon ground cinnamon

1. In large bowl, combine 1½ cups flour, ½ cup sugar, buttermilk, eggs, shortening, baking powder, baking soda, salt, and nutmeg. With mixer at medium speed, beat until smooth, about 1 minute, scraping bowl with rubber spatula. Stir in remaining 1½ cups flour. Cover and refrigerate at least 1 hour for easier handling.

2. In deep-fat fryer or 6-quart Dutch oven, heat 3 to 4 inches oil over medium heat until temperature reaches 370°F on deep-fat thermometer. In large bowl, combine sugar and cinnamon; set aside.

3. Meanwhile, on well-floured surface, with floured rolling pin, roll dough ½ inch thick. With floured 2½-inch doughnut cutter, cut out doughnuts. Reserve trimmings for rerolling.

4. Fry dough rings, four at a time, until golden, 2 to 3 minutes, turning once. With slotted spoon, transfer doughnuts to paper towels to drain. Toss in cinnamon-sugar mixture while still warm.

## Doughnut "Holes"

Prepare as directed in Steps 1 through 3; use centers cut from doughnuts. Or use small biscuit cutter instead of doughnut cutter to cut dough into small rounds. Fry and coat with cinnamon-sugar as directed.

**EACH DOUGHNUT AND HOLE:** About 213 calories, 2g protein, 30g carbohydrate, 10g total fat (1g saturated), 18mg cholesterol, 220mg sodium.

# Chapter 6

# Desserts

Americans have always been in love with dessert. In the original thirteen colonies, desserts were rich and often very English. The colonists enjoyed creamy custard, whipped syllabub, Indian pudding, blueberry buckle, steamed pudding with raisins, mince pie, and soft flummery fruit pudding flavored with sherry. In eighteenth-century America, when a dinner's main course was over, the tabletop was sometimes flipped over to the "clean pie side." Then a dessert, such as a freshly baked pie (made from stewed preserved fruits in the winter and fresh garden fruits in the summer) was offered.

In the nineteenth century in the wealthiest homes, the dessert course was served in the formal European style, often with twenty sweets to choose from, including ice-cream bombes, sponge cakes, fruit pastries, and fancy puddings. Chocolate was also growing in popularity, thanks to Baker's German chocolate, the introduction of cocoa, and America's first mass-produced chocolate bar: the Hershey Bar.

During the early 1900s, Americans still catered to their sweet tooth but with lighter desserts, such as gelatin molds and quick-to-mix pudding desserts. Strawberry shortcake also found favor, as did hand-churned ice cream, which was drizzled with fudge sauce.

By the end of World War II, cake mixes were turning novice cooks into proud bakers, many of whom mixed, measured, and baked their way to national fame in bake-offs. Our tastes became more sophisticated as Americans traveled abroad and visited European pastry shops, then came home to tackle their first puff-pastry desserts.

As the century came to a close, we returned to the homey desserts we first loved: pandowdies, buckles, slumps, and betties, sometimes served with vanilla-bean ice cream or a fruit sauce laced with liqueur. Americans will always treasure their desserts—homespun, homemade, or store-bought.

◄ *New Orleans Bread Pudding*

# New Orleans Bread Pudding

*(pictured on page 132)*

The bread puddings that appear in early American cookbooks are plain and simple: some are made with cracker crumbs; others use bread or biscuit crumbs or sliced bread. Often the bread puddings are baked plain with an egg-and-milk-custard, or they are layered with currants and citron or with grated lemon, then served with a sweet sauce. Annabella Hill, in her 1867 *Southern Practical Cookery and Receipt Book,* advises readers in her bread pudding recipe: "To ascertain whether a pudding is done, pierce it near the centre with a large straw or knife-blade; if no batter adheres to it, the pudding is done." Our bread pudding brings the spirit of New Orleans to the table with brown sugar–praline and toasted pecans.

**PREP:** 20 minutes plus standing and cooling
**BAKE:** 45 minutes ★ **MAKES** 8 servings

½ cup dark seedless raisins

2 tablespoons bourbon

⅓ cup granulated sugar

⅛ teaspoon ground nutmeg

⅛ teaspoon ground cinnamon

3 large eggs

2 teaspoons vanilla extract

1 pint half-and-half or light cream

3 cups (½ inch) day-old French bread cubes

¼ cup packed dark brown sugar

2 tablespoons butter or margarine

1 tablespoon light corn syrup

⅓ cup pecans, toasted and chopped

**1.** In a small bowl, combine the raisins and bourbon; let stand 15 minutes. Grease 8-inch square baking dish.

**2.** In large bowl, combine granulated sugar, nutmeg, and cinnamon. Whisk in eggs and vanilla until combined. In cup, set aside 1 tablespoon half-and-half. Add remaining half-and-half to egg mixture and whisk until blended. Stir in bread cubes. Let stand 15 minutes, stirring occasionally. Stir in raisin mixture.

**3.** Meanwhile, preheat oven to 325°F. Pour bread mixture into prepared dish. Bake until knife inserted near center comes out clean, 45 to 50 minutes. Cool on wire rack 30 minutes.

**4.** In 1-quart saucepan, combine reserved half-and-half, brown sugar, butter, and corn syrup; heat to boiling over medium heat. Reduce heat and simmer, stirring occasionally, 2 minutes. Remove from heat and stir in pecans. Serve pudding drizzled with praline sauce.

**EACH SERVING:** About 300 calories, 6g protein, 36g carbohydrate, 16g total fat (7g saturated), 110mg cholesterol, 175mg sodium.

# Peach-Noodle Kugel

Jewish immigrants settling in America formed communities reminiscent of their native European villages. These enclaves had food markets and restaurants that served traditional specialties, such as *kugel* (pudding), which could be savory or sweet. Savory kugels were usually made with potatoes, carrots, matzoh, or egg noodles. Sweet kugels could be very simple, containing egg noodles, eggs, and a touch of sugar. At other times raisins, grated apple, nuts, or spices were added. Dairy noodle pudding, which was rich and delicious, had a generous amount of sour cream and farmer (or pot) cheese added. Sweet kugels were often sprinkled with cinnamon sugar, which made the topping crunchy and the kitchen fragrant.

**PREP:** 25 minutes ★ **BAKE:** 45 minutes
**MAKES** 10 servings

- **1 package (8 ounces) wide egg noodles**
- **3 tablespoons butter or margarine**
- **3 large eggs**
- **½ cup sugar**
- **1½ tablespoons grated freshly lemon peel**
- **¼ teaspoon salt**
- **2 cups milk**
- **½ cup dark seedless raisins**

## STREUSEL TOPPING

- **2 tablespoons butter or margarine**
- **¼ cup plain dried bread crumbs**
- **½ teaspoon ground cinnamon**
- **1 can (16 ounces) sliced cling peaches, drained**

**1.** Preheat oven to 350°F. Grease 12" by 8" baking dish. Cook noodles as label directs; drain. In large bowl, toss hot noodles with butter.

**2.** In medium bowl, with wire whisk or fork, beat eggs, sugar, lemon peel, and salt until well mixed; stir in milk and raisins. Stir egg mixture into noodles; pour into prepared dish. Bake 30 minutes.

**3.** Meanwhile, prepare streusel topping: In small saucepan, melt butter over low heat. Stir in dried bread crumbs and cinnamon.

**4.** Remove dish from oven; arrange peach slices on top and sprinkle evenly with topping. Bake 15 minutes longer. Let stand about 30 minutes for easier serving.

**EACH SERVING:** About 289 calories, 7g protein, 43g carbohydrate, 10g total fat (5g saturated), 108mg cholesterol, 190mg sodium.

# Rice Pudding

In *American Cookery,* Amelia Simmons instructs her readers to bake rice pudding for at least one-and-one half hours, either in a buttered dish or in one that is lined with puff pastry. Our recipe for plain rice pudding bakes in just over an hour.

**PREP:** 10 minutes ★ **COOK:** 1 hour 15 minutes
**MAKES** 4 cups or 6 servings

- **4 cups milk**
- **½ cup regular long-grain rice**
- **½ cup sugar**
- **¼ teaspoon salt**
- **1 large egg**
- **1 teaspoon vanilla extract**

**1.** In heavy 4-quart saucepan, combine milk, rice, sugar, and salt; heat to boiling over medium-high heat. Reduce heat; cover and simmer, stirring occasionally, until rice is very tender, about 1 hour.

**2.** In small bowl, lightly beat egg; stir in ½ cup hot rice mixture. Slowly pour egg mixture back into rice mixture, stirring rapidly to prevent curdling. Cook, stirring constantly, until rice mixture has thickened, about 5 minutes (do not boil, or mixture will curdle). Remove from heat; stir in vanilla. Serve warm, or spoon into medium bowl and refrigerate until well chilled, about 3 hours.

**EACH SERVING:** About 234 calories, 7g protein, 37g carbohydrate, 6g total fat (4g saturated), 58mg cholesterol, 187mg sodium.

## Rich Rice Pudding

Prepare and refrigerate as directed. In small bowl, with mixer at medium speed, beat *½ cup heavy or whipping cream* until soft peaks form. With rubber spatula, gently fold into rice pudding. Refrigerate until ready to serve, up to 4 hours. Makes 8 servings.

# Indian Pudding

The settlers used cornmeal (Indian meal) to make an English-style pudding called Yankee hasty pudding, and later Indian pudding. Eliza Leslie offers A Baked Indian Pudding in *Directions for Cookery* that contains molasses, butter, milk, and sifted Indian meal. "Serve it up hot, and eat it with wine sauce, or with butter and molasses."

**PREP:** 30 minutes ★ **BAKE:** 2 hours
**MAKES** 8 servings

⅔ cup cornmeal

4 cups milk

½ cup light (mild) molasses

4 tablespoons butter or margarine, cut into pieces

¼ cup sugar

1 teaspoon ground cinnamon

1 teaspoon ground ginger

½ teaspoon salt

¼ teaspoon ground nutmeg

whipped cream or vanilla ice cream (optional)

1. Preheat oven to 350°F. Lightly grease shallow 1½-quart baking dish.

2. In small bowl, combine cornmeal and 1 cup milk. In 4-quart saucepan, heat remaining 3 cups milk to boiling over high heat. With wire whisk, whisk in cornmeal mixture; heat to boiling. Reduce heat and simmer, stirring frequently with wooden spoon to prevent lumps, until mixture is thick, about 20 minutes. Remove from heat; stir in molasses, butter, sugar, cinnamon, ginger, salt, and nutmeg until well blended.

3. Pour batter into prepared dish, spreading it evenly. Cover with foil. Place dish in small roasting pan; place in oven. Carefully pour enough *boiling water* into roasting pan to come halfway up sides of baking dish. Bake 1 hour. Remove foil and bake pudding until lightly browned and just set, about 1 hour longer.

4. Carefully remove baking dish from water. Cool pudding in pan on wire rack 30 minutes. Serve pudding warm with whipped cream or vanilla ice cream, if desired.

**EACH SERVING WITHOUT WHIPPED CREAM OR ICE CREAM:** About 255 calories, 5g protein, 35g carbohydrate, 11g total fat (6g saturated), 33mg cholesterol, 270mg sodium.

## Christmas Pudding

*Take three-quarters of a pound each of chopped suet, stoned raisins, currants, sugar and dried bread crumbs, one-quarter of a pound of sliced citron, two chopped sour apples and the grated peel of one lemon. Mix together with one-half teaspoon each of cloves and salt. Add six eggs and one gill of rum or brandy. Steam for four hours in two buttered molds. Turn out on a hot dish, sprinkle sugar over the pudding, garnish with a sprig of holly, pour one-half cup of warm brandy over it and set it on fire as it goes to the table. Serve with*

## German Sauce

*Mix the yolks of four eggs with one-eighth of a pound of sugar, add the grated rind of half a lemon. Stir over the fire until the mixture coats the spoon. Serve hot. The pudding may be made some days before the dinner and reheated.*

**—Good Housekeeping Everyday Cook Book,** 1903

# Oven-Steamed Figgy Pudding (Christmas Pudding)

**D**elicious figgy pudding was once an all-day activity of mixing ingredients then steaming anywhere from four to seven hours. We have shortened the ingredients list, used butter instead of suet, and have simplified the preparation and cooking (oven steaming is easy and foolproof). Of course we have retained the moistness and rich flavor expected of a fine pudding.

**PREP:** 45 minutes ★ **BAKE:** 2 hours
**MAKES** 12 servings

2 packages (8 ounces each) dried Calimyrna figs

1¾ cups milk

1½ cups all-purpose flour

1 cup sugar

2½ teaspoons baking powder

1 teaspoon ground cinnamon

1 teaspoon ground nutmeg

1 teaspoon salt

3 large eggs

½ cup butter or margarine (1 stick), melted and cooled slightly

1½ cups fresh bread crumbs (about 3 slices firm white bread)

2 teaspoons freshly grated orange peel

1 teaspoon freshly grated lemon peel

Brandied Hard Sauce, optional (opposite)

1. Preheat oven to 350°F. Grease 2½-quart metal steamed-pudding mold or fluted tube pan.

2. With kitchen shears, cut stems from figs, then cut figs into small pieces. In 2-quart saucepan, combine figs and milk. Cover and cook over medium-low heat, stirring occasionally, 10 to 15 minutes (mixture may look curdled). Do not let mixture boil.

3. Meanwhile, in medium bowl, combine flour, sugar, baking powder, cinnamon, nutmeg, and salt.

4. In large bowl, with mixer at high speed, beat eggs 1 minute. Reduce speed to low; add butter, bread crumbs, orange peel, lemon peel, and fig mixture. Gradually add flour mixture; beat just until blended.

5. Spoon fig mixture into prepared mold; smooth top. Cover mold with sheet of greased foil, greased side down. (If your mold has a lid, grease inside of lid and omit foil.) Place mold in deep medium roasting pan; place pan on oven rack. Pour enough *very hot water* into roasting pan to come 2 inches up side of mold.

6. Bake until pudding is firm and pulls away from side of mold, about 2 hours. Transfer pudding to wire rack. Remove foil; cool 10 minutes. Invert onto cake plate; remove mold.

7. Meanwhile, prepare Brandied Hard Sauce, if desired. Serve pudding warm with sauce on the side.

**EACH SERVING WITHOUT HARD SAUCE:** About 350 calories, 6g protein, 59g carbohydrate, 11g total fat (3g saturated), 58mg cholesterol, 430mg sodium.

# Brandied Hard Sauce

In small bowl, with mixer at medium speed, beat *1½ cups confectioners' sugar, ½ cup butter or margarine (1 stick)* softened, *2 tablespoons brandy*, and *½ teaspoon vanilla extract* until creamy. Refrigerate if not serving right away. Makes about 1 cup.

**EACH TABLESPOON:** About 105 calories, 0g protein, 11g carbohydrate, 6g total fat (4g saturated), 16 mg cholesterol, 75mg sodium.

# Gingerbread

One of the earliest recipes for gingerbread, known as common gingerbread was a stiff dough that was rolled out, cut into strips, then braided or placed flat in a baking pan. Recipes for soft gingerbread and gingerbread cake are more like our recipe: they contain a mix of warm spices and bake up into a dessert that is not quite a bread, not quite a cake but always simply delicious. Early recipes suggest serving gingerbread warm and plain. But it's even more special with whipped cream or your favorite lemon sauce.

**PREP:** 10 minutes ★ **BAKE:** 45 minutes
**MAKES** 9 servings

2 cups all-purpose flour

½ cup sugar

2 teaspoons ground ginger

1 teaspoon ground cinnamon

½ teaspoon baking soda

½ teaspoon salt

1 cup light (mild) molasses

½ cup butter or margarine (1 stick),
   cut into 4 pieces

¾ cup boiling water

1 large egg

whipped cream (optional)

**1.** Preheat oven to 350°F. Grease and flour 9-inch square baking pan.

**2.** In large bowl, combine flour, sugar, ginger, cinnamon, baking soda, and salt. Stir until blended.

**3.** In small bowl, combine molasses and butter. Add boiling water and stir until butter melts. Add molasses mixture and egg to flour mixture; whisk until blended.

**4.** With rubber spatula, scrape batter into prepared pan. Bake until toothpick inserted in center comes out clean, 45 to 50 minutes. Cool in pan on wire rack. Serve warm or at room temperature with whipped cream, if desired.

**EACH SERVING WITHOUT WHIPPED CREAM:**
About 350 calories, 4g protein, 59g carbohydrate, 12g total fat (7g saturated), 51mg cholesterol, 325mg sodium.

# Chapter 7

# Cookies
# & Candies

Springerles were one of the first *koekjes* ("cookies" or "little cakes") baked by the New York–Dutch colonists. By rolling out a rich cookie dough on wooden boards that were carved with animals, flowers, and figures, the designs were transferred to the dough. In the seventeenth and eighteenth

centuries, there were many other cut-out cookies that began with a rich dough and contained a variety of flavorings, such as coriander, caraway, benne seeds, or ginger. They were quickly baked on a hot griddle, in a brick oven built into the fireplace, or in a free-standing reflector oven placed near an outdoor fire. Baking cookies back then was a tricky business at best.

During the nineteenth century, America's cookie repertoire expanded to include large molasses cookies, hermits, oatmeal cookies, shortbread, sand tarts, macaroons, and delicate sugar cookies.

By the early twentieth century, reliable gas and electric stoves made baking cookies easier. Americans baked icebox cookies, Toll House cookies, peanut butter cookies, snickerdoodles, and bar cookies. And in the 1960s, Girl Scouts made their mark by popularizing s'mores.

Candies, known as sweetmeats in England, were also special treats the colonists enjoyed. They included maple-syrup candy, marzipan, and benne-seed candies. In the eighteenth century, caramels, pralines, and lollipops were all the rage, and by the twentieth century, candy jars were being filled with pulled taffy, almond nougats, gumdrops, fudge, divinity, and homemade chocolates.

In the twentieth century, we discovered fast-cook and no-cook candies, such as No-Fail Fudge, which started with a can of sweetened condensed milk and melted chocolate, and Rocky-Road Squares. But that's not all. Penny-candy stores, taffy shops, and fudge shops made it possible to purchase chocolate bars, saltwater taffy, and any kind of freshly made fudge.

Americans have never outgrown their love of cookies and candies—and probably never will.

◄ *Chocolate-Walnut Fudge*

# Good Housekeeping's Fudgy Brownies

**B**rownies are a twentieth-century creation. Although a recipe for them does appear in *The Boston Cooking-School Cook Book* of 1896, it doesn't contain chocolate and they aren't bar cookies. Instead, they are "browned" by the addition of Porto Rico molasses and are baked in fancy cake tins. Fanny Farmer's 1906 cookbook offers a recipe for brownies that uses two squares of (melted) Baker's chocolate. It may very well be one of the earliest recipes for chocolate brownies. Our recipe is *Good Housekeeping's* favorite when it comes to fudgy, superrich brownies that have deep chocolate flavor. To make them even more decadent, spread them with praline-pecan icing.

**PREP:** 10 minutes ★ **BAKE:** 30 minutes
**MAKES** 24 brownies

1¼ cups all-purpose flour

½ teaspoon salt

¾ cup butter or margarine (1½ sticks)

4 squares (4 ounces) unsweetened
　　chocolate, chopped

4 squares (4 ounces) semisweet
　　chocolate, chopped

2 cups sugar

1 tablespoon vanilla extract

5 large eggs, beaten

**1.** Preheat oven to 350°F. Grease 13" by 9" baking pan. In small bowl, combine flour and salt.

**2.** In heavy 4-quart saucepan, melt butter and unsweetened and semisweet chocolates over low heat, stirring frequently, until smooth. Remove pan from heat. With wooden spoon, stir in sugar and vanilla. Add eggs; stir until well mixed. Stir flour mixture into chocolate mixture just blended. Spread batter evenly in prepared pan.

**3.** Bake until toothpick inserted 1 inch from edge comes out clean, about 30 minutes. Cool completely in pan on wire rack. When cool, cut lengthwise into 4 strips, then cut each strip crosswise into 6 pieces.

**EACH BROWNIE:** About 206 calories, 3g protein, 26g carbohydrate, 11g total fat (6g saturated), 60mg cholesterol, 121mg sodium.

## Praline-Iced Brownies

Prepare brownies as directed; cool. In 2-quart saucepan, heat *5 tablespoons butter or margarine* and *⅓ cup packed brown sugar* over medium-low heat until mixture has melted and bubbles, about 5 minutes. Remove from heat.

With wire whisk, beat in *3 tablespoons bourbon or 1 tablespoon vanilla extract plus 2 tablespoons water*; stir in *2 cups confectioners' sugar* until smooth. With narrow metal spatula, spread topping over room temperature brownies; sprinkle *½ cup pecans*, toasted and coarsely chopped, over topping. Cut brownies lengthwise into 8 strips, then cut each strip crosswise into 8 pieces. Makes 64 brownies.

**EACH BROWNIE:** About 297 calories, 3g protein, 39g carbohydrate, 15g total fat (8g saturated), 66mg cholesterol, 147mg sodium.

# Cookie Jars & Biscuit Boxes

In England, biscuit boxes, biscuit jars, and cracker jars are often made of sterling silver and hand-cut crystal. Known as cookie jars in America, they can be as humble as plain pottery or as elaborate as brightly painted ceramic, wood, or tin. The decorations range from apples to grandmas to colorful, laughing clowns. But no matter how they're shaped, painted, and decorated, they all serve the same purpose: to keep crisp cookies crisp and moist cookies moist.

Visit an English mansion or a London antique fair, and you'll see some of the most elegant cookie containers ever created: an engraved Victorian biscuit box by London silversmiths Martin and Hall (ca. 1869); a crystal Sheffield biscuit jar with a thistle- and-diamond pattern and sterling swing-handle and lid (ca. 1898); cream-colored bisque Wedgwood biscuit jars with hand-painted floral motifs; a ceramic biscuit jar decorated in bright cobalt and topped with a molded pomegranate knob; or transferware cracker and biscuit jars painted with English country scenes by W. T. Copeland.

In America, cookies were generally stored in cardboard oatmeal boxes, coffee or cracker tins, and bread boxes (anything handy that would keep them fresh). But by the twentieth century, a whole new "cookie world" opened up. More and more, cookies were being baked at home, thanks to delicious recipes, the availability of baking chocolate, and reliable stoves. Ever since the Great Depression, when homemakers discovered that it was more economical to make cookies at home than to buy them at bakeries, the demand for containers to keep them fresh had been increasing. The Brush Pottery Company in Roseville, Ohio, came up with a solution in 1929: a green canister embossed with the word *cookies* on the front. It is thought to be the first pottery cookie jar ever made. In 1932, the Hocking Glass Company added a cookie jar with a screw top to its glass-paneled canister set. These early jars were simple, often made of stoneware, with a cylindrical or bean-pot shape, and decorated with leaves and flowers, if at all. But soon, two giants, the Nelson McCoy Pottery Company and the American Bisque Company, each made cookie-jar history by respectively designing approximately three hundred decorative cookie jars. The McCoy jars were often shaped like apples, strawberries, and kettles, while the American Bisque jars were often shaped like people.

From the 1940s on, made-in-America cookie jars have been extremely popular, both as practical containers and as valuable collectibles. Among the most recognizable (and marketable) are nursery-rhyme characters, such as Humpty Dumpty and Bo Peep; barnyard animals, Walt Disney's Mickey Mouse and Donald Duck and the Cookie Monster. Cookie jars in America "live" on, and hopefully always will, in kitchens, corner cabinets, museums, and cherished collections.

# Blondies

Sometime in the 1940s, recipes for bar cookies that were similar to brownies but didn't contain chocolate began appearing. Bursting with brown-sugar flavor, these blonde-colored cookies were delicious. Today's blondies often contain nuts; sometimes chocolate chips or butterscotch chips are added too.

**PREP:** 10 minutes ★ **BAKE:** 30 minutes
**MAKES** 24 blondies

1 cup all-purpose flour

2 teaspoons baking powder

1 teaspoon salt

6 tablespoons butter or margarine

1¾ cups packed light brown sugar

2 teaspoons vanilla extract

2 large eggs

1½ cups pecans (6 ounces), coarsely chopped

**1.** Preheat oven to 350°F. Grease 13" by 9" baking pan. In small bowl, combine flour, baking powder, and salt.

**2.** In 3-quart saucepan, melt butter over low heat. Remove from heat. With wooden spoon, stir in brown sugar and vanilla; add eggs, stirring until well blended. Stir flour mixture into sugar mixture just until mixed. Stir in pecans. Spread batter evenly in prepared pan.

**3.** Bake until toothpick inserted 2 inches from edge of pan comes out clean, about 30 minutes. Do not overbake; blondies will firm as they cool. Cool completely in pan on wire rack.

**4.** When cool, cut lengthwise into 4 strips, then cut each strip crosswise into 6 pieces.

**EACH BLONDIE:** About 159 calories, 2g protein, 21g carbohydrate, 8g total fat (2g saturated), 25mg cholesterol, 179mg sodium.

## Coconut Blondies

Prepare as directed, stirring in ¾ *cup flaked sweetened coconut* with pecans.

## Chocolate Chip Blondies

Prepare as directed but in Step 2, let batter cool 15 minutes; stir in *1 package (6 ounces) semisweet chocolate chips.* Proceed as directed.

# Lemon Bars

**E**arly American cookbooks often included recipes for shortbread and lemon curd. It wasn't until the mid-twentieth century that these two favorites were combined in a bar cookie. The contrast of a buttery shortbread-cookie base and a smooth and tangy lemon filling makes these bars a popular sweet treat. Be sure to cool the bars completely before cutting them. If they are still soft and tender, chill them in the refrigerator for a short while before serving.

**PREP:** 15 minutes ★ **BAKE:** 30 minutes
**MAKES** 36 bars

---

1½ cups plus 3 tablespoons all-purpose flour

½ cup plus 1 tablespoon confectioners' sugar

¾ cup cold butter or margarine (1½ sticks), cut into pieces

2 large lemons

3 large eggs

1 cup granulated sugar

½ teaspoon baking powder

½ teaspoon salt

**1.** Preheat oven to 350°F. Line 13" by 9" baking pan with foil, extending foil over rim; lightly grease foil.

**2.** In medium bowl, combine 1½ cups flour and ½ cup confectioners' sugar. With pastry blender or two knives used scissor-fashion, cut in butter until mixture resembles coarse crumbs. Transfer crumb mixture to prepared pan. With floured hand, pat firmly onto bottom of pan.

**3.** Bake until lightly browned, 15 to 17 minutes.

**4.** Meanwhile, from lemons, grate 1 teaspoon peel and squeeze ⅓ cup juice. In large bowl, with mixer at high speed, beat eggs until thick and lemon-colored, about 3 minutes. Reduce speed to low. Add granulated sugar, remaining 3 tablespoons flour, baking powder, salt, and lemon peel and juice. Beat, occasionally scraping bowl with rubber spatula, until blended. Pour lemon filling over warm crust.

**5.** Bake until filling is just set and golden around edges, about 15 minutes. Transfer pan to wire rack. Dust remaining 1 tablespoon confectioners' sugar over warm filling. Cool completely in pan on wire rack.

**6.** When cool, remove lemon bars from pan by lifting edges of foil and place on cutting board. Cut lengthwise into 3 strips, then cut each strip crosswise into 12 pieces.

---

**EACH BAR:** About 95 calories, 1g protein, 12g carbohydrate, 4g total fat (3g saturated), 28mg cholesterol, 85mg sodium.

# Grandma's Oatmeal-Raisin Cookies

Although Fanny Farmer's 1896 cookbook included a recipe for oatmeal cookies, they were quite different from the ones we bake today. Her cookies contained lots of flour, only a little oatmeal, and no raisins. The stiff dough was rolled and cut out. By the 1900s, drop oatmeal cookie recipes began appearing. The 1921 edition of *The Settlement Cookbook,* had two oatmeal cookie recipes. Both called for white sugar (not brown), and one of the recipes had raisins and hickory nuts. Like many oatmeal cookie recipes today, ours are made with butter and are brimming with raisins.

**PREP:** 15 minutes ★ **BAKE:** 15 minutes per batch
**MAKES** about 24 cookies

¾ **cup all-purpose flour**

½ **teaspoon baking soda**

¼ **teaspoon salt**

½ **cup butter or margarine (1 stick), softened**

½ **cup granulated sugar**

⅓ **cup packed brown sugar**

1 **large egg**

2 **teaspoons vanilla extract**

1½ **cups old-fashioned or quick-cooking oats, uncooked**

¾ **cup dark seedless raisins or chopped pitted prunes**

**1.** Preheat oven to 350°F. In small bowl, combine flour, baking soda, and salt.

**2.** In large bowl, with mixer at medium speed, beat butter and granulated and brown sugars until light and fluffy. Beat in egg and vanilla until blended. Reduce speed to low; beat in flour mixture just until blended. With wooden spoon, stir in oats and raisins.

**3.** Drop dough by heaping tablespoons, 2 inches apart, on two ungreased large cookie sheets. Bake until golden, about 15 minutes, rotating cookie sheets between upper and lower oven racks halfway through baking. With wide spatula, transfer cookies to wire racks to cool completely.

**4.** Repeat with remaining dough.

**EACH COOKIE:** About 113 calories, 2g protein, 17g carbohydrate, 4g total fat (2g saturated), 19mg cholesterol, 94mg sodium.

# Shortenin' Bread

Shortbread originated in Scotland and the British Isles. Traditionally it was served at Christmas but was also enjoyed throughout the year. Shortbread cookies are firm but temptingly rich. Sometimes they contain only three ingredients: butter, flour, and white sugar. Other recipes call for ginger, almonds, or brown sugar, as does ours. Originally shortbread dough was pressed into a decoratively carved mold, so that when the cookies were turned out, they were embossed. In Scotland, as far back as the twelfth century, shortbread was baked in round pans (sometimes with fluted edges) and cut into wedges that resembled the hoop petticoats worn by ladies of the court. In those days, they were known as *petty cotes tallis'*; today they are called petticoat tails. In our recipe the shortbread is cut into the traditional "fingers."

**PREP:** 20 minutes  ★  **BAKE:** 23 minutes
**MAKES** 24 wedges

¾ **cup butter or margarine (1½ sticks), softened**

⅓ **cup packed dark brown sugar**

3 **tablespoons granulated sugar**

1 **teaspoon vanilla extract**

1¾ **cups all-purpose flour**

1 **cup pecans (4 ounces), chopped**

1. Preheat oven to 350°F. In large bowl, with mixer at medium-low speed, beat butter, brown and granulated sugars, and vanilla until creamy. Reduce speed to low and beat in flour until blended (dough will be crumbly). With wooden spoon, stir dough until it holds together.

2. Divide dough in half. With hand, pat evenly onto bottom of two ungreased 8-inch round cake pans. Sprinkle with pecans; press lightly.

3. Bake until edges are lightly browned and center is firm, 23 to 25 minutes. Transfer pans to wire racks. With small sharp knife, cut each round into 12 wedges. Cool completely in pans or on wire racks.

**EACH WEDGE:** About 130 calories, 1g protein, 12g carbohydrate, 9g total fat (4g saturated), 16mg cholesterol, 60mg sodium.

# Peanut Butter Cookies

In the late nineteenth century, a physician developed a protein substitute for people who had poor teeth and therefore had trouble chewing; it was called peanut butter. In 1903, Ambrose W. Straub invented the first peanut butter machine, and a year after that, peanut butter was promoted as a health food at the St. Louis World's Fair. In 1923, J. L. Rosefield developed a process that prevented peanut butter from separating, which Swift and Company began using for its Peter Pan brand peanut butter. It was at this time that recipes for peanut butter cookies began showing up. Originally the dough was cut into shapes, but by the 1940s a stiffer peanut butter dough was being rolled into balls then crosshatched with a fork. Our cookies are rich, thanks to a generous amount of peanut butter. The dough is also soft enough to be dropped onto cookie sheets, which eliminates the need to roll the dough into balls.

**PREP:** 15 minutes ★ **BAKE:** 15 minutes per batch
**MAKES** about 36 cookies

1¼ **cups all-purpose flour**

1 **teaspoon baking soda**

¼ **teaspoon salt**

1 **cup creamy peanut butter**

½ **cup butter or margarine (1 stick), softened**

½ **cup packed brown sugar**

¼ **cup granulated sugar**

1 **large egg**

½ **teaspoon vanilla extract**

**1.** Preheat oven to 350°F. In small bowl, combine flour, baking soda, and salt.

**2.** In large bowl, with mixer at medium speed, beat peanut butter, butter, brown and granulated sugars, egg, and vanilla until combined, occasionally scraping bowl with rubber spatula. Reduce speed to low. Add the flour mixture and beat just until blended.

**3.** Drop dough by heaping tablespoons, 2 inches apart, on two ungreased large cookie sheets. With fork, press crisscross pattern into top of each cookie. Bake until lightly browned, 15 to 20 minutes, rotating cookie sheets between upper and lower oven racks halfway through baking. With wide spatula, transfer the cookies to wire racks to cool completely.

**4.** Repeat with remaining dough.

**EACH COOKIE:** About 100 calories, 3g protein, 9g carbohydrate, 6g total fat (2g saturated), 13mg cholesterol, 114mg sodium.

# Chocolate Chip Cookies

In 1930, Ruth Wakefield and her husband purchased a 1709 Cape Cod–style house near Whitman, Massachusetts. At one time it had been a toll house where travelers could get a bite to eat, change their horses, and pay their road tolls. Mrs. Wakefield had a large collection of recipes and loved cooking. Both she and her husband enjoyed having guests in their home, so they decided to open up the Toll House Inn. One day when mixing up a batch of her favorite Butter Drop Do cookies, she stirred two chopped up chocolate bars into the dough figuring that the chocolate bits would melt, thus saving her the task of melting the chocolate beforehand. To her surprise, the chocolate bits didn't melt. Her guests liked the cookies so much that she perfected the recipe, adding two bars of Nestlé semisweet chocolate that were chopped "into the size of peas" and some nuts. After the recipe was published in a Boston newspaper and in her first cookbook in 1930, the sales for Nestlé chocolate bars skyrocketed. By 1939, the Nestlé company was packaging chocolate chips and Ruth Wakefield's recipe was being printed on the back of every package.

**PREP:** 15 minutes ★ **BAKE:** 10 minutes per batch
**MAKES** about 36 cookies

1 1/4 **cups all-purpose flour**

1/2 **teaspoon baking soda**

1/2 **teaspoon salt**

1/2 **cup butter or margarine (1 stick), softened**

1/2 **cup packed brown sugar**

1/4 **cup granulated sugar**

1 **large egg**

1 **teaspoon vanilla extract**

1 **package (6 ounces) semisweet chocolate chips (1 cup)**

1/2 **cup walnuts, chopped (optional)**

1. Preheat oven to 375°F. In small bowl, combine flour, baking soda, and salt.

2. In large bowl, with mixer at medium speed, beat butter and brown and granulated sugars until light and fluffy. Beat in egg and vanilla until well combined. Reduce speed to low; beat in flour mixture just until blended. With wooden spoon, stir in chocolate chips and walnuts, if using.

3. Drop dough by rounded tablespoons, 2 inches apart, on two ungreased large cookie sheets. Bake until golden around edges, 10 to 12 minutes, rotating cookie sheets between upper and lower oven racks halfway through baking. With wide spatula, transfer cookies to wire racks to cool completely.

4. Repeat with remaining dough.

**EACH COOKIE:** About 80 calories, 1g protein, 11g carbohydrate, 4g total fat (2g saturated), 13mg cholesterol, 79mg sodium.

# White Chocolate-Macadamia Cookies

Prepare as directed but substitute ¾ *cup white baking chips* for semisweet chocolate chips and *1 cup chopped macadamia nuts (4 ounces)* for walnuts.

# Whoopie Pies

**T**his Pennsylvania-Dutch favorite is not a pie at all but two cakelike chocolate cookies that are sandwiched together with a fluffy white filling. According to Betty Groff, cookbook author and owner of Groff's Farm Restaurant, they may have been created by mothers using leftover cake batter to make a few cookies for their children. How they became known as whoopie pies is unclear. Perhaps it's the "whoop of glee" that children express when given such a treat. Our recipe uses a marshmallow crème filling that's reminiscent of moon pies, cookies "as big as the moon," which the Chattanooga Bakery in Tennessee has been making since 1917.

**PREP:** 30 minutes plus cooling ★ **BAKE** 12 minutes
**MAKES** 12 whoopie pies

## COOKIE DOUGH

**2 cups all-purpose flour**

**1 cup sugar**

**½ cup unsweetened cocoa**

**1 teaspoon baking soda**

**¼ teaspoon salt**

**¾ cup milk**

**6 tablespoons butter or margarine, melted**

**1 large egg**

**1 teaspoon vanilla extract**

## MARSHMALLOW CRÈME FILLING

**6 tablespoons butter or margarine,
  slightly softened**

**1 cup confectioners' sugar**

**1 jar (7 to 7½ ounces) marshmallow crème**

**1 teaspoon vanilla extract**

**1.** Preheat the oven to 350°F. Grease two large cookie sheets.

**2.** Prepare cookie dough: In large bowl, with wooden spoon, beat flour, sugar, cocoa, baking soda, salt, milk, butter, egg, and vanilla until mixture is smooth.

**3.** Drop 12 heaping tablespoons dough, 2 inches apart, on each prepared cookie sheet. Bake until puffy and toothpick inserted in center comes out clean, 12 to 14 minutes, rotating sheets between upper and lower oven racks halfway through baking. With wide spatula, transfer cookies to wire racks to cool completely.

**4.** When cookies are cool, prepare marshmallow crème filling: In large bowl, with mixer at medium speed, beat butter until smooth. Reduce speed to low; gradually beat in confectioners' sugar. Beat in marshmallow crème and vanilla until smooth.

**5.** Spread 1 rounded tablespoon filling on flat side of 12 cookies. Top with the remaining cookies, flat side down.

**EACH WHOOPIE PIE:** About 365 calories, 4g protein, 59g carbohydrate, 14g total fat (8g saturated), 51mg cholesterol, 290mg sodium.

# Black-and-Whites

Just which year these popular cookies began appearing in bakeshops in New York City and elsewhere on the East Coast (in Boston they are called Half Moons) is hazy. But by the mid-twentieth century, these large golden cookies (up to five inches in diameter) had become a regular feature in many neighborhood bakeries. They are rather cake-like, and the tops are half-coated with vanilla icing and half-coated with chocolate icing.

**PREP:** 20 minutes plus cooling
**BAKE:** 15 minutes per batch
**MAKES** about 14 cookies

2 cups all-purpose flour

1/2 teaspoon baking soda

1/4 teaspoon salt

10 tablespoons butter or margarine (1 1/4 sticks), softened

1 cup granulated sugar

2 large eggs

2 teaspoons vanilla extract

1/2 cup buttermilk

1 3/4 cups confectioners' sugar

2 tablespoons light corn syrup

8 to 10 teaspoons warm water

1/4 cup unsweetened cocoa

1. Preheat oven to 350°F. In small bowl, combine flour, baking soda, and salt.

2. In large bowl, with mixer at medium speed, beat butter and granulated sugar until creamy. Beat in eggs and vanilla until blended. Reduce speed to low; add flour mixture alternately with buttermilk, beginning and ending with flour mixture. Beat just until combined, occasionally scraping bowl with rubber spatula.

3. Drop dough by 1/4 cups, about 3 inches apart, on two ungreased large cookie sheets. Bake until edges begin to brown and tops spring back when lightly touched with finger, 15 to 17 minutes, rotating sheets between upper and lower racks halfway through baking. With wide spatula, transfer cookies to wire racks to cool completely.

4. When cookies are cool, prepare glazes: In medium bowl, mix 1 1/4 cups confectioners' sugar, 1 tablespoon corn syrup, and 5 to 6 teaspoons water, 1 teaspoon at a time, until smooth and of spreading consistency. Turn cookies flat side up. With small metal spatula, spread glaze over half of each cookie. Allow glaze to set 20 minutes.

5. Meanwhile, prepare chocolate glaze: In small bowl, mix remaining 1/2 cup confectioners' sugar, cocoa, remaining 1 tablespoon corn syrup, and remaining 3 to 4 teaspoons water, 1 teaspoon at a time, until smooth and of spreading consistency. With clean small spatula, spread chocolate glaze over remaining un-iced half of each cookie. Let glazes set completely, at least 1 hour.

**EACH COOKIE:** About 280 calories, 3g protein, 46g carbohydrate, 9g total fat (6g saturated), 53mg cholesterol, 190mg sodium.

# Snowballs

By the 1950s, buttery cookie balls covered with powdered sugar had become so popular that recipes for them began appearing in community cookbooks across America. They are known by several names: Mexican wedding cakes, Russian tea cakes, nut butter balls, and crispy nougats. Just where the recipe originated remains a mystery. These delicious cookies traditionally contain only a small amount of sugar because they are rolled twice in confectioners' sugar: once while still warm from the oven and again when cool.

---

**PREP:** 25 minutes ★ **BAKE:** 20 minutes per batch
**MAKES** about 4 dozen cookies

---

1 cup pecans (4 ounces)

1¾ cups confectioners' sugar

1 cup butter (2 sticks), cut into 16 pieces, softened (do not use margarine)

1 teaspoon vanilla extract

2 cups all-purpose flour

1. Preheat oven to 325°F. In food processor with knife blade attached, process pecans and ¼ cup confectioners' sugar until nuts are finely chopped. Add butter and vanilla and process until smooth, scraping down side of processor bowl with rubber spatula. Add the flour and process until the dough comes together.

2. With floured hands, roll dough into 1-inch balls. Place balls, 1½ inches apart, on ungreased large cookie sheet.

3. Bake until bottoms are lightly browned and tops are very light golden brown, 20 to 22 minutes. With wide spatula, transfer cookies to wire rack to cool slightly.

4. Place remaining 1½ cups confectioners' sugar in pie plate. While cookies are still warm, roll in sugar until coated; place on wire rack to cool completely. When cool, reroll the cookies in sugar until thoroughly coated.

5. Repeat with remaining dough.

---

**EACH COOKIE:** About 85 calories, 1g protein, 9g carbohydrate, 5g total fat (3g saturated), 10mg cholesterol, 40mg sodium.

# Coconut Macaroons

**M**acaroons that were most likely made with almonds were recorded as early as the eighth century and were very popular in Venice and other cities in Italy during the Renaissance. Their name comes from the Italian *maccherone* and *macarone* (fine paste), from which the word *macaroni* is also derived. These small, sweet egg-white puffs were often served with fine wine or liqueur as a light refreshment, particularly during Passover. As far back as the 1850s, American cookbooks contained recipes for both almond and coconut macaroons, including Eliza Leslie's 1848 edition of *Directions for Cookery.* Her Cocoa-Nut Maccaroons [*sic*] included instructions to grate loaf sugar over their tops before baking them in a brisk (hot) oven. Regardless of the recipe you're using, Fanny Farmer's advice in her macaroon recipe in *The Boston Cooking-School Cook Book* still holds true: "After removing [cookies] from oven, invert paper, and wet with a cloth wrung out of cold water, when macaroons will easily slip off."

**PREP:** 20 minutes ★ **BAKE:** 25 minutes
**MAKES** about 30 cookies

1 package (7 ounces) flaked
   sweetened coconut

¾ cup sugar

3 large egg whites

1 teaspoon vanilla extract

⅛ teaspoon almond extract

1. Preheat oven to 325°F. Line two large cookie sheets with parchment paper or foil. Spray with nonstick cooking spray.

2. In large bowl, stir coconut, sugar, egg whites, and the vanilla and almond extracts until well combined.

3. Drop batter by rounded teaspoons, 1 inch apart, on prepared cookie sheets. Bake until set and light golden, about 25 minutes, rotating cookie sheets between upper and lower oven racks halfway through baking. Cool 1 minute on cookie sheets. With wide spatula, transfer cookies to wire racks to cool completely.

**EACH COOKIE:** About 54 calories, 1g protein, 8g carbohydrate, 2g total fat (2g saturated), 0mg cholesterol, 22mg sodium.

## Chocolate-Coconut Macaroons

Prepare as directed, stirring *2 tablespoons unsweetened cocoa* and *1 square (1 ounce) semisweet chocolate*, grated, into coconut mixture.

## Chocolate-Dipped Coconut Macaroons

Melt *4 squares (4 ounces) semisweet chocolate* according to package directions. Dip bottoms of cooled macaroons in melted chocolate, scraping bottoms on edge of bowl to remove excess chocolate. Place macaroons on wax paper–lined cookie sheets, chocolate side up. Let stand until chocolate sets.

# Benne Seed Wafers

In the South Carolina low country you'll rarely hear folks call the main ingredient in these cookies sesame seeds. Instead they refer to them as benne seeds: the name the African slaves called them when the seeds were brought here in the seventeenth century. South Carolina cooks add the seeds to bread, candy, and to these traditional brown-sugar wafers. Be sure to let the cookies rest one minute (for easier handling) before transferring them to wire racks to cool and crisp.

**PREP:** 30 minutes ★ **BAKE:** 6 minutes per batch
**MAKES** about 120 cookies

½ **cup sesame seeds**

¾ **cup all-purpose flour**

¼ **teaspoon salt**

½ **cup butter (1 stick), softened (do not use margarine)**

1 **cup packed light brown sugar**

1 **large egg**

1 **teaspoon vanilla extract**

1. Preheat the oven to 350°F. Grease two large cookie sheets.

2. Spread sesame seeds in even layer in jelly-roll pan. Bake until light golden, 10 to 12 minutes. Cool in pan on wire rack.

3. In small bowl, combine flour and salt.

4. In medium bowl, with mixer at medium speed, beat butter and brown sugar until creamy. Reduce speed to low; beat in egg and vanilla until well blended. Beat in flour mixture and sesame seeds until combined, occasionally scraping bowl with rubber spatula.

5. Drop the dough by rounded half teaspoons, 3 inches apart, on prepared cookie sheets. Bake until light brown and lacy, 6 to 7 minutes, rotating cookie sheets between upper and lower oven racks halfway through baking. Cool on cookie sheet on wire rack 1 minute. With wide spatula, transfer cookies to wire rack to cool completely.

6. Repeat with remaining dough.

**EACH COOKIE:** About 20 calories, 0g protein, 3g carbohydrate, 1g total fat (1g saturated), 4mg cholesterol, 15mg sodium.

# Cookie-Press Cookies

Scandinavian immigrants introduced America to buttery spritz cookies. Half of the fun in preparing them is choosing a decorative disk (or disks) and pressing the cookies out onto cookie sheets. The name *spritz* comes from the German word *spritzen*, which means "squirt" or "spray." If you've never used a cookie press, you may need a little practice at first. Experts advise to shape the dough into a roll a little narrower than the diameter of the cookie-press tube. You can easily make hearts, wreaths, and trees by using the various metal disks. Tint the dough different colors if you wish, and sprinkle the cookies with decorating sugar.

**PREP:** 15 minutes ★ **BAKE:** 10 minutes per batch
**MAKES** about 60 cookies

1 **cup butter or margarine (2 sticks), softened**

¾ **cup confectioners' sugar**

1 **teaspoon vanilla extract**

⅛ **teaspoon almond extract**

2 **cups all-purpose flour**

⅛ **teaspoon salt**

1. Preheat oven to 350°F. In large bowl, with mixer at medium speed, beat butter and confectioners' sugar until light and fluffy. Beat in vanilla and almond extracts. Reduce speed to low; add flour and salt and beat until well combined.

2. Spoon one-third of batter into cookie press fitted with disk of choice. Press out cookies, 1 inch apart, on two large ungreased cookie sheets.

3. Bake until golden brown around edges, 10 to 12 minutes, rotating cookie sheets between upper and lower oven racks halfway through baking. With wide spatula, transfer cookies to wire racks to cool completely.

4. Repeat with remaining dough.

**EACH COOKIE:** About 48 calories, 0g protein, 5g carbohydrate, 3g total fat (2g saturated), 8mg cholesterol, 36mg sodium.

# Raspberry Linzer Thumbprint Cookies

From Linz, Austria, comes the famous linzertorte, a tart made with a nutty, shortbread-type crust that is filled with jam and topped with a pastry lattice. Thumbprint cookies, which became popular during the mid-twentieth century, were typically made from a buttery cookie dough that was mixed with ground nuts (often almonds), then formed into balls and rolled in more ground nuts. Before popping them into the oven, the baker would make an indentation in each cookie with his or her thumb, and then fill it with any favorite jam or jelly. Our thumbprint cookies resemble the classic linzertorte, as they are made with a rich shortbread dough and raspberry jam.

**PREP:** 45 minutes ★ **BAKE:** 20 minutes per batch
**MAKES** about 48 cookies

1⅓ cups hazelnuts (filberts, about 6 ounces)
½ cup sugar
¾ cup butter or margarine (1½ sticks), cut into pieces
1 teaspoon vanilla extract
¼ teaspoon salt
1¾ cups all-purpose flour
¼ cup seedless red-raspberry jam

1. Preheat oven to 350°F.

2. Place 1 cup hazelnuts in 9-inch square baking pan. Bake until toasted, about 15 minutes. Wrap hot hazelnuts in clean kitchen towel. With hands on outside of towel, roll hazelnuts back and forth to remove most of skins. Cool; separate hazelnuts from skins.

3. In food processor with knife blade attached, process toasted hazelnuts and sugar until nuts are finely ground. Add butter, vanilla, and salt; process just until blended. Add flour and process until evenly combined. Remove knife blade and press dough together with hands.

4. Finely chop remaining ⅓ cup hazelnuts; spread on sheet of waxed paper. Roll dough into 1-inch balls (dough may be slightly crumbly). Roll balls in hazelnuts, gently pressing to coat.

5. Place balls, about 1½ inches apart, on two ungreased large cookie sheets. With thumb, make small indentation in center of each ball. Fill each indentation with ¼ teaspoon jam.

6. Bake until lightly golden around edges, about 20 minutes, rotating cookie sheets between upper and lower oven racks halfway through baking. With wide spatula, transfer cookies to wire racks to cool completely.

7. Repeat with remaining dough balls and jam.

**EACH COOKIE:** About 75 calories, 1g protein, 7g carbohydrate, 5g total fat (2g saturated), 8mg cholesterol, 40mg sodium.

# Wooden Spoon-Lace Cookies

These delicate confections are called French lace cookies and *crepinettes* (almond lace cookies). When they first appeared is not clear, but there are recipes in mid-twentieth-century cookbooks. In France, the cookies are often made with sliced almonds and confectioners' sugar, while Swedish bakers use ground almonds and white sugar. Once the cookies are baked, they are sometimes rolled around a broom handle to give them a curved shape. In American recipes, the cookies are often made with uncooked oatmeal and brown sugar. Our cookies, however, are made in the Swedish manner. We suggest baking only a few cookies at a time, as they spread out on the cookie sheet.

**PREP:** 25 minutes plus cooling
**BAKE:** 5 minutes per batch
**MAKES** about 36 cookies

¾ **cup blanched almonds, ground**

½ **cup butter or margarine (1 stick), softened**

½ **cup sugar**

1 **tablespoon all-purpose flour**

1 **tablespoon heavy or whipping cream**

1. Preheat oven to 350°F. Grease and flour two large cookie sheets.

2. In 2-quart saucepan, combine ground almonds, butter, sugar, flour, and cream. Heat over low heat, stirring occasionally, until butter melts. Keep mixture warm over very low heat.

3. Drop batter by rounded teaspoons, about 3 inches apart, on prepared cookie sheets. (Do not place more than six on each cookie sheet.)

4. Bake until edges are lightly browned and centers are just golden, 5 to 7 minutes. Cool cookies 30 to 60 seconds on cookie sheet, until edges are just set. With long, flexible narrow metal spatula, flip cookies over quickly (lacy texture will be on outside after rolling up).

5. Working as quickly as possible, roll each cookie around handle (½-inch diameter) of wooden spoon or dowel. If cookies become too hard to roll, briefly return to oven to soften. As each cookie is shaped, slip off spoon handle and cool completely on wire rack.

6. Repeat with remaining batter.

**EACH COOKIE:** About 57 calories, 1g protein, 4g carbohydrate, 5g total fat (2g saturated), 7mg cholesterol, 26mg sodium.

## Maple Sugar Cookies

*One cup of sugar, one cup of crushed maple sugar, one cup of butter, two well beaten eggs, two tablespoons of water, two teaspoons of baking powder, and flour enough to roll out. Do not make too stiff. Bake in quick oven.*

—**Good Housekeeping Everyday Cook Book**, 1903

# Snickerdoodles

These rich cinnamon-sugar cookies were created in New England and Pennsylvania-Dutch communities in the nineteenth century. As they bake, the little balls of dough puff up, then quickly flatten out and crinkle on top. Recipes for these cookies differ: some contain chopped walnuts, hickory nuts, raisins, or currants; others, like ours, are simple and buttery, with only a little vanilla extract and a fine coating of cinnamon-sugar to flavor them. Craig Claiborne believed that the name is derived from the German word *schnecken* (sticky buns.) Early Hudson River Valley community cookbooks called them schnecken noodles, schneckenoodles, or snecke noodles, while in the Midwest, they are called snickerdoodles. Some historians credit this cookie's name to the fact that New England cooks often enjoyed giving dishes whimsical names.

**PREP:** 25 minutes ★ **BAKE:** 12 minutes per batch
**MAKES** about 54 cookies

3 cups all-purpose flour

2 teaspoons cream of tartar

1 teaspoon baking soda

1 cup butter or margarine (2 sticks), softened

1⅓ cups plus ¼ cup sugar

2 large eggs

1 teaspoon vanilla extract

1½ teaspoons ground cinnamon

**1.** Preheat oven to 375°F. In large bowl, combine flour, cream of tartar, and baking soda.

**2.** In large bowl, with mixer at medium speed, beat butter and 1⅓ cups sugar until light and fluffy. Beat in eggs, one at a time, beating well after each addition; beat in vanilla. Reduce speed to low; beat in flour mixture until well blended.

**3.** In small bowl, combine remaining ¼ cup sugar and cinnamon. Roll dough into 1-inch balls. Roll in cinnamon-sugar to coat evenly. Place balls, 1 inch apart, on two ungreased large cookie sheets.

**4.** Bake cookies until set and slightly crinkled on top, about 12 minutes, rotating cookie sheets between upper and lower oven racks halfway through baking. Cool cookies 1 minute on cookie sheet. With wide spatula, transfer cookies to wire racks to cool completely.

**5.** Repeat with remaining dough.

**EACH COOKIE:** About 81 calories, 1g protein, 11g carbohydrate, 4g total fat (2g saturated), 17mg cholesterol, 61mg sodium.

# Gingersnaps

Late-eighteenth-century recipes for gingersnaps called for rolling out the dough and cutting it into rounds. Nowadays some recipes suggest rolling the dough into logs, chilling it, then slicing the dough into rounds. Still other recipes (like ours) recommend rolling the dough into small balls, then spacing them well apart on cookie sheets. As they bake, they spread out flat. The derivation of the name for these cookies is hazy, though the word *snap* does come from the German *snappen,* which means "seize quickly" (easily). Indeed, these cookies are quick and easy to make as well as delicious.

---

**PREP:** 20 minutes ★ **BAKE:** 15 minutes
**MAKES** 10 large cookies or about 30 small cookies

---

**2 cups all-purpose flour**

**2 teaspoons ground ginger**

**1 teaspoon baking soda**

**$\frac{1}{2}$ teaspoon ground cinnamon**

**$\frac{1}{2}$ teaspoon salt**

**$\frac{1}{4}$ teaspoon ground black pepper (optional)**

**$\frac{3}{4}$ cup vegetable shortening**

**$\frac{1}{2}$ cup plus 2 tablespoons sugar**

**1 large egg**

**$\frac{1}{2}$ cup dark molasses**

**1.** Preheat oven to 350°F. In medium bowl, combine flour, ginger, baking soda, cinnamon, salt, and black pepper, if using.

**2.** In large bowl, with mixer at medium speed, beat shortening and $\frac{1}{2}$ cup sugar until light and fluffy. Beat in egg until blended; beat in molasses. Reduce speed to low; beat in the flour mixture just until blended.

**3.** Place remaining 2 tablespoons sugar on waxed paper. Roll $\frac{1}{4}$ cup dough into ball; roll in sugar to coat evenly. Repeat with remaining dough to make 10 balls in all. Place balls, 3 inches apart, on ungreased large cookie sheet. Or, for small cookies, roll slightly rounded tablespoons dough into balls and place 2 inches apart on two ungreased cookie sheets.

**4.** Bake until set, about 15 minutes for large cookies, or 9 to 11 minutes for small cookies, rotating cookie sheets between upper and lower oven racks halfway through baking. Cookies will be very soft and may appear moist in cracks. Cool cookies 1 minute on cookie sheets on wire racks. With wide spatula, transfer the cookies to wire racks to cool completely.

---

**EACH LARGE COOKIE:** About 323 calories, 3g protein, 42g carbohydrate, 16g total fat (4g saturated), 21mg cholesterol, 258mg sodium.

**EACH SMALL COOKIE:** About 108 calories, 1g protein, 14g carbohydrate, 5g total fat (1g saturated), 7mg cholesterol, 86mg sodium.

# Gingerbread Cutouts

Early cookbooks often offered several gingerbread cookie recipes. Among them was usually one for gingerbread that was rolled out thin, baked on an inverted drip pan, then cut into strips. It is possible that this recipe was the forerunner of the ever-popular gingerbread cutout cookies that are piled high on holiday cookie platters and often found hanging on Christmas trees. Nowadays gingerbread cookies are decorated with various colors, but in earlier times they were outlined with a thin zigzag of white icing.

**PREP:** 45 minutes plus cooling and decorating
**BAKE:** 12 minutes per batch ★ **MAKES** about 36 cookies

½ **cup sugar**

½ **cup light (mild) molasses**

1½ **teaspoons ground ginger**

1 **teaspoon ground allspice**

1 **teaspoon ground cinnamon**

1 **teaspoon ground cloves**

2 **teaspoons baking soda**

½ **cup butter or margarine (1 stick),
   cut into pieces**

1 **large egg, beaten**

3½ **cups all-purpose flour**

**Ornamental Frosting (opposite)**

**1.** In 3-quart saucepan, combine sugar, molasses, ginger, allspice, cinnamon, and cloves; heat to boiling over medium heat, stirring occasionally with wooden spoon. Remove pan from heat; stir in baking soda (mixture will foam up in pan). Add butter; stir until melted. Stir in egg, then flour.

**2.** On floured surface, knead dough until thoroughly blended. Divide dough in half; wrap one piece in waxed paper and set aside.

**3.** Preheat oven to 325°F. With floured rolling pin, roll remaining piece of dough slightly less than ¼ inch thick. With floured 3- to 4-inch assorted cookie cutters, cut dough into as many cookies as possible; reserve trimmings for rerolling. Place cookies, 1 inch apart, on two ungreased large cookie sheets. If desired, with drinking straw or skewer, make ¼-inch hole in the top of each cookie for hanging.

**4.** Bake until the edges begin to brown, about 12 minutes, rotating cookie sheets between upper and lower oven racks halfway through baking. With wide spatula, transfer cookies to wire racks to cool completely. Repeat with remaining dough and trimmings.

**5.** When cookies are cool, prepare Ornamental Frosting. Use frosting to decorate cookies as desired. Allow frosting to dry completely, about 1 hour.

**EACH COOKIE WITHOUT FROSTING:**
About 95 calories, 2g protein, 16g carbohydrate, 3g total fat (2g saturated), 13mg cholesterol, 100mg sodium.

# Ornamental Frosting

**PREP:** 8 minutes ★ **MAKES** about 3 cups

**1 package (16 ounces) confectioners' sugar**

**3 tablespoons meringue powder***

**⅓ cup warm water**

**assorted food colorings or food color pastes (optional)**

**1.** In bowl, with mixer at medium speed, beat confectioners' sugar, meringue powder, and warm water until stiff and knife drawn through leaves path, about 5 minutes.

**2.** If desired, tint frosting with food colorings. Keep tightly covered to prevent drying out. With small metal spatula, artists' paintbrushes, or decorating bags with small plain tips, decorate cookies with frosting. (You may need to thin frosting with a little warm water to obtain desired spreading or piping consistency.)

*Meringue powder is available in specialty stores wherever cake-decorating equipment is sold.

**EACH TABLESPOON:** About 40 calories, 0g protein, 10g carbohydrate, 0g total fat, 0mg cholesterol, 3mg sodium.

# Christmas Sugar-Cookie Cutouts

In Amelia Simmons's book *American Cookery*, there are two similar cookie recipes. One of them, Another Christmas Cookey, suggests: "…roll [dough] three quarters of an inch thick, and cut or stamp into shape and size you please, bake slowly fifteen or twenty minutes; tho' hard and dry at first, if put into an earthenware pot, and dry cellar, or damp room, they will be finer, softer and better when six months old." With today's recipes, sugar cookies can be enjoyed warm out of the oven. Or let them cool, then decorate them with icing and all the colorful holiday sugars and edible decorations you can find.

**PREP:** 1 hour 30 minutes plus chilling
**BAKE:** 12 minutes per batch
**MAKES** about 6 dozen cookies

3 cups all-purpose flour

½ teaspoon baking powder

½ teaspoon salt

1 cup butter (2 sticks), softened (do not use margarine)

1½ cups sugar

2 large eggs

1 teaspoon vanilla extract

Ornamental Frosting (page 167), optional

colored sugar crystals (optional)

1. In large bowl, combine flour, baking powder, and salt. In separate large bowl, with mixer at low speed, beat butter and sugar until blended. Increase speed to high; beat until light and fluffy, about 5 minutes. Reduce speed to low; beat in eggs and vanilla until mixed. Beat in flour mixture, just until blended, occasionally scraping bowl with rubber spatula.

2. Divide dough into four equal pieces. Shape each into disk; wrap each disk in waxed paper and freeze until firm enough to roll, at least 2 hours or refrigerate overnight.

3. Preheat oven to 350°F. On lightly floured surface, with floured rolling pin, roll one piece of dough until slightly less than ¼ inch thick; refrigerate remaining dough. With floured 3- to 4-inch assorted cookie cutters, cut out as many cookies as possible, reserving trimmings for rerolling. Place cookies, about 1 inch apart, on two ungreased large cookie sheets.

4. Bake cookies until golden around edges, 12 to 15 minutes, rotating cookie sheets between upper and lower oven racks halfway through baking. With wide spatula, transfer cookies to wire racks to cool completely. Use Ornamental Frosting or colored sugar to decorate cookies, if desired.

5. Repeat with remaining cookie dough and the trimmings.

**EACH COOKIE WITHOUT FROSTING OR SUGAR CRYSTALS:** About 60 calories, 1g protein, 8g carbohydrate, 3g total fat (2g saturated), 13mg cholesterol, 45mg sodium.

# Icebox Pinwheels

During the 1930s, a time when electric refrigerators were being installed in more and more American kitchens, recipes for icebox cookies began appearing in magazines and cookbooks claiming "… you can now quickly slice and freshly bake from rolls of chilled dough, at a moment's notice." The refrigerator cookies contained nuts, candied fruit, melted chocolate, or a few drops of almond extract or peppermint oil. Chocolate pinwheels were one of the first variations on icebox cookies, and they became an instant winner.

**PREP:** 35 minutes plus chilling
**BAKE:** 10 minutes per batch
**MAKES** about 48 cookies

2 cups all-purpose flour

1 teaspoon baking powder

¼ teaspoon salt

½ cup (1 stick) plus 1 tablespoon butter or
  margarine, softened

1 cup sugar

1 large egg

1 teaspoon vanilla extract

1 square (1 ounce) semisweet chocolate

3 tablespoons unsweetened cocoa

1. In small bowl, combine flour, baking powder, and salt. In medium bowl, with mixer at medium speed, beat ½ cup butter and sugar until creamy. Reduce speed to low; beat in egg and vanilla until blended. Beat in flour mixture just until combined, occasionally scraping bowl with rubber spatula. Transfer half of dough to sheet of waxed paper.

2. In 2-quart saucepan, melt chocolate and remaining 1 tablespoon butter over very low heat. Stir in cocoa until combined. Add chocolate mixture to dough in bowl, stirring until blended.

3. Roll chocolate dough between two sheets of waxed paper into 12" by 10" rectangle. Repeat with vanilla dough. Remove top sheets of waxed paper from chocolate and vanilla doughs. Using waxed paper, turn vanilla dough over onto chocolate dough. Peel off top sheet of waxed paper. Using bottom piece of waxed paper to help, roll up doughs together jelly-roll fashion. Wrap dough in plastic wrap and refrigerate until very firm, at least 4 hours or up to overnight.

4. Preheat the oven to 375°F. Grease two large cookie sheets.

5. Cut dough crosswise into ¼-inch-thick slices. Place the slices, ½ inch apart, on the prepared cookie sheets.

6. Bake just until golden, 10 to 12 minutes, rotating cookie sheets between upper and lower oven racks halfway through baking. Cool on cookie sheets on wire racks 5 minutes. With wide spatula, transfer to wire racks to cool completely.

**EACH COOKIE:** About 61 calories, 1g protein, 9g carbohydrate, 3g total fat (2g saturated), 10mg cholesterol, 46mg sodium.

# Penny Candy Store

In the late nineteenth century, hundreds of factories were busy producing candies destined to fill the glass bins and candy jars in mom-and-pop candy stores, corner ice-cream shops, and general stores. Such was the beginning of an American institution that would stand the test of time and be known as penny candy.

In 1880, the Wunderle Candy Company in Philadelphia was making one of the most beloved penny candies: orange, white, and yellow fondant candy corn. Eighteen years later, Gustav Goelitz began mass-producing candy corn. In 1886, in a candy kitchen in Lancaster, Pennsylvania, Milton S. Hershey was turning out high-quality caramels. Some time later, he purchased chocolate-making equipment and began chocolate coating his caramels. Around the same time, the Quaker City Confectionery Company was producing soft and chewy Good & Plenty licorice candies, the oldest branded candy in the United States. Their advertisements featured Choo-Choo Charlie, the engineer, who fueled his train with the pink-and-white candies and steered the confection into candy stores all across America.

In 1896, in a small candy shop in New York City, Austrian immigrant Leo Hirshfield began hand-rolling the first-ever wrapped penny candy in brown and red–striped paper. He named his chewy, chocolaty treat the Tootsie Roll, after his daughter Clara, whose nickname was Tootsie. Just four years later, Milton S. Hershey would once again make candy history by creating the first milk-chocolate bar. He also created chocolate kisses. In 1901, in California, the King Leo Company began making striped peppermint sticks.

In the candy shops of the early twentieth century, hard candies came in an array of colorful shapes and sizes: tiny cinnamon red hots; root beer barrels; wrapped butterscotch buttons; orange, lemon, lime, and cherry sour balls; peppermint Lifesavers, and crystalline rock candy on a stick in vivid colors. Chewy candies include bite-size peanut butter and molasses candies called Mary Janes, multicolored Jujyfruit, and honey-flavored taffy and almond bites named Bit-O-Honey. Fruit-flavored jelly candies were turned into sugared gumdrops, jelly beans, rippled rectangles called Chuckles. Licorice, too, was a regular feature.

Peanuts and peanut butter popped up in various guises, such as candy-coated peanuts called Boston Baked Beans, Reese's peanut butter cups, and chocolate-coated peanuts named Goobers. Naturally, penny-candy bins often held chocolate treasures: M&M's, Milk Duds, Rocky Roads, Goo Goo Clusters, and Sugar Babies. Other candies were simply silly and fun: tiny wax bottles filled with colorful sugar sips (now called Nik-L-Nips), Chupa Chups suckers in assorted flavors, candy cigarettes, six-inch-long chewy caramels called Cow Tales, and chewable, edible waxy lips.

Although old-fashioned penny-candy stores are a rare sight these days, penny-candy treasures can still be found.

# Chocolate-Walnut Fudge

*(pictured on page 140)*

As the story goes, in the late nineteenth century a batch of toffee was being manufactured and something went very wrong. The toffee crystallized, turning grainy instead of silky smooth. Surprisingly, it was a rich golden color—and delicious! What had been created was America's first batch of fudge, a mixture of sugar, milk, and butter. Over the years, lots of flavor variations have been developed: chocolate, the all-time favorite; peppermint; coconut; maple sugar; and vanilla nut. Fudge shops began popping up, too, especially in resort communities, such as Atlantic City. In the mid-twentieth century, making fudge became easier, faster, and practically foolproof thanks to sweetened condensed milk.

---

**PREP:** 25 minutes plus chilling ★ **MAKES** 64 pieces

---

**1 pound bittersweet chocolate or 16 squares (16 ounces) semisweet chocolate, chopped**

**1 can (14 ounces) sweetened condensed milk**

**1 cup walnuts (4 ounces), coarsely chopped**

**1 teaspoon vanilla extract**

**⅛ teaspoon salt**

1. Line 8-inch square baking pan with plastic wrap; smooth out wrinkles. In heavy 2-quart saucepan, melt chocolate with condensed milk over medium-low heat, stirring constantly, until smooth. Remove from heat.

2. Stir in walnuts, vanilla, and salt. Scrape chocolate mixture into prepared pan; spread evenly. Refrigerate until firm, about 3 hours.

3. Remove fudge from pan by lifting edges of plastic wrap. Invert fudge onto cutting board; discard plastic wrap. Cut fudge into 8 strips, then cut each strip crosswise into 8 pieces. Layer between waxed paper in airtight container. Store at room temperature up to 1 week, or refrigerate up to 1 month.

---

**EACH PIECE:** About 67 calories, 1g protein, 8g carbohydrate, 4g total fat (2g saturated), 2mg cholesterol, 13mg sodium.

# Creamy Penuche

**F**rom the Mexican word *panocha* (raw sugar) comes the name of this popular confection. It's also called Mexican fudge and brown-sugar fudge. Just when and where penuche was created appears to be a mystery. But we do know that authentic south-of-the-border versions contain raw, coarse Mexican sugar. Southern cooks claim that authentic penuche is made by caramelizing white sugar until nutty brown, but recipes often use brown sugar along with cream, butter, and nuts.

**PREP:** 15 minutes plus cooling ★ **COOK:** 25 minutes
**MAKES** about 64 pieces

4 tablespoons butter (do not use margarine)
2 cups heavy or whipping cream
2 tablespoons light corn syrup
1½ cups granulated sugar
1½ cups packed dark brown sugar
2 ounces white chocolate or white baking bar, chopped
1½ cups walnuts (6 ounces), toasted and coarsely chopped

1. Grease 8-inch square baking pan. Line pan with foil, extending foil over rim on two opposite sides; grease foil.

2. In heavy 4-quart saucepan, melt butter over medium heat. Add cream, corn syrup, and granulated and brown sugars; cook over high heat, stirring, until sugars have completely dissolved and mixture is bubbling. With pastry brush dipped in cold water, wash down sugar crystals on side of the saucepan.

3. Set candy thermometer in place; continue cooking, without stirring, until temperature reaches 234° to 240°F (soft-ball stage), 15 to 20 minutes.

4. Remove saucepan from heat. Without stirring, cool mixture to 210°F, about 8 minutes. Sprinkle chopped white chocolate over mixture; let stand 1 minute.

5. With wooden spoon, stir in walnuts just until mixed (do not overmix). Immediately pour mixture into prepared pan (do not scrape mixture from saucepan).

6. Cool in pan on wire rack until firm but still warm, about 30 minutes. Remove candy from pan by lifting edges of foil and place on cutting board. Cut into 8 strips, then cut each strip crosswise into 8 pieces. Cool completely on foil on wire rack. With spatula, lift candy away from foil. Layer between waxed paper in airtight container. Store at room temperature up to 3 weeks.

**EACH PIECE:** About 95 calories, 1g protein, 11g carbohydrate, 6g total fat (2g saturated), 12mg cholesterol, 14mg sodium.

# Pralines

**A**ccording to the 1951 edition of *The Original Picayune Creole Cook Book,* these delightful confections originated in the old Creole kitchens of New Orleans. The word *praline,* however, did not. It's of French origin and means "sugared." Numerous recipes (and variations) for these dainty, delicious candies exist. Pralines can be made with white or brown sugar, almonds or peanuts, or coconut and cochineal, which turns the candies pink. If you ever get to the French Quarter in New Orleans, be sure to look for *pralines aux pacanes* (pralines with pecans); they are one of the most authentic versions you will find.

**PREP:** 15 minutes ★ **COOK:** 25 minutes
**MAKES** about 40 pralines

½ cup butter (1 stick), cut into pieces (do not use margarine)

2 cups granulated sugar

1 cup packed light brown sugar

1 cup heavy or whipping cream

2 tablespoons light corn syrup

2 cups pecans (8 ounces), toasted and coarsely chopped

1 teaspoon vanilla extract

**1.** Grease two or three cookie sheets.

**2.** In heavy 3-quart saucepan, combine butter, granulated and brown sugars, cream, and corn syrup; cook over medium heat, stirring occasionally, until sugars have dissolved and syrup is bubbling.

**3.** Set candy thermometer in place and continue cooking, without stirring, until temperature reaches 230° to 234°F (thread stage), about 8 minutes.

**4.** Add pecans and vanilla; stir until bubbling subsides. Heat to boiling. Continue cooking until candy temperature reaches 244° to 248°F (firm-ball stage).

**5.** Remove saucepan from heat and stir vigorously until syrup has thickened and turns opaque, about 3 minutes.

**6.** Working quickly, drop mixture by tablespoons, at least 1 inch apart, on prepared cookie sheets (stir briefly over low heat if mixture gets too thick). Cool pralines completely. Layer between waxed paper in airtight container. Store at room temperature up to 1 week, or freeze up to 3 months.

**EACH PRALINE:** About 144 calories, 1g protein, 17g carbohydrate, 9g total fat (3g saturated), 14mg cholesterol, 29mg sodium.

# Popcorn Balls

Some historians believe that it is likely that the Native Americans brought popping corn to the first Thanksgiving feast. The colonists called it by several names, including popped corn and parched corn; by 1820 the name popcorn was commonly used. Before long, cooks were adding molasses to the popped corn and shaping it into sweet, crunchy balls. In 1886, candy maker Milton S. Hershey opened the Lancaster Caramel Company in Lancaster, Pennsylvania. About ten years later, he began adding chocolate and vanilla to his caramels. Just when the idea of melting caramels to make popcorn balls occurred isn't clear, but it quickly became the fastest and most foolproof way to make these ever-popular treats.

**PREP:** 10 minutes ★ **COOK:** 10 minutes
**MAKES** 15 balls

16 cups salted popped corn

1 cup salted cocktail peanuts

1 bag (14 ounces) caramels, unwrapped

2 tablespoons water

**1.** Pick over popcorn and discard any unpopped kernels. Grease large deep roasting pan or bowl. In pan, combine popcorn and peanuts

**2.** In medium microwave-safe bowl, combine caramels and water. Cook in microwave according to package directions, stirring frequently, until smooth. Pour over popcorn; with large spoon toss until evenly coated. Grease hands and shape by cups into 15 balls.

**EACH BALL:** About 207 calories, 5g protein, 28g carbohydrate, 10g total fat (4g saturated), 2mg cholesterol, 291mg sodium.

# Peanut Brittle

Around the turn of the twentieth century, recipes for peanut brittle began appearing; it didn't take long for Americans to embrace it as a favorite candy treat. In the original recipe, raw peanuts are slowly poached in hot sugar syrup, which infuses the candy with lots of peanut flavor. In our recipe, roasted peanuts are stirred into the candy just before it is removed from the heat. The bubbling-hot candy mixture is poured onto a cookie sheet and stretched into a thin rectangle. Traditionally, confectioners use a slab of marble for this step, as the cool temperature of the marble gives more time to stretch the hot mixture before it turns to brittle. Once it hardens, the brittle is broken into pieces just right for eating out of hand.

**PREP:** 5 minutes plus cooling ★ **COOK:** 30 minutes
**MAKES** about 1 pound

1 cup sugar

½ cup light corn syrup

¼ cup water

2 tablespoons butter or margarine

1 cup salted peanuts

½ teaspoon baking soda

1. Lightly grease large cookie sheet.

2. In heavy 2-quart saucepan, combine sugar, corn syrup, water, and butter; cook over medium heat, stirring constantly, until sugar has dissolved and syrup is bubbling.

3. Set candy thermometer in place and continue cooking, stirring frequently, until temperature reaches 300° to 310°F (hard-crack stage), 20 to 25 minutes. (Once temperature reaches 220°F, it will rise quickly, so watch carefully.) Stir in peanuts.

4. Remove saucepan from heat and stir in baking soda (mixture will bubble vigorously); immediately pour onto prepared cookie sheet. With two forks, quickly lift and stretch peanut mixture into 14" by 12" rectangle.

5. Cool brittle completely on cookie sheet on wire rack. With hands, break brittle into small pieces. Layer between waxed paper in airtight container. Store at room temperature up to 1 month.

**EACH OUNCE:** About 146 calories, 2g protein, 22g carbohydrate, 6g total fat (2g saturated), 4mg cholesterol, 103mg sodium.

## Gold Rush Nut Brittle

Prepare as directed but use only ¾ *cup salted peanuts;* stir in ¾ *cup sliced blanched almonds* and ¾ *cup pecans,* coarsely broken, with peanuts. Makes about 1¼ pounds.

# Index